P9-APY-055

LOVE AND LIMERENCE

The Experience of Being in Love

DOROTHY TENNOV

STEIN AND DAY/*Publishers*/New York

Also by Dorothy Tennov

Psychotherapy: The Hazardous Cure
Super Self: A Woman's Guide to Self Management

THIRD PRINTING, 1980

First published in 1979
Copyright © 1979 by Dorothy Tennov
All rights reserved
Designed by Ed Kaplin
Printed in the United States of America
Stein and Day/*Publishers*/Scarborough House,
Briarcliff Manor, N.Y. 10510

Library of Congress Cataloging in Publication Data

Tennov, Dorothy.
  Love and limerence.

    1. Love.   I. Title.
BF575.L8T46   152.4   77-20117
ISBN 0-8128-2328-1

FOR HELEN PAYNE

and in memory of
Stendhal
(Marie Henri Beyle, 1783–1842)

Acknowledgments

I gratefully acknowledge the contributions of the many—thousands in all—who provided personal data through questionnaires, anonymous phone calls, interviews, diaries, letters, or specially prepared written materials, and whose personal experiences guided the development of the conceptions presented here. Included were students at the University of Bridgeport, in particular, Nora Budzilik, Larry Kravitz, and Meir Hadar, who interviewed and administered questionnaires to other students in the early days. A special note of thanks must be sounded for Elinor Carlson, who helped with questionnaire administration and supplied me with helpful materials from the popular press from time to time; to Norma MacDaniel, whose generous aid took various forms; and to Leland Miles and Henry Heneghan, who probably did not realize the importance to me and to my work of the faith I felt they had in me at critical times. And deep gratitude goes to Lillian Wachtel, who generously provided me with numerous important items, but especially, in 1976, with the now worn and dog-eared copy of Stendhal's *Love;* to Jonas Trinidad, who contributed enthusiasm, time, data, and insights; to Michelle Vian, who assured me that "limerence" works well in French; to Alexandra Nelson, Cecelia Rosenberg, Joan Farcus,

Daniel Tennow, Virginia Newlin, Jean Veta, Kay Woodard, Maureen Lecht, and Lolly Hirsch for general support and for reading manuscript drafts; to Marilee Talman, my editor, who worked both long and hard organizing material and rendering it increasingly readable, and, above all, who made me feel that she understood and appreciated the concepts in much the same way that I did.

I would also like to make grateful acknowledgment to those who allowed me to reprint portions of copyrighted material: From the *Sexual Code* by Wolfgang Wickler, translated by Francesca Garvie. Translation Copyright © 1972 by Doubleday & Company, Inc. Reprinted by permission of the publisher. Excerpts from *Love, Sex and Being Human* by Paul Bohannan. Copyright © 1969 by Paul Bohannan. Reprinted by permission of Doubleday & Company, Inc.—From *Stendhal* by Matthew Josephson. Copyright © 1946 by Matthew Josephson. Copyright renewed 1973. Reprinted by permission of Harold Ober Associates.—From *On Love* by José Ortega y Gasset, translated by Toby Talbot. Copyright © 1957 by Toby Talbot. Reprinted by arrangement with The New American Library, Inc., New York, N.Y.—From *The Summer Before the Dark*. Copyright © 1973 by Doris Lessing. Reprinted by permission of the author and her agent, James Brown Associates, Inc.—Penguin Books, for material from *On Love* by Stendhal. Translation copyright © 1957 by The Merlin Press. Introduction copyright © 1975 by Jean Stuart and B.C.J.G. Knight.—Random House, for portions of *Intimate Behavior* by Desmond Morris, 1971.—Grove Press, for material from *Rationale of the Dirty Joke* by G. Legman, 1968 and *The American Sexual Tragedy* by Albert Ellis, 1958.—Columbia University Press, for material from *The Art of Courtly Love* by Andreas Capellanus, 1941.—Harper and Row, for material from *The Art of Loving* by Erich Fromm. Copyright © 1956 by Erich Fromm.—Liveright Publishing, for material from *My Life* by Isadora Duncan, 1955.—Maurice Valency, for material from *In Praise of Love* by Maurice Valency, Macmillan, 1958.—Delacorte Press, for an excerpt from *Sartre: His Philosophy and Existential Psychoanalysis* by Alfred Stern, 1967.—Arno Press, Inc., for material from *Seven Faces of Love*, by André Maurois. Reprinted by Books for Library Press. Distributed by Arno Press, Inc.—Morton Hunt, for material from *The Natural History of Love* by Morton Hunt. Alfred A. Knopf, 1959.—John Wiley & Sons, for material from *Exchange and Power in Social Life* by Peter Blau, 1964.—William Morrow & Company, Inc., for *The Dialectic of Sex* by Shulamith Firestone, 1971.—*Ms. Magazine*, for material from Feb., 1978 article about Mary Wollstonecraft and material from "Being a Boy" by Julius Lester. David Norton, for "Toward an Epistemology of Romantic Love," by David Norton, *The Centennial Review*, 1970.—For material in *Quest: A Search for Self* by Sarah Cirese. Copyright © 1977 by Holt, Rinehart and Winston. Reprinted by permission of Holt, Rinehart and Winston.—St. Martin's Press for permission to quote from *Love Between Women* by Charlotte Wolff, 1971.—The American Sociological Association, for material from "The Theoretical Importance of Love" by William J. Goode, *American Sociological Review* 1959.—David McKay & Company, for permission to quote from *Pairing* by George R. Bach and Ronald M. Deutsch, 1971.—Jonathan Cape, Ltd., for excerpt from *The Diary of Nellie Ptashkina*, edited by M. Jacques Povolotsky, 1923.

Preface

You think:

I want you.

I want you forever, now, yesterday, and always. Above all, I want you to want me.

No matter where I am or what I am doing, I am not safe from your spell. At any moment, the image of your face smiling at me, of your voice telling me you care, or of your hand in mine, may suddenly fill my consciousness rudely pushing out all else.

The expression "thinking of you" fails to convey either the quality or quantity of this unwilled mental activity. "Obsessed" comes closer but leaves out the aching. A child is obsessed on Christmas Eve. But it's a happy prepossession full of excitement, curiosity, and expectation. *This* prepossession is an emotional roller coaster that carries me from the peak of ecstasy to the depths of despair. And back again.

I bear the thought of other topics when I must, but prolonged concentration on any other subject is difficult to tolerate. I must admit that it has happened on occasion that some entertainment or distraction overwhelmed thought of you, and I was suddenly freed from my pain and for an instant viewed you from a new perspective. (On those occasions I glimpsed reality usually closed from my view.) I don't seek "distractions." I'm too afraid that they won't distract after all and I'll be imprisoned somewhere saying polite nothings while I long to give myself up to desiring you with all my passion; to Tin Pan Alley's "burning desire."

Everything reminds me of you. I try to read, but four times on a single page some word begins the lightning chain of associations that summons my mind away from my work, and I must struggle to return my attention to the task at hand. Often I give up easily, leave my desk, and throw myself down on my bed, where my body lies still while my imagination constructs long and involved and plausible reasons to believe that you love me.

Or I remember. After the weekend in Vermont my brain replayed each moment. Over and over. You said you loved me, at dusk by the waterfall: Ten thousand reverberations of the scene sprinkled my succeeding days with happiness. . . .

You remember the state, do you? It's what this book is about. If you don't remember, that's okay, too. Some of you do and some of you do not. That fact is itself an important aspect of the story.

Contents

Contents

It is not love. It is the force of evolution expressed as the compulsion for the particular, this particular one above all others. Often, it is called love. . . .

1

The Beginning

My decision to pursue the systematic study of romantic love came—as love itself so often does—suddenly. Also, as is frequently true in love, I remember the moment.

It was an autumn afternoon in the mid-1960s that Marilyn Weber, a student who had favorably impressed me with her alertness and intelligence, was waiting for me as I returned to my office from class. Her posture sagged, her head hung forward, and when we had entered the office and seated ourselves, I saw that her eyes were red rimmed and swollen. She struggled with herself to keep from bursting into renewed tears.

"Dr. Tennov, I want you to know that I meant to get this week's assignment in on time but have not been able to do anything for the past two days. May I have an extension until next week? I'm sure I can finish it by then. I think. . . ."

1

At that point, her control foundered, and she began to weep. She took one of the tissues I pushed toward her, blew her nose, took another, and pressed it to her eyes.

"I'm sorry. Things are getting me down. Various family problems. A number of things have happened at once, and I don't know why I'm acting this way, but I'm sure it will be over soon. I wanted to see you before. I didn't want you to think I was neglecting my work out of lack of interest. I'm going to stay in the dorm all weekend and catch up. I really don't know what's the matter with me. It's very silly. I suppose I take things too hard."

She straightened up and began to gather her things as if afraid that if she stayed longer she might lose the composure she had regained. I said she could turn in the assignment when she had finished it and added that I was free to discuss whatever it was that was bothering her if she felt it would help. She hesitated slightly, but declined, saying, "There is nothing anyone can do." Still a little shaky, she thanked me and rose to leave. I almost let her go.

About three weeks earlier, the students in one of my graduate courses had held a spontaneous debate on the issue of whether lower animals experience emotion. After class, in my office over coffee, Fred Johnson argued that certain emotions, love, for example, were strictly human experiences. Bill Golding, on the other hand, felt that not only do animals experience emotion, but that dogs, at least, experience love, and he cited the case of his own dog, Scruffy. Fred conceded that Scruffy probably felt something positive toward Bill, but insisted that "love" was not the appropriate label for it. I wondered whether Fred would like to try to explain the difference between what Scruffy feels for Bill and what a human being might feel for another human being. We forgot about canine emotions and began to focus on the human experience of romantic love.

Both Fred and Bill had had severe bouts with erotic passions. Fred described his breakup with Carol during his sophomore year in college.

"I dropped out of three of my five classes because I was spending hours every day lying on my bed thinking about Carol. It was all I wanted to do. Just lie around, think about her, and try to figure out ways to get her back. Every few days I would telephone her, until finally she told me to stop calling."

"Are you saying that love is a painful thing?" I asked.

"Yes. But not always. Right now Brenda and I have got this really beautiful thing going."

Bill, too, had had a similar, and more recent, experience.

"Fred's situation really sounds like mine with Lisa. If we hadn't broken off in the summer, I'll bet I would have missed some school, too. As it was, on my job at the gas station, I was able to operate with half a mind on gas and half a mind on Lisa, except that sometimes my mind was completely on Lisa and then it got a little rough. It took a long time to get over, about six or eight months; and even now, if I heard that Lisa was in town, or if I saw her, I don't know how I would react."

Although I did not realize it at the time, Fred and Bill can be counted as my first two interviewees. They had described an experience both extreme and banal, a pain whose source lay in completely uncharted regions of the human psyche. In essence their experiences resembled those portrayed daily on the television screen. They resembled the experiences I myself had undergone in past years. I had assumed that my own personal experiences with love were unlike those of other people. And, of course, they were, as any experience or any situation is a unique event in the life of one individual. But the tales of Fred and Bill contained elements of such striking similarity to each other, to my own past experience, and to that reported in fiction and in autobiography that my assumption of uniqueness gave way to the consideration of the possibility that these elements constituted, at least in part, aspects of a more universal phenomenon. This thought kept racing through my head as I drove home from campus after the discussion. I wondered if there were a definite progression of events in romantic love, a progression that tended to occur in similar if not identical form among individuals and in situations that otherwise differed greatly from each other.

Busy as I was at that time with classes and other projects, Marilyn Weber's visit a few weeks later took me unawares but as she was going out the door, I found myself asking her, "Does it have anything to do with a disappointment with love?"

At my question, Marilyn sat down again.

"Oh, Dr. Tennov, how did you know? When Mark's letter came last Monday, my world fell apart. I've been a wreck ever since. I can't believe he did it. We were supposed to be married in June, but in his letter he said he was going to marry someone else next month. How could he do that? I just can't pull out of it. I can't believe it. I can't stop these awful feelings. I can't think about anything else. That's why I didn't work on the paper. Since the letter came on Monday, I have spent most of my time lying on my bed weeping. Just last week I thought I was really happy, and now, no one could be more miserable than I am."

For the next hour Marilyn cried and talked about Mark, how they met, what he was like, what she liked about him, how she could not believe that he no longer cared for her, and how she had read his letter over and over again looking for some sign of hope between the lines.

I listened transfixed. It was not that I had never heard of such feelings as she was describing. What amazed me was that I suddenly realized that probably all around me, among colleagues and friends as well as students, was a form of suffering that is usually hidden.

Hidden, yet easily revealed. Although I might have missed Marilyn's story, and Fred and Bill might never have told about themselves had it not been for the class discussion, it had not really required much encouragement for any of them to speak openly about their experiences.

After Marilyn left, I sat in my office for a long time, just thinking. From time to time, I'd take a book from my bookcase, turn to the index, look up "love," "romantic love," "erotic love," or "passionate love." They were mostly textbooks in general psychology; some were advanced texts in behavior, emotion, or perception; none contained any reference to the experience described by Marilyn, Fred, and Bill. In many books, "love" was not even listed. In others, the discussion was brief and did not relate to such experiences. When writers were not vague, they tended to contradict each other, disputing even the basic nature of love. Was it an emotion, an attitude, a sentiment, a personality type, a neurotic manifestation, a way of looking at the world, a means of emotional manipulation, a sublime passion, a peak experience, a religion, a desire, a mental state, a perversion of thought, a prepossession, a biological urge, a type of mystical experience, a weakness of the will, an obsession, an aesthetic reaction, a sacred state, a universal thirst, a glimpse of heaven? All were suggested.

The illustrious and influential Sigmund Freud dismissed romantic love as merely sex urge blocked. Pioneer sexologist Havelock Ellis provided his famous and entirely incorrect mathematical formula: sex plus friendship. (It seems to be neither.) Contemporary sex researchers seldom discuss love since they view sex and love as quite distinct from each other. Psychoanalytic writers have disagreed with each other as well as with the master, Freud. Theodore Reik asserted that sex and love are quite different, although the usual interpretation of Freudian concepts is that they are fused. Psychoanalyst Robert Seidenberg comments that the only similarity he could think of is that neither makes sense. In books with the word "love" in their titles, two of the most widely read writers on mental and emotional life managed to virtually avoid the subject of romantic love: Erich Fromm, in the *Art of Loving*, dismisses "falling in love" as a clearly unsatisfactory, as well as "explosive," way to overcome "separateness"; and Rollo May, in his best-selling book *Love and Will*, forces the reader to search for romantic love in the interstices between sexual, procreational, friendly, and altruistic loves. The general view seemed to be that romantic love is mysterious, mystical, even sacred, and not capable, apparently, of being subjected to the cool gaze of scientific inquiry.

Some writers disparaged the "myth of love," in which two healthy, normal, and attractive people, each of whom is of that gender to which the other is attracted, meet, most often by accident, and realize that they are "right" for each other. The "love story" concerns their increasing attraction and desire for each other and the difficulties they encounter—whether internal or external in origin. Eventually, in the words of a sociologist, "Believing that love is a panacea, that the future holds only goodness for them, they marry and form a new nuclear family." [1] A psychologist described the "True Romance Package":

> A man and a woman, young and beautiful, are drawn together by a strong physical attraction that tells them that they are meant to satisfy one another's erotic and affectional needs. They are tossed about by the fury of passion and excitement and pain and fear, the two of them alone against the world and others who will intrude, forever and everlasting. Obsessed with one another to addiction, they are willing to risk all to retain the feeling of being in love. They are scornful of reason or harsh realities—the two of them, in love with love.[2]

The implication of the article was that the pattern is culturally induced and not quite real, a mental aberration.

I turned over in my mind the prospect of conducting research myself on the subject of romantic love. It was an exciting idea. The subject was both unexplored and important. What additional justification was required? There were obstacles, of course. As an experimental psychologist, I felt convinced of the importance of using objective methods. But by what methods can private human feelings be studied?[3] From that day of Marilyn's visit and my examination of the psychology textbooks, I wanted to know what causes people to fall in love, whether some people are more likely than others to fall in love, what is the incidence of unhappy love, and how can we help people who are unhappy because of love. Two points of view guided the course of my work. The first was that I would look for aspects common to the romantic experience, particularly those aspects of what was termed "love" that produced distress. I count myself lucky that Fred and Bill had not, by chance, been Lucy and Vivian; otherwise, I might have wasted effort looking for sex differences instead of an underlying pattern that was obviously shared by members of both sexes. The second orientation was that this "thing" I aimed to study was a normal condition, not a pathological state, or sign of a weak or "neurotic" personality. Whatever else Marilyn, Fred, Bill, myself, and the writers of innumerable popular stories and songs had in common—and any sociologist would be quick to point out that the students and I shared a largely similar culture—we also appeared to be psychologically ordinary individuals.

While I was reading everything I could find about love in all fields, and especially published autobiographies and unpublished personal journals, I began to give a series of questionnaires, both individually and in classrooms, that asked for true or false responses to approximately 200 statements about romantic love, sex, and personal relationships.

Although most of the first 79 students who answered the first questionnaire reported that they obtained great pleasure from love, more than half said that they had been emotionally depressed, and more than 25 percent said that they had had suicidal thoughts. Some of the statements described extreme social difficulties as well as emotional insecurity, depression, and suicide attempts. Such statements were selected particularly by those who were "getting over a broken love affair" at that time.

Since the strong correlation between getting over a broken love affair and scoring high in statements concerning insecurity, depression, and difficulty in social relationships was a pattern more consistent with drama and with such popular expressions as "lovesick" and "heartbreak" than with the writings of many social scientists, it seemed that many people in the past have tended to understate the extent of their suffering in the traumatic aftermath of romantic love. Perhaps the anonymity of the responses made it easier for my students to speak up.

A group of older women who answered the questionnaire complained that they had difficulty deciding whether or not the statements were true. Many of them had been true at one time in these women's lives but not at other times. As one 41-year-old woman said, "At one time or another in my life almost every statement would have applied but today almost none apply."

Ultimately the first questionnaire was administered to approximately 400 people, henceforth referred to as "The Group." Subsequent versions were given to another 400 persons.

Notices about my interest in romantic love at meetings, on bulletin boards, and in various newsletters and other publications brought many people to me with their individual tales—some only by telephone and anonymously. Others let me read their private and sometimes very intimate diaries. In addition, I obtained interviews from more than 300 people who volunteered to report their love experiences. I brought the subject up with virtually all of my acquaintances—friends of years' standing, colleagues from across the world encountered at professional meetings, clients who came for other problems but stayed on without fee to tell their love stories for my research, women who were participants in the consciousness-raising groups of the early 1970s, and business executives who telephoned in response to a request announced at a convention.

Altogether, more than 500 people heard of my interest and supplied me with information in various forms other than questionnaires. With rare exceptions, everyone I asked agreed to be interviewed and many others volunteered unsolicited. The interviews, of course, were not anonymous, and many of those interviewed swore me to absolute secrecy. It is embarrassing when Jimmy taunts his classmate without mercy in the schoolyard by calling out, "Lydia loves Joseph." The mature person who falls in love with an associate on the job may be no less concerned, and many a diary has been burned lest hidden loves be revealed. Whatever the motives of those who provided testimonies— whether it was because they wished to assist the scientific effort or simply because they enjoyed talking about their feelings to another person—they trusted me to guard their secrets.

As I listened to people tell of love experiences, I often worried that they would read the book and think that I had used their individual stories unaltered. The fact is that although any given example might seem to be the story of one person, it is also the story of others because I adopted the procedure of including only material that had occurred in the same way in at least three different testimonies. In one sense my task was far simpler than the interviewees anticipated. A major finding was the great similarity among many of the tales told me. All accounts given are fictionalized in that names, places, and all other specific details have been altered to render them untraceable to their actual sources.

Each story, of course, had unique aspects. They were usually fraught with dangers, decisions, separations, reunions, quarrels, jealousies, regrets. Most also described joy. And some contained memorable moments of pure and unforgettable ecstasy. I heard tales to rival the *grands amours* of fiction. They ranged in duration from a three-day spree in Naples to a fifty-year unrequited yearning. But the more "case histories" I encountered, the more mysterious the process appeared. Although everyone had some story to tell, the more I heard, the less certain I became about what questions to ask. People fell in love. Sometimes things went well; sometimes they did not. Was I learning anything not already well known? This kind of intense experience had been described brilliantly in the yearnings of Anna Karenina for Count Vronsky, in the fanaticism of the middle-aged man obsessed by attraction for a youth before his death in Venice, and in the works of Proust, Rousseau, Hazlitt, and thousands of others, great and not so great. Story, drama, verse, and song provided a picture consistent with what many people told me about their own lives.

The Browns—Lou and Jim—were typical of early interviewees, who described the events that transpired in the course of a relationship. Lou told how she and Jim had met during their first college class because they happened to be sitting next to each other. An urgent summons that caused the instructor to depart in the middle of the session produced an atmosphere of conviviality among students, who suddenly found themselves with half an hour of free time. Lou reported:

"It was totally a matter of that circumstance, and the general excitement and uncertainty of being in a new situation. I think our first few dates were also mainly a matter of, well, almost convenience. I enjoyed being with Jim, but it was a very nonserious, friendship sort of relationship until Thanksgiving, when suddenly he announced that his girlfriend from back home would be visiting him during the holiday. I really didn't know what struck me, but I found myself at loose ends. At first I just thought it was loneliness, but when I went to a dance with a group of friends and met some other male students, especially Dave, who took me to a movie, I realized that it was Jim I was missing."

As it turned out, Jim had also undergone an intensification of feeling, especially after Lou told him of her expanded social circle. "After that, we were serious. It was obvious. By Christmas we were writing each other letters, and spring was about 60 percent being in love with Jim, 40 percent being a student." Although there were several stressful periods of one sort or another, they mostly concerned minor matters, such as which movie to see or whether faithfulness had been preserved during times of physical separation. There was never a complete break between them, and they were married soon after graduation. When I interviewed Lou, she was a part-time graduate student. Jim had taken a master's degree in business, and they had two children.

Their major concerns were repairing the new house they had bought in the fall—an old one at a good price—and the rearing of their daughters.

"I decided to go back to school because, well, I always planned, to. It gets me out of the house, Jim doesn't mind sitting with the girls two evenings a week, and although Jim's career seems to be doing all right, we'll do a lot better if I can get a job in a couple of years when the children are in school."

When I asked whether Lou felt that she was in love with Jim, she said:

"I'm tempted to say, of course, and I do love him tremendously. My whole life is built around him, and I'm sure that if you'd asked me that question during our most unsettled, if not actually stormy, second year, I'd have said yes without hesitation. But my feelings for Jim are not the kind of thing you read about in romantic stories. I don't know how I'd feel if I suspected he was having an affair with his secretary, or losing interest in me, but as things stand, I say I am not 'in love' with Jim, but rather feel a very deep, very solid love and affection for my husband and the father of my precious babies."

At the other extreme of the scale from the ordinary and relatively peaceful tale of Lou and Jim was Terry's story of her unilateral passion for Norman Altern.

For as long as she could remember, even as a child of eight or ten, Terry had always been in love with someone. In sixth grade, she had had a "terrible crush" on Smithy Adams, the most popular boy in the school, and the valedictorian at graduation. Although she hardly knew Smithy and had only one date with him, and that more or less by accident, she had filled her diary with descriptions of the clothes he wore, the "way he smiled," and what he said to her during "chance" encounters on the street. In fact, she had found a long and out-of-the-way route to and from school which increased the probability of those meetings, although, despite her efforts, they happened infrequently. "He doesn't know I exist, but yes I love him with all my heart," she wrote in her diary at age 16. Eventually, of course, there were others who followed each other in close succession, since the pain of one love seemed only to cease with the advent of the next.

"I was always more or less in love. Even when the man showed little interest, I would find myself totally involved. It wasn't as painful as it probably sounds, because whenever I knew I would see him, even if only at a public gathering, I would spend my time imagining things that *might* happen and doing everything I could think of in the way of preparation—hairdressers, shopping for clothes, trying out a new lipstick. Those activities made me feel really happy in a way. Sometimes I was happier when something *might* happen, like when Bill *might* be at the skating rink on Saturday night—than when I was actually with whichever man was 'right' at that time."

Norman Altern was the "right" person from the moment Terry heard him speak at a meeting about seven years prior to the interview. For a time he seemed to agree, and they enjoyed an intense and passionate relationship in which they were together every evening, talked on the phone once or twice daily as well, and gave every evidence to themselves, to each other and to their friends, of beginning an enduring match. Then gradually, very gradually at first, Norman became less available. His work load was getting heavy, he said he didn't have time. There was someone important he had to see, there might be a job in it; he had to get a paper finished; and so on. After each defection, Norman would, at least in the early days, return to Terry the next night or, later on, the next week with excuses, promises, and declarations of love and affection. But as time passed, their relationship drastically altered. Finally, Terry saw Norman only every two or three weeks, and sometimes those meetings were only for lunch or to attend a meeting together. Rumors of other women in Norman's life were eventually confirmed by her own eyes when she happened on him and "his latest" in a restaurant.

"Someone else might have kicked and screamed, or threatened suicide, or something, but I knew it was already too late for that. If I had complained, that would have been the complete end. I left the restaurant and cried for three days, but never said a word. When he called a week or so later, I acted as if nothing had happened, as if I didn't care, and as if I had other interests, too. I was desperately trying to win him back but I felt the only way I had a chance was by not making a scene, by keeping our friendship, and by being good in bed for him. It's been like that ever since. As far as he is concerned, I'm a really good friend, understanding, sympathetic, fun to be with. He doesn't know how I feel and never will if I can help it, because if he did, I'd simply lose him forever. I know him. In a way, he's my whole life. As things stand, even if he married I wouldn't lose him completely. I'm important to him. It's not what I want. Sometimes, if I let myself, I almost go crazy longing for him. It's a real physical ache. I feel as if I'd like to tear myself in two. Sometimes I use a tranquilizer to relieve the pain of it. I don't dare drink. I did once and found myself telephoning him. I'd have told him how I really felt if he'd answered the phone. Thank God he was out. I shook with fear next day when I realized what I'd almost done."

Interviews with people like Terry, whose involvement was "unrequited," encouraged me to focus on the individual experience of being in love rather than on whatever interactions were occurring between the lovers. Today I count that strategy as another very lucky break.

Although I had rejected the idea that romantic love as Terry, Marilyn, Fred, Bill, and so many others had experienced it was the result of pathology in their personalities, I still more or less expected that there would be certain discernible temperaments or other characteristics more closely associated with a tendency to fall in love than others. But as the interviews continued, so many people who differed greatly from each other described such similar subjective states, that I was more and more inclined toward the opposite generalization: that the state of being in love could happen to anyone regardless of other aspects of their situations or personalities. On that score I was in for a real surprise.

What I have come to look back on as a kind of "theoretical breakthrough" took place during a transatlantic flight from Paris to New York. I had just finished filming an interview with the French writer, Simone de Beauvoir. My friend and traveling companion, Helen Payne, was considering writing about the lifelong relationship between Beauvoir and existentialist philosopher, Jean-Paul Sartre. Since Beauvoir had written romantic novels and essays that dealt with love, it seemed an appropriate topic of conversation. I must confess that Helen gave evidence of considerably less interest in romantic love than I. In retrospect, I am quite sure that the conversation would never have taken place had it not been for the unusual combination of circumstances that included her being more or less trapped with me for several hours.

As I recounted the details of some of my interviews and compared them with characters in Beauvoir's novels, I became increasingly aware of Helen's distaste for the topic. I am forced to admit a certain social insensitivity on my part, as I allowed my enthusiasm to override her growing discomfort. Finally, unable to tolerate it longer, she blurted out what had been troubling her. This person whom I had known for many years and with whom I had had many conversations on topics of common interest, had never experienced a reaction that resembled what I had been describing, and this despite two marriages, several children, and an active sex life with various partners following her divorce. She said that she had always found puzzling what appeared to her as extravagant exaggeration in the media portrayal of romantic love. Furthermore, she had on many occasions been annoyed and inconvenienced by pressures on her to conform to the demands for attentiveness and exclusivity of husbands and lovers. "They seemed to care excessively about everything I did, as if I were going to run off or something. I always kept appointments and hoped we would have a good time together, but nothing was ever enough for them."

Describing the intricacies of romantic attachments to Helen was like trying to describe the color red to one blind from birth. "It doesn't make sense," she would say. "I simply don't understand how anyone could feel like that, how anyone could be so important to another person." She described her confusion over the strange "positive" behavior of persons in love with her. Their claims of ecstasy were as incomprehensible as was their obvious suffering. At one point she consulted a psychotherapist, who assured her that if she were only able to conquer her "neurosis," love would some day come to her as to others. That experience left her feeling no better, only more perplexed.

Had Helen not been a person with whom I had many times before held serious, honest, and problem-solving conversations, I might never have recognized the implications of what she told me. What Helen described was for me at that time inconceivable: a person who showed no signs at all of having experienced a complex reaction that others had described in very similar ways. The "interview" with Helen rendered suspect much other data that had been collected, but, above all, by discovering someone who admitted to no experience whatsoever with what would be called "limerence," I discovered the state itself. It was not the first time in human thought that the existence of an entity was clearly revealed for the first time under the special conditions of its absence.

Actually, Helen's failure to experience the phenomenon of romantic love, even in a mild or partial degree, turned out not to be rare at all. In the months to follow, such individuals began to appear regularly among interviewees. That they had not done so before was the joint result of my having been blinded by my expectations and of the problem of terminology.

What I really had discovered was a certain state that some people were in much of the time, others in some of the time, but still others never in, or at least not yet. Because of my high regard for Helen Payne, the first person I knew who had not experienced this state, I adopted the view that never being in this state was neither more nor less pathological than experiencing it. I wanted to be able to speak about this reliably identifiable condition without giving love's advocates the feeling something precious was being destroyed. Even more important, if using the term "love" denoted the presence of the state, there was the danger that absence of the state would receive negative connotations. People like Helen Payne also referred to their relationships, and to their feelings for persons important to them, as "love affairs" with persons whom they "loved." There was no way around it; a new term had to be found.

Many writers on love have complained about semantic difficulties.[4] The dictionary lists two dozen different meanings of the word "love." And how does one distinguish between love and affection, liking, fondness, caring, concern, infatuation, attraction, or desire? The Group was overwhelmingly of the opinion that loving and liking refer to quite different feelings, but what, precisely, constitutes the difference? Acknowledgment of a distinction between love as a verb, as an action taken by the individual, and love as a state is awkward. Never having fallen in love is not at all a matter of not loving, if loving is defined as caring. Furthermore, this state of "being in love" included feelings that do not properly fit with love defined as concern. As de Rougement said, being in love is not the same. One is a state; the other, an act, and an act is chosen, not something merely endured.[5]

I coined the word "limerence." It was pronounceable and seemed to me and to two students to have a "fitting" sound.[6] To be in the state of limerence is to feel what is usually termed "being in love." It appears that love and sex can coexist without limerence, in fact that any of the three may exist without the others. Human beings are extremely sensitive to each other and easily bruised by rejection or made joyful when given signs of appreciation. When a friendship runs into difficulties, we suffer; when we are able to share our lives with others in the pleasure of what is perceived as mutual understanding and concern, we are strengthened. The person who is not limerent toward you may feel great affection and concern for you, even tenderness, and possibly sexual desire as well. A relationship that includes no limerence may be a far more important one in your life, when all is said and done, than any relationship in which you experienced the strivings of limerent passion. Limerence is not in any way preeminent among types of human attractions or interactions; but when limerence is in full force, it eclipses other relationships.

2

The Individual Experience of Limerence

Limerence enters your life pleasantly. Someone takes on a special meaning. It may be an old friend unexpectedly seen in a new way. Or it may be a new person, someone who only a week before, perhaps just yesterday, was unknown to you.

Many of my interviewees recalled the first moment of limerent feeling. Sometimes the reaction was so clear that it is no wonder the ancients believed it was brought about through the intervention of a magical or supernatural force—a love potion, a dart from Cupid's bow, the enchantment cast by a sorcerer. When I asked those who had experienced the state, they could only say *when* it began; on the score of why, the answer was "I must have been ready for it," or, even more often, "I have no idea." I don't mean to imply that they were uninterested in the answer. As Marvin, a mathematics student from a major university in the Northeastern United States said:

"I guess it was time. For one thing, it was spring. Maybe that really does affect things. I've heard there are more suicides in

April. I had been literally submerged in work all winter, I had pretty much got over the affair with Joyce, and I looked up from my books and there was Marilyn. It was an immediate reaction—on both parts, or so it seemed at the time. I would say that within a week—less than that, within three days—my whole world had been transformed. It had a new center, and that center was Marilyn."

Why limerence occurs at one time and place and has one person rather than another as its object could not be determined either by questionnaires or by retrospective accounts given in interviews. Some informants found themselves in love at a time when, by their accounts, it was furthest from their thoughts or expectations or even hopes. Some act on the part of the other person, some look or word or gesture that is interpreted to indicate possible responsiveness, seems necessary, even if it is only imagined. Limerence is, above all else, mental activity. It is an interpretation of events, rather than the events themselves. You admire, you are physically attracted, you see, or think you see (or deem it possible to see under "suitable" conditions), the hint of possible reciprocity, and the process is set in motion.

A young man whom I will call Teddy told of the first evening of his limerence for Sue:

"I think I noticed Sue and felt physically attracted the minute I entered the room that evening. When I saw her dance, I was also impressed with her extraordinary talent. At that point I was ripe, and when she gave me that look, I succumbed totally. We danced together several times and I was in seventh heaven. At the time, I wasn't thinking, I'm in love with Sue. I was just thoroughly enjoying the situation. I was also noticing everything about her. And everything was beautiful, especially the fact that she seemed to be having the same experience."

You suddenly feel a sparkle of interest in somebody else, an interest fed by the image of returned feeling. Maybe the eyes lock. The eyes, as we shall see again and again, are so important in limerence that they, not the genitals or even the heart, may be called the organs of love. In any case, the beginning is a transformation that is sometimes so distinct that the French use the term *coup de foudre,* or thunderbolt.

Sometimes, on the other hand, limerence sneaks up on you. At the time, you insist that it has not in fact occurred, and it is only later, in ever repeated retrospection, that *the moment* is recognized for what it was: the beginning of a state of consciousness that, if experienced for the first time, is utterly unlike anything else that has ever happened.

A middle-aged professor, whom I will call Dr. Vesteroy, recounted the following:

"Dr. Ashton had remained in my office after the faculty meeting, apparently writing out some of her thoughts. I thought absolutely nothing of it at the time except to note, in an entirely detached manner, the way one regards a painting or an impressive landscape, that she was an attractive woman and we were quite fortunate to have her as a new addition to the department, not only because of her superb professional credentials but because of the aesthetic uplift she provides as well. I was amused at the thought but that was all. I was much more interested in her research findings than in the way the sunlight caused those little sparkles in her hair. (Obviously I had noticed them.) And I was rather taken by the intensity of her concentration as she wrote. That was all. I mean I wasn't actually staring at her. I was merely waiting for her to finish so I could put through a telephone call to that publisher whose textbooks in American history still had not come in. It was already the third week of the semester.

"Suddenly, Dr. Ashton—Elena her name is—looked up and seemed startled to find herself the only leftover from the meeting. She flushed a bit and gathered her things saying that she hoped she had not kept me. Then just before she went out, she looked at me and smiled! It was that smile and that look that started the whole thing off, and I still find the whole thing embarrassing to speak of; but I had this flash, this thrill, a running sensation of excitement, and I don't even remember what I said. It was not, and I emphasize, it was not a matter of actually believing either then or now that she had *on that occasion* deliberately delayed her departure or had any romantic ideas of me. It was ridiculous to think anything at all, but the fact was that I felt strongly at the time, even that first time, that some spark of communication had passed between us and that it was communication of a very personal and delightful sort. But I forgot it. By the time I had the publishers on the line, Dr. Ashton was entirely out of my mind, at least for the moment. It was only much later that I recognized that that smile had actually been the beginning."

Although I can only speculate on the mystery of what makes limerence strike here rather than there, or at this time rather than another, what happens during limerence, what it feels like, and what it makes you do and desire are clear. A constellation of features constitute an experience that has a certain "wholeness" about it. One thing is certain. Limerence is not mere sexual attraction. Although something you may interpret as sexual attraction may be, or seem to be, the first feeling, sometimes nothing you would label sexual interest is ever consciously felt. Sex is neither essential nor, in itself, adequate to satisfy the limerent need. But sex is never entirely excluded in the limerent passion, either. Limerence is a desire for *more* than sex, and a desire in which the sexual act may represent the symbol of its highest achievement: reciprocation. Reciprocation expressed through physical union creates the ecstatic and blissful condition called "the greatest happiness," and the most profound glorification of the achievement of limerent aims.

ECSTATIC UNION

It is surely limerence that has caused writers to expound in passages like these:

And Jacob served seven years for Rachel; and they seemed unto him but a few days, for the love he had for her.

—Genesis 1:6–14 [1]

The speaking in a perpetual hyperbole is comely in nothing but in love.

—Francis Bacon [2]

[Love is] the greatest happiness that can exist.

—Stendhal [3]

The face of all the world is changed, I think,
Since first I heard the footsteps of thy soul
Move still, oh still, beside me, as they stole
Betwixt me and the dreadful outer brink
Of obvious death, where I, who thought to sink,
Was caught up into love, and taught the whole
Of a new rhythm.

—Elizabeth Barrett Browning [4]

Love is a human religion in which another person is believed in.

—Robert Seidenberg [5]

I felt as though the clouds were not on the horizon but under my feet. How sweet it was.

—Liv Ullmann [6]

Yearned for, dreamed about, and, for the fortunate, reveled in, limerence inspires even ordinary persons to verbal excess. It is called the "supreme delight," "the pleasure that makes life worth living," "the experience that takes the sting from dying." It has been said to power the very revolution of the planet.

A young woman who allowed me to tape-record our talk said:

"I remember that Simone de Beauvoir used the term 'ecstatic union' and I kept thinking those words at the time. Almost from the very first moment when Rick looked into my eyes—so deeply, he didn't merely look *at* me—I thought that word. 'Ecstasy.' After our first night together, I woke up with this strange and wonderful feeling like nothing describable or nothing I had ever felt before. Problems, troubles, inconveniences of living that would normally have occupied my thoughts became unimportant. I looked at them over a huge gulf of sheer happiness. I even enjoyed the prospect of dealing with them—with Rick. The landlord had given me notice and the bank loan had not gone through, and I could not bring myself to care! Whatever happened, it would be wonderful somehow.

"My delight in simply existing eclipsed everything else, and I literally could scarcely feel the ground as I walked. In some ways, my perceptions grew stronger. Colors seemed more brilliant. The warmth of the sunlight on my arm as I drove to work was so acutely pleasurable that I marveled at never before appreciating it. I relived our moments of intimacy as I drove—the loving pressure of Rick's arms around me, the softness of his lips, and, most of all, his eyes. His look was an embrace.

"I could recall every word he had said, even the most ordinary things. I glowed and the world glowed back at me. When I stopped for a red light, I waved at children playing in the street and they waved back. It was as if they somehow shared my experience, almost as if in some way, they—everyone—*knew*.

"At the office, I could hardly keep from shouting out how deliriously happy I felt. The work was easy; things that had annoyed me on previous occasions were taken in stride. And I had strong impulses to help others; I wanted to share my joy. When Mary's typewriter broke down, I virtually sprang to my feet to assist. Mary! My former 'enemy'! No one was an enemy anymore! My affection included the universe. I loved every single creature. A fly landed on my desk, I hadn't the heart to brush it away."

A similar reaction viewed by another was reported in an interview with a client whose son's severe depression had been one of her chief concerns. Now he had become "involved" with a woman. Ms. Verne described the situation:

"Mary was a little dumpy 35-year-old with two children, just about the last person I would have wanted or expected Ted to have anything to do with. I didn't see what they could have in common. I didn't even ask. Whatever it was he liked about her, she was obviously responsible for a highly beneficial change in him. It was undeniable. For the first time in years, he was actually cheerful! He whistled as he got dressed in the morning, and when he came into the kitchen he almost bounced. He'd put his arm around me and say, 'What's good for breakfast, Mom? I'm famished.' "

"While he ate, he chatted about the garden, the cat, what he planned to do that day. It was a metamorphosis. He changed almost overnight from a morose and sullen child to a happy, mature, and responsible adult. And how could I be jealous when he treated me so lovingly? It was like magic."

The Group tended to agree with this inflated evaluation of "love." Ninety-five percent called love "a beautiful experience." Eighty-six percent said that "the support and companionship of a member of the opposite sex is very important to me," and "I enjoy being in love." Eighty-three percent felt that "anyone who has never been in love is missing one of life's most pleasurable experiences," and 61 percent were "happiest" when in love. Even 42 percent were willing to go as far as agreeing that "being in love is like living on top of a cloud."

Limerence may begin as a barely perceptible feeling of increased interest in a particular person but one which if nurtured by appropriate conditions can grow to enormous intensity. In most cases, it also declines, eventually to zero or to a low level. At this low level, limerence is either transformed through reciprocation or it is transferred to another person, who then becomes the object of a new limerent passion. Under the best of conditions, the waning of limerence through mutuality is accompanied by the growth of the emotional response more suitably described as love. In either case, as the poets have acknowledged, the state is an inconstant one.

Limerence has certain basic components:
• intrusive thinking about the object of your passionate desire (the limerent object or "LO"), who is a possible sexual partner
• acute longing for reciprocation

- dependency of mood on LO's actions or, more accurately, your interpretation of LO's actions with respect to the probability of reciprocation
- inability to react *limerently* to more than one person at a time (exceptions occur only when limerence is at low ebb—early on or in the last fading)
- some fleeting and transient relief from unrequited limerent passion through vivid imagination of action by LO that means reciprocation
- fear of rejection and sometimes incapacitating but always unsettling shyness in LO's presence, especially in the beginning and whenever uncertainty strikes
- intensification through adversity (at least, up to a point)
- acute sensitivity to any act or thought or condition that can be interpreted favorably, and an extraordinary ability to devise or invent "reasonable" explanations for why the neutrality that the disinterested observer might see is in fact a sign of hidden passion in the LO
- an aching of the "heart" (a region in the center front of the chest) when uncertainty is strong
- buoyancy (a feeling of walking on air) when reciprocation seems evident
- a general intensity of feeling that leaves other concerns in the background
- a remarkable ability to emphasize what is truly admirable in LO and to avoid dwelling on the negative, even to respond with a compassion for the negative and render it, emotionally if not perceptually, into another positive attribute.

It occasionally occurred, although rarely, that an attraction was described to me which seemed to fit the limerent pattern in all ways except that the informant felt no initial inclination toward physical union. Despite those few exceptions, I am inclined toward the generalization that sexual attraction is an essential component of limerence. This sexual feeling may be combined with shyness, impotence or some form of sexual dysfunction or disinclination, or with some social unsuitability. But LO, in order to become LO, must stand in relation to the limerent as one for whom the limerent is a potential sex partner.

Sexual attraction is not "enough," to be sure. Selection standards for limerence are, according to informants, not identical to those by which "mere" sexual partners are evaluated, and sex is seldom the main focus of limerence. Either the potential for sexual mating is felt to be there, however, or the state described is not limerence.

Limerents (those who are experiencing the state at a given time) sometimes vacillate between two or more possible LOs during the earliest stages. Jill, for example, thought for a time that she might be in love with both Al and Rudi:

"Whether 'it' was Al or Rudi depended on their actions. Like the song goes, I preferred the one I was with. There was definitely something special with both of them, but they were running neck and neck for a long time, a time which was really quite pleasant. But one weekend, the situation was shifted. Al was out and Rudi was in. The scales had tipped. After that, it was a matter of only about two weeks before I really had it bad.

"On Friday I was supposed to go out with Al, but he called to say he couldn't make it. He sounded strange and didn't give a reason. I was a little disappointed, but that was okay. I spent the evening watching TV with Mom and Dad. Then around eleven o'clock—we were watching the news—the doorbell rang. Al was there with his brother, and both were very drunk. They seemed to have no idea of the time and acted as if it were perfectly okay to come to the house at that hour. I was glad I was the one to answer the door, because it would have embarrassed me to have my parents see them.

"It seems that Al had lost a lot of money gambling and had had an opportunity, he thought, to win some of it back. That was why he had broken the date. Instead, he lost even more. He was very upset over this—as well as drunk—and he pleaded with me to say it was okay and that I'd marry him anyway."

Jill recoiled.

"Standing there looking at him, suddenly all I could think of was Rudi. I finally got them to leave, and as I closed the door, I knew that I was no longer attracted to Al at all. The next night, Rudi and I had an especially lovely evening."

Actually, the lovely evening had, as if by the design of a malevolent fate, included running into one of Rudi's old girlfriends, Meriam.

"I had never seen her before, although I knew about her. Rudi had told me that their relationship had been 'important' to him. I was unprepared, however, for her beauty. I noticed her instantly when we entered the room because she was so attractive. It really shook me up, and it might have had something to do with the intensity of the reaction I began to have."

For the process to develop fully, some form of uncertainty or doubt, or even some threat to reciprocation appears necessary. There is considerable evidence that an externally imposed obstacle, such as Romeo and Juliet met in the resistance of family and society, may also serve.

Several persons described the rejections they encountered when "throwing caution to the wind" and "wearing their hearts on their sleeves," they took the honest course of immediate, open declaration. Said one:

"I should have held back. I can see that now all too clearly. I was scared, but I felt I owed it to Fran to be honest. I was honest, and it was a mistake."

Indeed, too early a declaration on the limerent's part or, on the other hand, too early evidence of reciprocation on LO's part may prevent the development of the full limerent reaction. Something must happen to break a totally positive interaction. Not that totally positive reactions are without highly redeeming features in themselves; it is only that they stop the progression to full or maximum limerence.

In a situation similar to Jill's, Teddy's reaction intensified when Sue's lover, Gerald, arrived at the dance later that same evening.

"We were dancing together when I felt Sue sort of stiffen in my arms. She was looking at a tall blond and rather good-looking man who had just arrived. He marched right over to us with an air of ownership which seemed to make Sue feel conflicted. She introduced us, then excused herself to dance with him, and I was left for most of the rest of the evening to watch her from a distance. Every once in a while she seemed to search out my eyes, and just before they left, she gave me this long look which could only mean that her interest had not died completely just because Gerald had arrived on the scene."

That look was the flicker of hope that sustained, and even intensified, Teddy's limerent response to Sue; without Gerald's presence and the threat he posed, the initial pleasantness might have remained just that.

The degree of objective attractiveness necessary to initiate limerence varies considerably. The relative admiration you feel for your LO as compared with others may be based on peripheral, even trivial factors, which, however, like the moment of initial interest, tend to be remembered. The question "What did you especially admire in _____?" or "What particularly attracted you?" generally yielded a definite and specific response. Here are some samples:

"I liked Betty's hair. It was long and very dark brown with waves, the kind of hair that moved when she turned her head. I was always in love with her. That *was* love at first sight, even before I knew anything else about her. Then, and don't laugh, I know this will sound even more ridiculous, but I liked her white blouses. She was always wearing white, which was terrific against her hair. Of course, there were a lot of other things. The more I got to know her, the more things I found to like. She has a great sense of humor. She's poised and confident, even in tough situations. She's really bright. But when you asked just now, the first picture that came into my mind was that wonderful hair and those white tops she always wore."

"This is going to make me sound a bit daft, I know, but the first thing that attracted me—and I never stopped being attracted by it—was his height. Barry was exactly the same height I was, and I loved it. I don't care what they say about 'the man's supposed to be taller,' etc. I think being the same size—of course, he's heavier—is nice. It feels so close and, I don't know, equal. I also liked the fact that he played jazz piano and had a lot of friends who were musicians."

"I think I was attracted to Ruth because she, well, she isn't ugly, but she isn't what you'd call pretty, either. I guess you'll think I'm one in a million to feel that way, but it wasn't that I was attracted to her looks. Here was a woman who had made her way up the ladder to a pretty important position, and obviously she didn't do it on the basis of a pretty face. That meant there had to be a lot more to her than what met the eye, and I was intrigued. I wasn't disappointed, either. And maybe—after all, I'm no Clark Gable—I hoped that there was a better chance she'd go for me, too. That may have been part of it. It's hard to tell."

And so on. Some mentioned general character traits like "honesty," "forthrightness," or "intelligence"; others stressed physical characteristics. The certainty and specificity of many of the replies were impressive.

What features of LO are *truly* important? Can you become limerent about someone who is objectively *not* attractive? Although my interviewees tended to speak in glowing terms of their LOs, physical attractiveness was not always mentioned.

"I had known Phil for almost seven years without ever thinking of him as more than a friend, and not even as a close friend. But I had a good feeling about him as far as it went. He was cheerful and dependable—the kind of person you felt you could go screaming to if the world started crashing in. Knowing him, even slightly, was something of a comfort, Phil was what you'd call a natural leader. Everybody looked to him whenever they didn't know what to do. 'Lets go see what Phil thinks,' they'd say. I thought that was a marvelous trait. It really impressed me."

Typically, I did not meet my informants' LOs. But the importance of "visible features of the loved one" has frequently been discussed in the literature on love. Researchers John Money and Anke Ehrhardt found that sight of the face may alone elicit the reaction but that no aspect of a potential LO is indispensable, This, they note, helps to make human beings flexible so that attractiveness may be differently defined from society to society and from time to time—as well as from person to person.[7] Some psychologists stress the evidence that it is not absolute attractiveness but the match between you and your potential LO that matters.[8] In fact, Hilary claimed that it was his ugliness that attracted her to Bernard.

"It wasn't that I liked his homeliness per se. I didn't. Or, rather, I didn't see it as homeliness, but as an indication that he might become attracted to me. I fell in love with Bernard because I thought he might love me in return. I must also admit that his money and success and all the power that seemed to go with them probably also played a role."

PERCEPTION OF THE LIMERENT OBJECT

In 1822, French novelist Marie Henri Beyle, better known by his favorite pseudonym, Stendhal, published his highly personal, yet precisely analytical collection of essays on love, *De l'Amour.* Despite his attempts to disguise the actual people of whom he wrote, scholars easily discovered that Stendhal produced the work amid an enduring and hopeless passion for a Milanese woman named Métilde. His aim was to describe the experience of what he called "passionate love," partly in a search for explanation, partly perhaps to exorcise the painful emotion through literary dissection. The most renowned conceptualization from

De l'Amour was of the manner in which the object of passionate love was perceived, a process to which he gave the metaphorical term, "crystallization."

A branch of a tree, he said, if tossed into a salt mine and allowed to remain there for several months undergoes a metamorphosis. It remains a branch, or even just a twig, but the salt crystals transform it "into an object of shimmering beauty." In an analogous manner, although more quickly, the characteristics of the LO are crystallized by mental events in which LO's attractive characteristics are exaggerated and unattractive characteristics given little or no attention. According to Stendhal, you interpret LO in the most favorable light. You do not exactly misperceive, but rather focus your attention on the positive.[9] You seem unconcerned about the defects in what appears to the concerned outsider—friends and family—to be quite an unsuitable individual. Popular tradition has attributed this process to blindness (as in "love is blind"); it is really a matter of emphasis. The good qualities endlessly revisualized in the limerent consciousness are not pure inventions, but as the salt crystals on a twig magnify the attractive features of the twig,

... the original naked branch is no longer recognizable by indifferent eyes, because it now sparkles with perfections, or diamonds, which [others] do not see or which they simply *do not consider to be perfections.*[10]

Similarly you may seize on objectively trivial aspects of LO's appearance or behavior—a look in the eye, a way of walking, a hesitation in speech or a dialect, an article of clothing—and imbue it with meaning. LO's eyes reflect "intense concentration," "impassioned concern for the welfare of others," "empathic sorrow," "lively wit," "extreme intelligence," or "deep understanding." LO's walk suggests "gaiety," "seriousness of purpose," or "savoir faire." LO's manner of speech may seem aesthetically pleasurable; the way LO is attired reveals favorable aspects of character that might range from sophistication to disdain for current fashion or else it might suggest or reveal pleasing aspects of the underlying anatomy. However LO may appear to others, the limerent bias brings forth the positive and plays down the unfavorable.

Not only does limerence overemphasize and exaggerate what is actually positive, but neutral aspects of the person are perceived as charming and delightful. Said Terry:

"Once I fall, really fall, everything about her becomes wonderful, even things that would otherwise mean nothing at all are suddenly capable of evoking curiously positive reactions. I love her clothes, her walk, her handwriting (its illegibility would seem charming, or if it were clear and readable, that would be equally admirable), her car, her cat, her mother. Anything that she liked, I liked; anything that belonged to her acquired a certain magic. *Her* handbag, *her* notebook, *her* pencil. I abhor the sight of toothmarks on a pencil; they disgust me. But not *her* toothmarks. Hers were sacred; her wonderful mouth had been there. Did I worship the ground on which the woman I loved walked? You know, it's almost that bad!"

The "misperception" of the person experiencing romantic passion has been discussed by writers prior to and following Stendhal, who most often refer to "idealization."[11] But idealization differs from crystallization in its implication that the image is molded to fit a preformed, externally derived, or emotionally needed conception. In crystallization, the actual and existing features of LO merely undergo enhancement. Idealization implies that unattractive features are literally overlooked; in limerence these features are usually seen, but emotionally ignored. In a study of 2,000 couples, two-thirds of the men and three-fourths of the women were able to indicate their partner's character defects, physical defects and bad habits, e.g., nail-biting. Obviously, perception of these defects was not an impediment.[12] As Lenore said of Michael:

"Yes I knew he gambled, I knew he sometimes drank too much, and I knew he didn't read a book from one year to the next. *I knew* and I didn't know. I knew it but I didn't incorporate it into the overall image. I dwelt on his wavy hair, the way he looked at me, the thought of his driving to work in the morning, his charm (that I believed must surely affect everyone he met), the flowers he sent, the considerations he had shown to my sister's children at the picnic last summer, the feeling I had when we were in close physical contact, the way he mixed a martini, his laugh, the hair on the back of his hand. Okay! I know it's crazy, that my list of 'positives' sounds silly, but those *are* the things I think of, remember, and, yes, want back again!"

When crystallization has occurred, says Stendhal, "even the asperities of [LO] have an infinite grace."[13] It is not, as some contend, a blindness or self-deception,[14] but rather a taking of the person whole, even "loving in advance every disclosure which awaits there."[15] Because LO *is* LO, every feature is "divinely perfect,"[16] not perhaps in objective terms, but as measured by the emotional reaction. A character in one of Stendhal's novels felt sorry for LO's deficiencies as time went on.[17] The point is not how the deficiencies are perceived; they might be seen quite readily. It is the limerent's capacity to react positively to them once the limerence is in full swing and the gates of the mind have been closed to the possibility of a limerent reaction to anyone else.

Bill, a creative writing instructor, struggled with his images of Greta, a student:

"She is essentially invisible to me. I see my own construction, and sometimes my image of Greta alters without her doing anything, without my even seeing her or hearing anything new about her. I cannot assess the reasonableness or unreasonableness of my reactions to her literary compositions. How can I continue to feel so strongly when it seems apparent by objective standards, by the standards I would apply to anyone else, that her work is mediocre? But as soon as I say that, my head fills with objections to the idea. I make excuses—she has had an inadequate background, and the potential is there. I take anything that is less than terrible and blow it up into something of genius. But part of me knows that this glowing image is my own construction."

Those of you who have been an object of limerence, especially if you were unable to return the feeling, and those of you who have "recovered" from limerence only to find that the former objects of your passion had acquired previously underappreciated imperfections, realize that the limerent reaction may miss by a wide mark the truly important features of LO.

In the beginning I expected a degree of understandable resistance to referring to a person as an "object," although "love object" seems far less objectionable than does "sex object." I once mentioned my concern about using the word "object" in presenting limerence theory to a workshop group. One of the participants said that if ever the word "object" was appropriate it was here, because to the degree that your reaction to a person is limerent, you respond to *your construction* of LO's qualities.

INTRUSIVE THINKING

Limerence is first and foremost a condition of cognitive obsession. Stendhal wrote:

The most surprising thing of all about love is the first step, the violence of the change that takes place in [the] mind. . . . A person in love is unremittingly and uninterruptedly occupied with the image of [the] beloved.[18]

During the earliest stages of limerence, those who are experiencing it may sense only a general longing for love and may vacillate between two or more possible LOs. For example, Isabella, one of my interviewees, estimated that she spent almost two-thirds of her time desiring a "love." But the kind of speculation this desire produced was spread over five different men. She was "very attracted" to both Gary and Bill and thought she might be falling in love with either of them. She also admired Jim and Al in a special way, although she was not really attracted romantically. She was somewhat more interested in Lou. A week later, after a special moment with Bill, her limerence for him developed fully. Bill was now the only one of the five to occupy her mind, and he did so almost totally. She no longer thought of the others as potential partners; in fact, she rarely thought of them.

Just as all roads once led to Rome, when your limerence for someone has crystallized, all events, associations, stimuli, experience return your thoughts to LO with unnerving consistency. At the moment of awakening after the night's sleep, an image of LO springs into your consciousness. And you find yourself inclined to remain in bed pursuing that image and the fantasies that surround and grow out of it. Your daydreams persist throughout the day and are involuntary. Extreme effort of will to stop them produces only temporary surcease.

In a diary I was given, someone complained,

"This obsession has infected my brain. I cannot shake those constantly intruding thoughts of you. Every thought winds back to you no matter how hard I try to direct its course in other directions."

It is not entirely pleasant, this obsession. Mary Wollstonecraft wrote in a letter to William Godwin, "Get ye gone, Intruder!" [19]

If you encounter objects, people, places or situations associated with LO, those associations are vivid. "There was the park bench we sat on." An ad in the newspaper recalls the department store in which you met. "That was the song we danced to last year." "Ah, yes, that was [LO]'s favorite topic, wine, composer, sport or perfume."

The connections need not be logical or even close. It is not the "other thing" that reminds one of LO, but rather that the perpetual presence of LO in your head defines all other experience in relationship to that presence. If a certain thought has no previous connection with LO, you immediately make one. You wonder or imagine what LO would think of the book in your hand, the scene you are witnessing, the fortune or misfortune that is befalling you. You find yourself visualizing how you will tell about it, how LO will respond, what will be said between you, and what actions will—or might—take place in relation to it. As you engage in the ordinary tasks that constitute your daily activities, you invent intricate scenarios for possibly upcoming events. Endlessly, you plan the next encounter going over every detail of exactly what you will do in order to improve your image in LO's eyes. You imagine LO's reaction and your further responses. The widely acclaimed movie *Rocky* portrays this feature of limerence well in the scene in which actor Sylvestor Stallone stands before a mirror in his room rehearsing a joke about turtles he has invented to impress Adrienne, the young woman who works in the pet shop.

You hope and you anticipate. You recall with vividness what LO said and did. You search out alternative meanings of those behaviors. It's as if each word and gesture is permanently available for review, especially those which can be interpreted as evidence in favor of "return of feeling."

When Larry walked Margaret home one evening, they paused for a few moments before her door while she searched for her key. He observed her mild frustration as she rummaged among the jumble of items in her handbag. Finally successful, she looked at him, held the key up for him to see, and complained, "I'm so disorganized. Tomorrow I am going to get rid of some of this junk that's getting in my way all the time." Then she grinned and playfully poked him in the side with her elbow. "Hey," she said, "it was a great concert. I really enjoyed it." And then she turned and left him.

All during the following day, Larry found himself reviewing the events of the night before. Margaret's face was almost as clear to him in his daydreams as it had been in the reality of her presence. He could smell her perfume. But above all, he recalled that final moment, that wonderful touch of her arm in his ribs, and the way she looked at him when she found the key. He tried to analyze the feelings behind her comments. Why had she not asked him in for a cup of coffee or a drink? She had to go in to work early. Her mother had not been feeling well, and she wanted to telephone. She was afraid of appearing too forward, too eager. Every thought of Margaret made her more beautiful, more admirable, more desirable in Larry's eyes.

To others, his behavior that next day appeared quite normal, but in fact Larry's mind was so totally occupied with thoughts of Margaret, with reviewing and analyzing the events of the previous evening, and with anticipating events that might occur in the future, that only his external actions could in any sense be considered ordinary.

In his limerence, Larry's preoccupation was almost 100 percent. Only the most habitual actions were easily accomplished. It was near torture to wrench his mind free of Margaret in order to deal effectively with his work. As soon as he could, he returned to his limerent mooning. He sought out moments of solitude in which he could pursue his daydreams undisturbed.

The compulsive daydreams that dominate the limerent's consciousness are clearly directed toward a goal. You imagine a possible meeting, the conversation that might take place and your fantasies all lead toward a moment of mutuality, of the expression of returned feelings, and it is this and not any particular action that is the goal or "moment of consummation" of the limerent fantasy.

Because limerent fantasy depends on how you actually perceive reality, its content, which leads up to and renders plausible the ecstatic finale, varies not only from person to person, but from day to day as new knowledge becomes available. A young man told of his limerent reaction to a co-worker, Evelyn:

"It was like you read about but I never thought really happened. Her first day on the job and boom! Just like that. I took one look, as they say . . . Oh, well, maybe that is not entirely accurate. That's how it seems as I look back on it. Maybe at first it was just, wow, what a doll! Maybe it took a couple of looks. Maybe a couple of days, but it wasn't long. It was certainly a fixed thing by the time she'd been working in the office a week. I couldn't believe it and I tried to deny it. I'd had attractions before, but this thing was something that was in my head every minute—even before we had ever spoken to each other.

"Every night I planned a whole campaign for the next day. Evelyn sat three desks away, and I could see her without being too obvious when I turned sideways to my file cabinet. You wouldn't believe what a file keeper I became! And after I had watched her for a while, I calculated just when to get up and leisurely arrive at the coffee machine just before she got there. I was very concerned about not appearing stupid and overeager.

"After the third or fourth day, we had our first conversation when the machine ran out of cream and I recommended the hot chocolate. The next day, she asked me if I had any spare change because she only had dollar bills, and it continued that way for a few weeks—casual, but friendly.

"That was on the outside. In my mind I was rehearsing the big moment when I'd suggest we have dinner together and imagine these complex situations that would bring it off. Every time I learned something more about her, I'd incorporate that into my daydream. For example, I first thought of, you know, inviting her to my place to listen to jazz records, and we'd be off and running from there. Then I found out she was a classical musical student and I went into this big idea about getting a pair of super concert tickets through my brother-in-law whose uncle plays the oboe in some orchestra."

Limerent fantasies do not necessarily cease when an actual relationship begins. They may diminish *or increase* in frequency, depending on circumstances. Hilda and Stu had been seeing each other for several months, during which her limerence had not diminished at all.

"Really, it got worse. Stu and I would usually spend the weekend together at his place, and he'd call on Wednesday or Thursday to finalize the plans. My week was spent thinking about what had happened during the previous weekend and trying to plan what would happen during the next one. I don't mean that all I did was lie around thinking about it, but it was a constant part of my thinking no matter what else was going on.

"A lot of it was planning conversations. If I saw a movie or read a book, I'd think about telling Stu about it, actually work out impressive sentences which I'd try to memorize. As I drove to work, I'd imagine that he was in the seat next to me and I'd comment on the scenery, on how I felt about various things. Sometimes I'd sing—I really have a good voice, I think, but I've *never* sung when anyone else could hear me—and I'd pretend that Stu was listening and admiring and falling more in love with me every minute."

During limerent's height of intensity, thoughts of LO are both persistent and intrusive. Martin, a business executive in his early fifties, found himself enamored of a young woman in the office. It was an unwanted condition. Not only was he married, even happily so, although no longer "in love" with his wife, but his good sense told him that however desirable and lovely Emily might be, their lives could not be joined. She was 25 years younger and surely wanted to have her own family. In addition, she had not responded with any indication of romantic interest in him. He wrote in his diary, the only outlet for his turmoil at the time:

"I am advancing toward the thesis that this attraction for Emily is a kind of biological, instinct-like action that is not under voluntary or logical control. I don't mean to imply that it is a purely sexual attraction. I only wish it were! That would be easy—well, relatively easy—to take care of.

"But I don't direct this thing, this attraction, to Emily. It directs me. I try desperately to argue with it, to limit its influence, to channel it (into sex, for example), to deny it, to enjoy it and, yes, dammit, to make her respond! Even though I know that Emily and I have absolutely no chance of making a life together, the thought of her is an obsession. I am in the position of passionately wanting someone I don't want at all and could find no use for if I had her.

"And as irrational as is my desire, it is then compounded by her doing little things that drag me even deeper into the quagmire. Her look when we pass each other in the hallway can send me into an ecstasy of belief that she feels as I do. Then I begin to long for her so intensely that only fantasy, that thief of work and time, that treacherous devil, can give me the barest moment of relief. And so I moon about when I should be conducting the serious affairs of my position. On top of this incessant desire is guilt. I can't shake the feeling that I have a choice even though I persist in not exercising it. The illogic of my state screams at me, but the force of it always overpowers my feeble attempts at resistance. How dumb it all is! How imperative!

"And when I read back in my diary and am forced to recall how much hopefulness and energy I had put into upcoming events that turned out to be without significance, I embarrass myself in my own eyes. I am forced to see Emily realistically. A nice young woman, but not for me. But it does no good. A few minutes later I am lost again in romantic daydreams.

"And a very strange aspect of my fantasies, beside their persistence against my will, is that they often leave me suspended, paralyzed, as it were, just at the very moment before my goal is achieved. I never quite "get there." Although I enjoy the fantasy enormously, it is not necessary to imagine, for example, sex with Emily (in fact, it is almost distasteful, as if it would be disrespectful of her). My pleasure in the daydream reaches its culmination at the point at which some word or look or touch indicates that all else is possible, that it will happen. It is not necessary that I imagine its actually occurring."

This was repeatedly expressed during the interviews. The "moment of consummation," the goal, the climax of the limerence fantasy, is not sexual union but emotional commitment on the part of LO. Even when the limerent fantasy included sexual elements, it retained characteristics that distinguished it clearly from a sexual fantasy per se.

A classic limerent fantasy involves an unusual, often tragic, event. The following are the thoughts of a high school sophomore in love with Vera, a girl he has secretly been limerent about all year, a week before the annual spring picnic:

"At the picnic a bunch of the guys decide to scare the girls with their motorbikes. About six of them come barreling down in the direction of the picnic area. At this moment, Vera is returning from a walk with her five-year-old cousin, Nancy. Just as the bikes approach, the child runs in the direction of the picnic area and into the path of the bikes. Vera screams and I rush forward, pick up Nancy, and run. Before I reach Vera, I step into a snake's nest and am fatally injured. With Nancy still in my arms, I limp toward Vera. I put Nancy on the ground with care and then collapse at Vera's feet. She takes my head in her lap while others rush for aid. Tears are streaming down her face. Although I am in great pain, and know it is hopeless to try to save me because doctors have told me that any snake bite would kill me because of an allergy, I manage just one sentence: 'Vera, I love you.' As I breathe my last breath, I hear her answer, 'I love you, too, Jim, I always have.' "

It is very hard to explain to one who has never been limerent how such a tragic daydream can provide a kind of pleasure, but it can. In another recurrent limerent fantasy, the limerent receives news that death is near. LO learns of this and rushes to the limerent's side to confess mutuality. In more sophisticated form, such fantasies are the stuff of fiction. Cathy and Heathcliff are mutual limerents prevented a life together by circumstances. Her death scene recalls the limerent fantasy given above. A similar death scene occurs in the opera *La Traviata*.

In summary, limerent fantasy is, most of all, intrusive and inescapable. It seems not to be something you do, but something *that happens.* Most involuntary are the flash visions in which LO is reciprocating. Compelling, seductive, tempting, or even, as one man described them, "tantalizing," the longer limerent fantasy is a deliberate attempt to achieve relief of the limerent yearning through imagining consummation in a context of possible events. Limerent fantasy is unsatisfactory unless firmly rooted in reality. Sometimes it is retrospective; actual events are replayed in memory. This form predominates when what is viewed as evidence of possible reciprocation can be reexperienced. Otherwise, the long fantasy is anticipatory; it begins in your everyday world and climaxes at the attainment of the limerent goal. The intrusive "flashes" may be symbolic; you find LO's indication of returned feelings expressed by a look, a word, a handclasp, or embrace. The long fantasies form a bridge between your ordinary life and that intensely desired ecstatic moment. The two types of fantasy are ends of a continuum, not mutually exclusive. The duration and complexity of a fantasy often seem to depend on how much time and freedom from distraction is available. The bliss of the imagined moment of consummation is greater when events imagined to precede it are believed in. In fact, of course, they often represent grave departures from the probable, as an outside observer might estimate them.

THE COURSE OF LIMERENCE

The course of true love never did run smooth [20]

Scientific analysis is greatly aided by quantification, even when numbers are merely used to indicate subjective evaluations.[21] People are surprisingly good at making such evaluations and at expressing them numerically. Try, for example, greeting people with the following question: "On a ten-point scale, where perfect health, maximum vitality, and ecstatic joyfulness are represented by the number ten and suicidal depression by the number one, how do you feel today?" You will undoubtedly find as I have that although the question gives rise to amusement, an answer is often given readily, sometimes with instantaneous refinement of the scale, as in "Oh, I would say, maybe, six-and-a-half."

Using a similar approach, I have asked people to describe their current degree of limerent intensity: "If every moment of your waking day not by necessity consumed by other matters is spent in limerent fantasy, let that be 100 percent. At the other end of the scale, call it zero if regardless of how much free thinking time you have in a day, not one moment of it is so engaged." From the results of such inquiries, it appears that limerence percentage is as readily assessed as is a feeling of general well-being.

During most of the period from the beginning of his limerence for a young Frenchwoman, Laura, until his departure for the United States, one of my first interviewees estimated that his limerence consistently averaged 85 percent. As Fred put it:

"Thinking thoughts of Laura intruded while I was working, and it was that struggle with myself that, I suppose, was one of the most unpleasant aspects of the thing. As far as free time was concerned, while shaving, walking about, waiting for sleep to come at night—this was often at 100 percent. On a couple of occasions, especially after Laura had been particularly unfriendly, my limerence would take a sharp, unfortunately temporary, drop, sometimes going as low as 20 percent. When I got back home, the average went down, gradually, to maybe 60 percent the first month, 50 percent the second, and it leveled off, by the time I met Linda, to 10 percent or less. But don't get the impression that it was a consistent downward progression. Sometimes, even after I had been back in the United States for four months, I would occasionally have days at 90 percent."

Other informants also had no trouble at all describing their limerence intensity in numbers. Limerence's most reliable attribute, the characteristic that more than any other differentiates it from other states of attraction and affection that are also described by the phrase "being in love," is the intrusiveness of the preoccupation with LO. Judging by my interviewees' estimate of how much time they spent thinking about LO, I could describe their limerence as varying from zero to 100 percent.[22] It appears that although the direction of feeling—happy vs. unhappy—shifts rapidly, the intensity of limerence, measured through intensive reverie, alters less rapidly, and alters only in response to an accumulation of experiences with the particular LO.

For example, Margrit, a 36-year-old sportswriter, met Bert on March 6th, and by the next day, her preoccupation percentage had gone up to 15 percent (she thought about him 15 percent of the time). He telephoned her that day. The day after that, on the 8th, it rose to 20 percent. That evening they had their first date, which was successful enough to bring her preoccupation up to 55 percent the next day and to 65 percent on the three days after that.

The second date, on the 12th, raised her preoccupation percentage even higher, to 80 percent. However, Bert broke the date they had scheduled for the 15th. At this point, Margrit's preoccuaption percentage was still at 80 percent. After he broke the date, it went even higher.

Up to this point, everything had been on the plus side; Margrit had been not only preoccupied, but pleasantly so. After the broken date, she found her attraction had intensified and her preoccupation increased to 90 percent, but the next three days consisted of unhappy intense limerence. These were days in which she did not hear from him. Then he called again and sounded really interested in her after all, at which time her preoccupation went up to 100 percent, this time a happy 100 percent.

Bert, in fact, was vacillating. On the 21st he broke the next date leaving her this time in more intense misery than she had felt before. During the next three days, both her preoccupation level and her intensity of unhappiness diminished but did not reach neutrality.

Then while driving on her way to an interview, she happened to see Bert on the street walking arm in arm with Ginny. She immediately returned to intense and miserable limerent longing. Her recovery had been based on hopes that were smashed by the sight on Main Street, and she suffered several days of unhappiness at the 100 percent level. On the 31st of March her limerence level dropped slightly (to 90 percent), then even more (to 75 percent) on the 1st of April. Following that, her limerence declined even further and felt less unpleasant.

But Bert called again, and the result of this renewed attention from him was to send her higher on the limerent scale and also to make her happy, a state which lasted for two days, when, true to form, he disappointed her again by breaking a date. Her limerence spiked to a negative 100 percent, where it stayed for about four days until she attended a professional convention. Although she did not feel up to going, and even tried to get out of it, to Margrit's surprise, her negative preoccupation went down to about 30 percent, seemingly because of the distractions from other people and activities at the convention.

Margrit's feelings fluctuated in relation to whether Bert's behavior was interpreted as indicating interest or rejection. The intensity of her feelings—at least as measured by preoccupation percentage—and the direction of her feelings—positive or negative—represent two different aspects of her experience. When Bert was rejecting Margrit, the intensity of her limerence would sometimes actually increase.

The course of limerence is, then, a rise, often very rapid, to a more intrusive thinking pattern than you may ever have experienced. This is invariably an expectant, even joyous period. It is what Stendahl termed the *first* crystallization, the initial focusing on LO's admirable qualities. Then, under appropriate conditions of hope and uncertainty, the limerence intensifies further. At the peak reached by the first crystallization, perhaps 30 percent of your waking thoughts revolve around LO; at the height of limerence, after what Stendhal called the second crystallization, the figure soars to virtually 100 percent. Subsequently your reaction may remain at that height for days or weeks, with only small and temporary respite, or it may begin to undergo a final decline, or, as is most typical, it may drop and then rise again one or more times before the decline that almost always follows sooner or later. The astounding thing is that the pleasantness or unpleasantness of the state seems almost unrelated to the intensity of the reaction. Limerence at 100 percent may be ecstasy or it may be despair, and it may change from positive to negative at any level of intensity. Joan described her experience:

"When I was intensely in love with Barry, I was intensely in love. When I felt he loved me, I was intensely in love and deliriously happy; when he seemed rejecting, I was still intensely in love, only miserable beyond words.

"Later, when my feelings were less intense, I could still flip-flop depending on how I perceived his feelings for me, only I'd go from mildly in love, and therefore happy, but not ecstatic, when I thought he cared, to unhappy, but not overcome with grief, when he seemed cool."

The transitions may be so abrupt that people seem emotionally volatile although they may be generally of stable temperament. Phil's reaction was similar to that described by a number of informants:

"Just when everything was going really well, Jane's letter arrived telling me she wanted to break the engagement, and my world fell apart. Just like that."

I don't mean to imply that limerence is the sole determiner of the person's emotional well-being. Even at its height, you carry on your ordinary activities and are affected by other events in expected ways. But a portion of your mentality is in its control. When limerence is at its peak, the other things in life are shunted off to the side and thought about only to the extent that limerence leaves room for them.

As it was repeatedly described to me, the course of limerence is as follows:

1. The limerent reaction begins, usually at a point discernible at the time and later recalled. Sexual attraction as such need not be experienced, although (a) the person is someone you view as a possible sexual partner, and (b) the initial "admiration" may be, or seem to be, primarily physical attraction.

2. Once limerence begins, you find yourself thinking about LO and receiving considerable pleasure from the process. There is an initial phase in which you feel buoyant, elated, and, ironically, for this appears to be the beginning of an essentially involuntary process, free. Free not only from the usual restraints of gravity,

but emotionally unburdened. You may be attracted to more than one potential LO. You feel that your response is a result of LO's fine qualities.

3. With evidence of reciprocation from LO, you enjoy a state of extreme pleasure, even euphoria. Your thoughts are mainly occupied with considering and reconsidering what you may find attractive in LO, replaying whatever events may have thus far transpired between you and LO, *and* appreciating qualities in yourself which you perceive as possibly having sparked interest in you on the part of LO. (It is at this point in *West Side Story* that Maria, the contemporary Juliet, sings *I Feel Pretty.*)

4. Your degree of involvement increases if obstacles are externally imposed or if you doubt LO's feelings for you. Only if LO were to be revealed as highly undesirable might your limerence subside. Usually, with some degree of doubt its intensity rises further, and you reach the stage at which the reaction is virtually impossible to dislodge, either by your own act of will, or by further evidence of LO's undesirable qualities. This is what Stendhal called crystallization. The doubt and increased intensity of limerence undermine your former satisfaction with yourself. You acquire new clothes, change your hairstyle, and are receptive to any suggestion by which you might increase your own desirability in LO's eyes. You are inordinately fearful of rejection.

5. With increases in doubt interspersed with reason to hope that reciprocation may indeed occur, everything becomes intensified, especially your preoccupation percentage. At 100 percent you are mooning about, in either a joyful *or* a despairing state, preferring your fantasies to virtually any other activity unless it is (a) acting in ways that you believe will help you attain your limerent objective, such as beautifying yourself and, therefore increasing the probability that you will impress LO favorably during your interaction, or (b) actually being in the presence of LO. Your motivation to attain a "relationship" (mating, or pair bond) continues to intensify so long as a "proper" mix of hope and uncertainty exist, as it did for Margrit when Bert showed interest but seemed to act on it unpredictably.

6. At any point in the process, if you perceive reciprocation, your degree of involvement ceases to rise—until, of course, you

become uncertain again. Usually, however, what might be an obvious sign of interest to an observer is not so obvious to you. "Lover's spats," games in which the timid partners attempt to conceal from each other the full nature of the reaction that has seized them, as well as the inevitable differences between their interests, prevent full reciprocation in each other's eyes and allow the intensity to continue to increase.

Philip's limerence toward Harriet lasted several months and included their engagement. Philip experienced longer periods of happiness than did Margrit because Harriet did show some return of feelings for him. During the first weeks of Philip's attraction, his limerence level rose slowly but steadily, with only minor fluctuations, and by the fourth week his preoccupation averaged 55 percent, a level at which it remained for only two weeks before they became engaged and a decline began. Over the next six weeks, Philip's preoccupation percentage declined to 30 percent. Thus far Philip's mood in relation to Harriet has been consistently positive; *i.e.*, no fluctuation downward was so extreme or persistent that a single day could be counted as negative.

During the tenth week, this picture of contentment was altered when Harriet announced that she was considering breaking their engagement, something that Philip was totally unprepared for. He had two negative days (the days after the announcement) that week, and his average preoccupation level shot up. Over the next month, Philip did not manage a single good day, and his average preoccupation level rose steadily. This was the period of "taking a break from each other for a while" that Harriet insisted on. When he saw her again and she appeared less rejecting than he had feared, up went his involvement and his joy. The next two months were blissful, and all days were positive as preoccupation declined. Preoccupation is not quite the same thing as intensity of feeling. During this time, Philip felt that he loved Harriet consistently; but he did not find thoughts of her intruding constantly. Still the low point of this period, 40 percent is a lot of thinking about one person.

Then disaster struck in the form of Harriet's unexpected and abrupt termination of the relationship. (Unexpected to Philip;

others might have seen it coming.) For a month he was distraught (no plus days and 100 percent involvement). This was the sort of misery Marilyn had been experiencing that day in my office on campus.

More than two months after Harriet walked totally out of his life, Philip had still not succeeded in getting her out of his mind. In fact, he had reached a level at which his preoccupation was down and his mood was generally positive. He sorely wished that someone would come along to bring him to the heights of ecstasy he had known during the intensely positive days with Harriet. Indeed, Jane came into his life, and nine and a half months after his first attraction for Harriet, he began to transfer his limerence to a new person.

FEAR OF REJECTION

The pleasures of love are always in proportion to the fear.[23]

Along with the emphasis of positive qualities perceived in LO, and preoccupation with the hoped for return of feelings, you fear that your limerence will be met by the very opposite of reciprocity: rejection. Physiological reactions associated with fear were described 2,500 years ago in a famous poetic fragment attributed to Sappho:

> For should I see thee a little moment,
>   Straight is my voice hushed;
> Yea, my tongue is broken, and
>   through and through me
> 'Neath the flesh, impalpable fire
>   runs tingling;
> Nothing see mine eyes, and a
>   voice of roaring
> Waves in my ear sounds;
>   Sweat runs down in rivers, a
>   tremor seizes

All my limbs, and paler than
    grass in autumn,
Caught by pains of menacing
    death, I falter,
Lost in the love-trance.[24]

The most frequently reported physiological correlates of limerence are heart palpitations, trembling, pallor, flushing, and
general weakness. Awkwardness, stammering, and confusion pre-
dominate at the behavioral level. And shyness. When limerent,
you are fearful, apprehensive, nervous, anxious—terribly worried
that your own actions may bring about disaster. Many of the
commonly associated physiological reactions are the result of this
fear, and there are other consequences as well. Stendhal, who
speaks of himself in the third person, describes some of these:

> [The man in love] is aware of the enormous weight attaching to every
> word he speaks to his beloved, and feels that a word may decide his
> fate. He can hardly avoid trying to express himself well, ... From
> that moment candour is lost.
>
> In your beloved's presence even physical movements almost cease
> to be natural, although the habit of them is so deeply ingrained in the
> muscles. Whenever I gave my arm to Leonore, I always felt I was
> about to fall, and I had to think how to walk.[25]

Philip, a 28-year-old truck driver summed up what many others
had said:

"I'd be jumpy out of my head. It was like what you might call
stage fright, like going up in front of an audience. My hand
would be shaking when I rang the doorbell. When I called her on
the phone I felt like I could hear the pulse in my temple louder
than the ringing of the phone, and I'd get into such a panic
listening to the ring and expecting Nelly's voice at the other end
that I'd have a moment of relief if no one answered. And when
she did answer, I wouldn't know what to say even if I'd gone
over the whole thing in my head beforehand. And then whatever
I did say never seemed to come out right.

"I was awkward as hell. It really got to me. And I don't mean the kind of nervousness that any man feels asking for a date. I'd got over that in my teens. There's maybe always a bit of that whenever it's somebody new, but this was different. It was much worse, and it lasted a long time, as long as I knew her. I had a really bad case, I guess, because I never felt sure of her or sure of myself."

Or as Ginny, a married woman having an extramarital affair with Herb, described it:

"About 90 percent of the whole affair was by mail. In the interest of secrecy, we obtained postal boxes just for each other. When I wrote to him I weighed every word. Sometimes I'd go through a dozen drafts until I got it right, and then I still wasn't sure. I had a vague image of wanting to appear gay, knowledgeable, intelligent, witty—everything that would make him love me more. Sometimes I'd get weak as I placed the letter in the box, and then go all jittery after I'd dropped it in and wish I could get it back to read over one more time.

"And when he'd telephone and I'd hear his voice on the other end, I'd get this sinking feeling in my stomach. Sometimes it would happen when the telephone rang even when I knew it couldn't be him. When it was him I'd breathe faster and my hands would get cold and start to perspire. I had trouble controlling my voice."

When I gave the first 175-item questionnaire to The Group, I had not developed questions that made a distinction between love and limerence, and the respondents answered according to their own, subjective definition of being "in love." Although a confident 68 percent of The Group claimed they felt "free, unself-conscious, and uninhibited in the presence of their lovers," responses to other statements indicated that a substantial minority of them became distinctly nervous when LO was around. More than a third agreed that "I do (did) not want _____ to see me when I am (was) not looking well." One quarter said, "I am afraid to have _____ see any flaw in me," and "I am afraid of making mistakes when I am with _____." Sixteen percent said, "I am afraid to be myself with _____."

Ingrid Bengis, in her book, *Combat in the Erogenous Zone*, portrays the limerent dilemma of "dependency and immobilization."

> "Despite the fact that I could live alone for years at a time, support myself in banal as well as curious ways, travel alone all over the world, drive a motorcycle at 70 miles an hour, have sex with whomever I chose, I was still capable of sitting by a telephone, unable to think of anything beyond whether or not a man I loved was going to call and feeling the most common hurt and frustration when he didn't." [26]

She would wander about her apartment unable to sustain interest in the usual pleasures and friends, literature or music, having little interest in any activity. This was particularly likely to occur when she felt that she had overstepped the boundaries of the permissable and made an "excessive or inappropriate" request that she feared might lead to rejection. She bewailed her loss of freedom as she found herself waiting endlessly.

> Certainly it was not a question of being liberated enough to make phone calls myself. I had made those calls many times. It was a question of security (a word I have always looked upon with contempt). No Female Bill of Rights could give me that kind of security. What I needed to know at those particular moments was whether it mattered enough to the man for him to do the calling.[27]

Some informants reported that their limerent fear of rejection was not confined to shyness in the presence of LO, but also spread to situations involving other potential LOs. Twenty-year-old Danny described the problem:

"I used to be fairly confident about my ability to attract and handle myself with girls. I was not especially nervous or fearful. But with Rachel that completely changed. Not only was I a wreck when she was around, but I lost my former confidence with other girls as well. After Rachel and I had stopped seeing each other, I called Nan to ask for a date and found my voice stuck in my throat. I pretended something was wrong with the phone. This went on for a long time, and it occurred in almost all situations in which I felt on the spot like that. I am just now beginning to regain some of my old confidence.

"Fortunately, the nervousness was confined to those situations. I have never been particularly shy. In fact, I'm something of a ham. I like speaking or performing in front of a group. It's only in the presence of someone I'm attracted to that it happens, and it never happened before Rachel. It's really strange."

Unlike Danny, most people are shy in LO's presence without it affecting other spheres of their lives (unless LO appears unexpectedly—or expectedly—in one of those "other" spheres).

Sherie tried to control her actions and not let the anxiety interfere with carrying out what the "rational part" of her mind dictated.

"I decided I was being silly and that I would simply stop being silly. Here I was, all worked up and indecisive, and, worst of all, Jim would never see the real me if I was always acting like a scared rabbit whenever I was around him. I decided to take myself in hand and let the chips fall where they would. Instead of being the timid soul I always turned into in his presence, I would behave the way I did with others—talkative, assertive, even maybe a little bold. If he didn't like me that way, well. . . .

"But it was all in vain. When the time came I froze. I lost all my will. My preparations did no good. The truth was, and I hated myself for it, I just couldn't take the chance. Not yet. I decided to give it a little more time. I set a deadline for myself. Three more weeks. Six more weeks. But I never went through with it, not even when I was pretty sure it was "over" and I had nothing to lose.

"But I never *believed* I had nothing to lose. It's hard to explain. I knew it logically, but my emotions never accepted the fact. But I don't think it was something in me. I'm not that way now with Gary. It was something about the way Richard acted, feeding out just enough attentiveness to keep me on the hook, but never quite enough to let me relax. I don't say that was his intention, although at the time I even imagined that his unreliability was a deliberate plot. I saw his lack of real interest in me, but kept believing that all that would change if he "really" knew me. Since I was always too up-tight when he was around to be myself, he never really knew me at all. It was extraordinary the way I went around in circles like that. I'd see him and freeze. At least I was still seeing him once in a while. If I made any sort of move, or change, or demand, I might lose even that."

A surprising proportion of persons who wanted to be interviewed were caught in a similar state, and sometimes the situation would remain relatively unchanged for long periods of time. Gregory had been married to Beatrice for 25 years and had feared that she would leave him at any moment throughout almost the entire period. This uncertainty perpetuated his limerence, providing both fear—and joy.

"I lived in constant fear of divorce. The only times I even felt at all safe were when she was pregnant or had a small child. It just didn't seem likely that she would walk out under these conditions. Not that walking out was really the issue. I'd feel uncertain and "put out" even when there was nothing I could quite put my finger on, nothing I could actually accuse her of. I would do everything I could think of to try and win her affection. I'd buy flowers, take the kids out, mow the lawn, paint the kitchen, just about anything I thought she'd like. Sometimes she'd give me a look of real appreciation; other times she'd get angry. She was unpredictable. I could never be sure of how she'd react, whether something I'd do to please her would have the right effect or its opposite.

"And it was all done very subtly, no fighting or screaming or anything crude like that. And another thing, she was always beautiful. From the day I met her until the day she died, she was the most beautiful woman on earth. And she really was. Other men thought so, too. She never got fat or let herself go, and she wore clothes with elegance. She was a real queen and she ruled my emotions for a quarter of a century. It's completely different now with Beth. She and I are more like equals, like really good friends.

"I would have to say I'm more content with Beth than I ever was during those years with Beatrice. But I also have to admit that with all the worry she caused me, she also gave me some great moments. They call it ecstasy, and I'd agree with the term. My feelings for Beth—and hers for me—are more solid and dependable. I'm not saying I wish she were like Beatrice, but maybe if just a little bit, it would put some spark into it. It's only five years, and things are comfortable, as I said, and I love her, but maybe they're getting just a little dull. I'm afraid I take her for granted."

Once again, limerence appears to develop and be sustained when there is a certain balance of hope and uncertainty. However unappealing it may be in a universe conceived as orderly and humane, the fact is undeniable; fear of rejection may cause pain, but it also enhances desire. A man who kidnapped his girlfriend tearfully explained that her rejection of him made him want and love her more. Stendhal described the conflict of desiring above all to be in the presence of LO and at the same time fearing what will happen:

> If you are sensitive you know very well that, in the contest about to begin as soon as you see her, the least negligence, the least lack of attention or of courage will be punished by a snub which would poison your imagination for some time, and indeed would be humiliating outside the realm of passion, if you were tempted to withdraw there. You reproach yourself for lack of wit or boldness; but the only way to show courage would be to love her less.[28]

Or in the words of one of my interviewees:

"It was just a little thing. Except it wasn't a little thing. She forgot to wear the pin I had given her, even though I had asked her to be sure to wear it. I wouldn't have minded so much if she had been angry and left it home to get even with me over something. But to forget? There's no way I could have forgotten if she had asked me for anything. It meant I wasn't in her thoughts the way she was in mine. I hoped that she was teasing, that she really was mad at me. Anything but forgetting. Being forgotten was like being dead. I wanted to die. I felt it was all over in that second. I prayed for a sign that she was playing with me. She wasn't. It was ended, but it took me about six more months before I could tolerate believing it."

When you are limerent, you experience considerable self-doubt and uncertainty about your own reactions. You wonder "Am I 'paranoid' to be so concerned about trivia?" And yet you find you cannot help noticing "little things" and endlessly analyzing them for meanings that are not apparent. The explanation is that reciprocation requires a reaction by LO similar to yours. As Heather said:

"If Joe forgets to call, it means I am not in his thoughts the way he is in mine. That's why it hurts so. It's not 'logical.' It's the way it is, however, and I can't help it. Into perfectly ordinary actions on his part, I read an indication that he's losing interest—and I panic."

Although it appears that love blossoms under some forms of adversity, extreme caution, even immobility, and shyness based on fear of giving LO an undesirable view can prevent a relationship from occurring even when both people are interested. According to Ted, an accountant in his mid-thirties:

"Joan and I knew each other slightly in high school, and here's the incredible part: We were in love with each other but were both too shy to make the first move or to do *anything* that would lead the other to suspect what was going on inside us. I wouldn't ask for a date, because she didn't seem to act as if she liked being with me. She'd walk off when she'd rather have stayed so as not to appear unduly interested. Even more incredible was that we had been married several years before we even found out about how we had felt back then. After high school, we didn't hear anything about one another for five years. Then we met again, after college, through mutual friends. We each still felt like idiots about our great adolescent infatuation and almost never even mentioned the high school days.

"How did we ever find out? It was strictly by sheer accident. Joan found an old school notebook of mine in which I had scribbled her name. She thought that was just an accident, but it gave her the courage to tell me about her big crush. At least I knew her. She thought I hadn't noticed her at all! Well, when she confessed, I did, too."

What is important here is that the uncertainty required by the limerent reaction may often be merely a matter of perception—either of one's own inadequacies or of a lack of response in LO. In the case of Ted and Joan, there were no external obstacles to their relationship, and the perception of each of them that the other was not interested was not accurate. On the other hand, their inaccurate perceptions probably increased their limerent reaction to each other.

The recognition that some uncertainty must exist has been commented on and complained about by virtually everyone who has undertaken a serious study of the phenomenon of romantic love. Psychologists Ellen Bersheid and Elaine Walster discussed this common observation made, they note, by Socrates, Ovid, the *Kama Sutra,* and "Dear Abby," that the presentation of a hard-to-get as opposed to an immediately yielding exterior is a help in eliciting passion. Ovid remarked that nobody wants what is easily acquired. And twentieth-century mathematician and philosopher, Bertrand Russell, was even more emphatic. According to Russell, "The belief in the immense value of the lady is the psychologic effect of the difficulty of obtaining her, and I think it may be laid down that when a man has no difficulty in obtaining a woman, his feeling toward her does not take the form of romantic love." [29] He was only stating what mothers have passed down to their daughters for centuries.

Of course, the uncertainty necessary to limerence may indeed be the result of external obstacles visible to the disinterested observer, such as those stemming from parental objections, spouses, or social customs. The barriers faced by Romeo and Juliet were so crucial to their mutual limerence that psychologists speak of "the Romeo and Juliet effect," in which parents who attempt to interfere in the romance of their children may in fact intensify it.[30] Another traditional barrier that often plays a role in limerence is the deceived spouse who, according to Suzane Brøgger in *Deliver Us from Love,* can keep things at a boiling point.[31]

HOPE

The objective that you as a limerent persistently pursue, as is clear in the fantasy that occupies virtually your every waking moment, is a "return of feelings." The ecstatically blissful moment, toward which your long fantasies progress and your short fantasies depict in living color, is the moment in which LO gives what you accept as clear indication that the limerent goal has been achieved. But what actions on LO's part are required? What, truly, does "return of feeling" mean?

Uncertainty about LO's true reaction is an essential aspect of your own limerence. Removal of the uncertainty is the goal, and because your desire is so unrelenting, so imperative, you continually search for the meanings underlying events. This brings us to the matter of hopefulness, as essential to the development of a full limerent reaction as uncertainty. Since limerent fantasy is rooted in the limerent's actual life situation, it would seem to follow that hopefulness must be similarly grounded. Well, yes and no. The problem is once again that it is not objective reality, but reality *as it is perceived* that provides the base for limerent hopefulness. Just as lack of confidence and fear of no response in LO may be based on misperceptions of reality, so hope of reciprocation of feeling turns out to require little foothold in actuality once the limerent reaction has fixed itself. It is primarily the true nature of LO's reaction to yourself that is obscure to your limerent eye, and it is this confusion that causes so much stress and anxiety over how to behave, what to say, how much to reveal, or how fast to move.

The inclination to sift through nuances of speech and subtleties of behavior for evidence of limerent hope presented itself repeatedly in the interviews. Dr. Vesteroy, the professor mentioned earlier, recalled his increased sensitivity to his colleague's behavior after that first smile:

"It might have ended there, too, if I had not thereafter felt I noticed other things in her behavior—the way she greeted me in the hall, always friendly but nothing out of line, except well, really, all I had to go on for the first few months was a certain look. Our eyes seemed to meet and linger together just a fraction of a second longer than they should. I puzzled over it. Was it really happening? And if so, which of us was the initiator? Was she going out of her way to meet me in the hall, or was I the one who was doing it? When that business came up over changing the grades of students who missed the exam because of the snowstorm, did she and I find ourselves on the same side of the issue accidentally, or was it an unconscious—or conscious—ploy, and on whose part, to throw us together?"

As he reported it, Dr. Vesteroy spent the entire academic year uncertain, increasingly limerent, and immobilized. He and his wife had been talking of divorce off and on for the past ten years, but he had never really considered the prospect seriously.

Dr. Ashton was married, too, but her husband had remained behind in Chicago when she accepted the new position and it seemed not unreasonable to infer that theirs was also a shaky relationship. It would therefore not have been entirely out of the bounds of propriety for him—or for her—to have made some tentative overt gesture. Yet neither did. Nor did their contacts with each other increase. Despite this, Dr. Vesteroy's limerence remained strong.

"Despite all logic, I could not shake off the feeling—the hope as well—that Elena's totally circumspect behavior was *itself* an indication that her feelings were not unlike my own. How could she know that my wife and I were having marital difficulties? Her very circumspection became proof of inner turmoil. When, unlike that first time, she hurried away with the others after a business meeting, could it have been lest she give herself away?

"In the meantime, my admiration of her work and appreciation of her beauty grew more and more intense. Without ever a word passing between us, I became—there's no other way to put it—lovesick! My mind was filled with her, my knees trembled when I saw her, and I fashioned all manner of elaborate schemes whereby I could test the ground before taking a step. I felt I had to do something, but I was completely paralyzed by fear that the whole affair existed only in my imagination and that I would make an utter fool of myself and destroy any chance of success that might possibly exist.

"At first, I'd set up little tests. I'd say that if at the next meeting she elects to sit beside me *or* facing me, I will count it as proof that this madness is not unilateral. But when she chose a seat farthest from me, or one which made it very difficult for us to look at one another, I realized that the test was not a test at all. *No matter what she did,* I could interpret it in my favor. Her remote position in the room could serve the function of helping her to hide feelings as intense as my own. She was as afraid as I was of overt interaction! Of course, if I had been certain of *that* conclusion, I'd have found it possible to take a positive step, but my thinking on the matter oscillated like a seesaw. Up and down, back and forth, my reactions went, but always with the same final result: I dared not advance."

Margot Strickland reports that Annabella admitted to extreme agitation at the sight of Lord Byron, the husband-to-be who never really loved her, taking his pallor as a sign that he was equally moved—which may have been romantic fancy, since he was normally pale.[32] Similarly, biographer Matthew Josephson observes that when Stendhal was in love with Madame Daru, he believed that she chose her gown according to what would be particularly pleasing to him.[33] To make an interpretation, especially a "tentative" one, is easy; to retain faith in it is another matter. Unless Dr. Vesteroy could be quite certain that his favorable interpretation was correct, his fear would prevent him from acting.

Hilda, the woman mentioned earlier who spent each week fantasizing about her upcoming weekends with Stu, was an example of a limerent who maintained her "hope against hope" long after objective behavior on the part of her LO should have made it clear that he did not return her feelings:

"The frustrating thing was that the scenes I'd play out in my imagination *never* worked out in reality. Something always went wrong. One time, just as a for instance, I worked out this whole Sunday morning brunch thing. I had bought this really fantastic orange dressing gown and I was going to absolutely knock him out with it over an omelet I had been perfecting. So what happened? Last thing he does before we go to sleep on Saturday night is set his alarm clock for six A.M.—it was already long after midnight—and say, 'Sorry, Hilda, I knew you'd understand. I've got to put in a couple of business hours at the golf course tomorrow, but I'll be back around two in the afternoon. At least *you* can get a good sleep!'

"Well, my great plan was out of the window, but I was undaunted. I spent the morning imagining that he was out pulling off the business deal of his life and finally clearing away the one barrier to our getting married, his financial future. I visualized him bursting in precisely at two with this glowing look in his eyes, rushing up to me, taking me in his arms and saying, 'Hilda, darling, I just closed a fantastic deal. Let's get married.'

"Actually, all the time Stu and I were lovers, it was like that. Even when we were together every week without fail, I'd be consumed with hopes and plans and visions of him really showing love, and he'd always pull something unexpected. If I gave up and planned to break it off, that would be the weekend he'd start off with flowers 'just for my Hilda' and be especially nice. The next week when I'd work myself up to expecting a big response from him, there would be the inevitable letdown.

"The only thing I could really count on from Stu was unpredictability. For the whole three years, I was filling up my head with plans and schemes and visions of hope, but all I got was disappointment.

"Actually, our idyllic weekends (idyllic in comparison with

what was to come) lasted less than a year, and after that it was sheer, unrequited misery."

This grasping for hope when by all rational indications hope is groundless is described by Simone de Beauvoir in *The Second Sex:*

> I recall a friend who said in reference to a long silence on the part of her distant lover: "When one wants to break off, one writes to announce the break"; then, having finally received a quite unambiguous letter: "When one really wants to break off, one doesn't write." [34]

And in the same section of the book, Beauvoir discusses the psychiatric phenomenon of "erotomania" in a manner that blurs the distinction between the psychologically pathological and the psychologically nonpathological:

> ... one of the constant characteristics of erotomania is that the behavior of the lover seems enigmatic and paradoxical; on account of this quirk, the patient's mania always succeeds in breaking through the resistance of reality. A normal woman sometimes yields in the end to the truth and finally recognizes the fact that she is no longer loved. But so long as she has not lost all hope and made this admission, she always cheats a little. [35]

Columbia sociologist William J. Goode comments:

> On the psychological level, the motivating power of ... love ... is intensified by this curious fact (which I have not seen remarked on elsewhere): Love is the most projective of drives; only with great difficulty can the attracted person believe that the object ... does not and will not reciprocate the feeling at all. Thus the person may carry [the] action quite far, before accepting a rejection as genuine. [36]

The limerent endures painfully intense suffering as daydreams smash against the rocks of events, until hope can only be built from the rubble through interpretation.

THE BODY SPEAKS

The limerent person develops a condition of sustained alertness, a heightening of awareness, and an enormous fund of energy to deploy in pursuit of the limerent aim. You are ever ready to perceive LO's most minute actions at any time when it is conceivable that they have meaning in relation to the goal.

Such attentiveness is not unwarranted. It has been estimated that the larger proportion of communication between two people in a face-to-face situation takes place through nonverbal means. Scientific studies on "body language" have found that such seemingly inconsequential behaviors as the position of the limbs, the general stance of one person with respect to the other, the rhythm of inhalation and exhalation, movements of the hands and, particularly of the eyes, all have significance.[37] If you are feeling favorably disposed and receptive, you are more likely to sit crossing your feet at the ankles rather than at the knees, to hold your palms outward rather than clenching your fists, occasionally to sigh (softly rather than sharply), to look at the person directly and openly rather than shiftily, and to allow your face to be fully exposed rather than partially hidden, either with a hand or by turning your face to the side.

Many actions of which you are quite unaware may communicate distaste for the person with whom you are conversing. These include clenching your teeth, holding your lips tight together, rubbing your nose or making brisk and repetitive movements such as flicking the ash of a cigarette or drumming your fingers. Thus the limerent's seemingly excessive concern over trivia may not be entirely unfounded.

The receipt of mixed messages may in fact provide just the combination of hope and uncertainty that feeds the reaction. One young man described his conflict:

"I could find no fault with anything Gladys did. She was prompt, cooperative, and aggreeable. But there was something about the *way* she did things that I could not quite put my finger on, but that bothered the hell out of me. They were such little things that I tried to talk myself out of my reactions, except that they kept happening, and kept bothering me. Things like the way she would hold herself when we sat beside one another in the theater, or the slight hesitation that preceded her response to an affectionate gesture on my part, and the way she looked at me— or rather, the way she rarely did."

Scientific research has emphatically confirmed the age-old suspicions concerning the importance of gaze.[38] When we are experiencing intensely pleasurable emotions, our pupils dilate and become larger. Unconsciously and involuntarily, this pupillary reflex can betray feelings. In addition, a small increase in the secretion of the tear ducts causes the eyes to glisten producing "shining eyes of love," which, when combined with dilation of the pupil, emit signals of amatory interest. Not only that, the eyebrows, once thought designed by nature to keep perspiration from running into our eyes, are now believed at least by some scientists to have as a basic function the indication of mood change. When we are surprised they rise; when we are angered, they lower; and when we are anxious, they knit together. To arch them means to question, and to flick them quickly once up and down is to acknowledge another person in an attitude of friendliness.[39]

One woman whom I interviewed based her belief that her limerent feelings were returned solely on her interpretation of the man's eye movements.

"I knew he loved me because of the way he looked at me. No words could be as eloquent; words were not even necessary. If you could have seen his eyes, those two limpid pools. . . . They told all, and I drowned in them."

It will surely surprise no one that a recent carefully conducted psychological experiment, using sophisticated recording apparatus, reported that couples whose questionnaire responses indicated greater intensity of love were found to look into each other's eyes for durations significantly longer than did couples less in love.[40]

I found surprisingly consistent support for the ancient wisdom that associates love with the heart. When I asked interviewees in the throes of the limerent condition to tell *where* they felt the sensation of limerence, they pointed unerringly to the midpoint in their chest. So consistently did this occur that it would seem to be another indication that the state described is indeed limerence, not affection (described by some as located "all over," or even in "the arms" when held out in a gesture of embrace) or in sexual feelings (located, appropriately enough, in the genitals).

Another recent study suggests the heart's probable importance in the physiology of limerence. Examining what they call "two-way communication" between the heart and the brain, Beatrice and John Lacey found that the hearts of experimental subjects slowed down when they tried to detect signals or perform a simple motor task.[41] It might be that the limerent's intrusive thinking results from a process of mutual feedback between the heart and the brain. Perhaps thoughts of LO trigger a change in heart rate, which in turn augments or transforms the thought.

On the other hand, unfortunately, the supersensitivity that is heightened by fear of rejection can get in the way of interpreting LO's body language and lead to inaction and wasted "opportunities," such as the mutual, but secret attractions of Joan and Ted during high school, or the miscommunication encountered by the two people depicted in the following poem, given to me by an informant:

The tree-fringed lake stretched before them
And although her gaze was directed
Outward with the water,
She was more aware of the blurred figure
To her left
Which was all she could see
Of him.

Conscious that the edge of his sleeve brushed her hand
Lightly
While she pretended concern with the lake and the
    trees as was usual

She was more aware
Of what she believed his behavior implied than
Did she hear his words.

"There's really nothing else to it,"
He was saying
"It's as simple as that. And all that was
        left was for me
To explain it to them.
That wasn't as easy as I had anticipated
But . . . "
He had warmed up
To his subject now and spoke rapidly.
She specifically noticed the rapidity with
        which he spoke. Soon, now,
He would pause
And she would feel the terror that came when
It would be absolutely
Necessary
For her to
Say
Something.
To show her capacity to meet his expectations.
That she knew he would
Look at her
Increased her
Anxiety.

"Don't you agree?" he said,
"Or maybe you see it differently. . . . "
"I . . . think . . . you are right,
No other explanation appears so reasonable . . . "
She thought she had been able to follow the gist
        of his story
And, fortunately, his question
Appeared to permit an ambiguous answer.

But his looking at her questioningly told her
        she had failed again.

The distance between them, all too perceptible
    during the afternoon, had
Widened.
A child appeared.
She wanted to pick up the child and run with it,
    to sit with it under a tree
And play peek-a-boo. To be barefoot with long hair
    blowing and getting in the way.
The baby would grab at her hair and she would
    scream and giggle and
They would roll over and over in the grass together
    hair flying
Skirt flying
Legs flying
Laughing and laughing
And finally lying still on her back with only
    his face in her
World
As he bent to kiss her beautiful smiling face
With beads of sweat and half-closed eyes.

But in the real world the panic and the fantasy
    produced only a small
Change
In the elevation of her
Shoulders
Which he interpreted as indicating boredom. He
    flushed at the thought of having
Forced her to listen to his boasting.

Thus the limerent person may emit bodily signals that confuse and interfere with attaining the object of desire. When the body speaks to others, it is not always understood.

PLOYS AND PLAYS

When you are limerent, no matter how intensely you desire reciprocation you cannot simply ask for it. You cannot simply inquire as to whether or not it exists. To ask is to risk premature self-disclosure. The interplay is delicate, with the reactions of each person inextricably bound to the behavior of the other. Like a hunter for whom the crackle of a twig in the bush measures the presence of the hunted, you subject LO's seemingly ordinary postures, movements, words, and glances to incessant analysis in quest of "true" meanings obscured beneath an ambiguous surface. Here, where the path is treacherous and possible consequence profound, face values cannot be trusted. Things may be what they seem or, again, they may in fact be just the opposite of what they seem. Despite ideals and philosophy, you find yourself a player in a process that bears unquestionable similarity to a game. The prize is not trifling; reciprocation produces ecstasy. Whether it will be won, whether it will be shared, and what the final outcome may be, depend on the effectiveness of your moves and those of your LO; indeed on skill.

The rocky course of progression toward ecstatic mutuality may involve not externally created difficulties, but the feinting and parrying, the minor deceptions, and the falsehoods of the lovers themselves that are so frequent as often to have been viewed as a "natural" aspect of the romantic love pattern.[42] (They also occur in sexual seduction and in many other forms of human interaction.) The lovers' fears lead them to proceed with a caution that they hope will protect them from disaster. Rather than commit themselves, they flirt. They send out ambiguous signals more or less as trial balloons. Reason to hope combined with reason to doubt keeps passion at fever pitch. Too-ready limerent availability cools them.[43] Andreas Capellanus, medieval author of *The Art of Courtly Love*, was neither the first nor the last to advise lovers to. erect artificial barriers and if necessary conceal their true feelings. When Stendhal began to fall in love himself, he feared the failure that certainty could bring and so, for "effect," he avoided his LO and walked about alone, brooding.[44]

You may lose your love through open declaration of your true feelings. As Ginny said:

"I was in love and I wanted to tell about it. I wanted to tell Vinny how I felt about him. I adored him, and it seemed only right that he should know. I wanted to give my love to him. *And I didn't want to play games!*

"But now I can see that was how I lost out. I should have slowed up and hidden my feelings. I overwhelmed him, and he couldn't take it, and that was the end. I'd probably have done the same thing in his place."

Peter, whose "affair" was more successful, used a different tactic:

"I knew, I don't know how, but I knew I had to be careful, that this was not the time to let her know how I was feeling. I deliberately canceled a date even though I wanted to be with her more than anything else in the world, and I spent the evening worrying—and even weeping—because I was afraid that she would be angry, that maybe this play would fail, that she'd go out and meet someone else. If I had been a nail biter, I'd have bitten off all my nails that night. I was going crazy inside but playing it cool outside, and I guess we have to say it worked. Maybe she would have fallen in love with me anyway, I'll never know, but my instincts told me to watch out and I obeyed them for a change. With other women, I had been more open, and they always lost interest and left me."

In the *Second Sex*, Simone de Beauvoir discusses this quandary in the chapter on "The Woman in Love."

It is almost impossible for a woman in love to play this game well. . . . To the extent that she still has regard for her lover, she will feel it repugnant to dupe him; how could he remain a god in her eyes? If she wins the game, she destroys her idol; if she loses it, she loses herself. There is no salvation.[45]

A similar conflict was expressed by a young graduate student in love with her professor:

"I had begun by simply having incredible respect for his mind. Even before I felt anything else, I could sit for hours and listen to him talk about his research. He was so intelligent, so enthusiastic! After a while, I recognized that I had begun to feel attracted to him in other ways and I sensed from little things that would happen, the way he would stay in the cafeteria and continue to talk with me alone after the other students had left, or how he would remember to bring a copy of one of his research reports for me, that he might feel the same way I did.

"They were small things, but I couldn't help reading a message in them. I was also experienced enough to know that the surest way to get someone to run away was to run after them. After a while, I was completely in love and more or less hanging on by a thread. I was so afraid of losing by showing my feelings that I actually did things that could be interpreted as uninterest.

"On the other hand, controlling myself as I was trying to do, took something away from my feelings for him. I really saw him as a kind of god, a perfect individual. That meant that if I could *manipulate* his feelings through my actions, he sank just a little lower in my eyes. There was no way to win."

Another informant, Virginia, was unusually frank:

"The man I am in love with is really silly. If he knew how I felt, he'd leave instantly. He'd feel insulted, and I wouldn't blame him in the least. What do you think I want him for? What scenes do I imagine with such delight? Do you think that I ponder his favorable qualities? Well, I do some of that, but my favorite fantasies have him struck dumb in rapt admiration of me! He is like a mirror that follows me about. I imagine him witnessing everything I do. I imagine his heart bursting with the delight that being in *my* presence brings. Every action of mine is cause for his rejoicing—the way I step into my bath, the wicked look in my eye as I apply my mascara, my intelligent contribution at the school board meeting.

"I find it strange that they say the person in love magnifies the qualities of the loved one; in my case I would say that the image of him magnifies my value. Being in love for me is being very self-involved, at least at certain stages. At any stage, being in love means wanting *his* love. I may be hating him and wishing he would come back so I could reject him, but I still want him to come back. Wanting him to want me is what it's all about. That's what one yearns for. The agony—it's so trite but it is agony, there's no better word—comes with doubt. To think that he might not be interested is to feel as if I've been stabbed with a knife. It hurts so sharply and inescapably."

Writing in 1964, totally from a male perspective, sociologist Peter Blau says:

The woman who impresses a man as a most desirable love possession that cannot easily be won and who simultaneously indicates sufficient interest to make ultimate conquest not completely beyond reach is likely to kindle his love.

To safeguard the value of her affection, a woman must be un-generous in expressing it and make any evidence of her growing love a cherished prize that cannot be easily won ... if she dispenses [sexual] favors readily—to many men or to a given man too soon—she depreciates their value and thus their power to arouse an enduring attachment.[46]

Simone de Beauvoir notes that a woman can lose her attraction to a man in the same way:

The knight departing for new adventures offends his lady, yet she has nothing but contempt for him if he remains at her feet. This is the torture of the impossible love. . . .[47]

Games, playacting, subterfuge, coyness, the sending of ambiguous messages and trial balloons that can be retracted or denied if such seems a wiser course: Such deviations from straightforward honesty become essential limerent strategies.

What is natural? The ploys of lovers are described in ancient writings; those whose modern philosophy dictates openness do so in a fear that sometimes proves to be justified by the turn of events. The limerent aim of return of feeling is an obsession that so overrides all other considerations that, as Ovid warned in the famous *Ars Amatoria (The Art of Love),* written almost 2,000 years ago, the lover and beloved are "shy predator and wily prey" and the nature of their love is "conquest." [48]

Is this deplorable state of affairs a necessary aspect of love? It does seem essential to *limerence;* hence the need for a new term. It appears, sadly enough, that limerent demands are contrary by nature when a limerent response in the other person can be killed by too early or blatant a display of affection. "Love," in most of its meanings, involves concern for the other person's welfare and feelings. Affection and fondness have no "objective"; they simply exist as feelings in which you are disposed toward actions to which the recipient might or might not respond. In contrast, limerence *demands* return. Other aspects of your life, including love, are sacrificed in behalf of the all-consuming need. While limerence has been called love, it is not love. Although the limerent feels a kind of love for LO at the time, from LO's point of view limerence and love are quite different from each other.

It is limerence, not love, that increases when lovers are able to meet only infrequently or when there is anger between them.[49] No wonder those who view limerence from an external vantage are baffled by what seems more a form of insanity than a form of love. Jean-Paul Sartre calls it a project with a "contradictory ideal." He notes that each of the lovers seek the love of the other without realizing that what they want is *to be* loved. His conclusion is that the amorous relation is "a system of infinite reflections, a deceiving mirror game which carries within itself its own frustration," a kind of "dupery." [50]

It should also be clear now that limerent uncertainly as well as projection can be viewed as the consequence of your limerent inclination to hide your own feelings: If you hide *your* true reactions, then LO, if indeed limerent, can be expected to do the same. When LO *appears* not to be eager, or even interested, it is not unreasonable to interpret that behavior as evidence itself of limerence; and a kind of "paranoia" becomes an entirely *logical* consequence of a situation that may indeed be what Simone de Beauvoir has called it: "impossible."

Because one of the invariant characteristics of limerence is extreme emotional dependency on LO's behavior, the actual course of the limerence must depend on the actions and reactions of both lovers. Uncertainty increases limerence; increased limerence dictates altered action which serves to increase or decrease limerence in the other according to the interpretation given. The interplay is delicate if the relationship hovers near mutuality; a subtle imbalance, constantly shifting, appears to maintain it. Each *knows* who "loves more."

If limerence were measurable by an instrument that enabled its intensity to be read by the points on a dial, one could imagine that, if lovers sat together reading each other's degree of reciprocation, the dials would rarely if ever set themselves at the same point on the scales. For instance, if you found yourself more limerent than your partner, then your limerence might decline through reduced hope, or if your partner's were higher, it might decline through reduced uncertainty. Perhaps such true awareness would provide a means of controlling the reaction.

SEXUALITY

The relationship between limerence and sex is one of the most baffling aspects of the entire subject. It has already been suggested that awareness of physical attraction plays a role in the development of limerence. Indeed, many writers define passionate or romantic love as "love between members of the opposite sex," or they use the terms "romantic love," "sexual love," and "erotic love" interchangeably. But the relationship is by no means a clear one.

Psychologists have observed a clear separation between sexuality on the one hand and "pure love," or "aesthetic components," on the other during adolescence, even speaking of a "collision between intimacy need and lust," or between the "sensual" and the "spiritual" aspects of "sexuality." [51] It has also been asserted that although sexual play and falling in love may occur during the so-called latency (prepubescent) period, they are not likely to be associated with each other.[52]

A teenaged male, Frankie, described his feelings about the distinction between sex and limerence, where he and LO had not had a physical relationship.

"Although I was attracted to Jennifer in a love way—in fact, I would say I was in love with her—I did not think about her sexually. What I mean is, I did not have fantasies about what it would be like to have sex with her. I don't mean that I didn't *want* to—I did want to—but only as it would follow naturally if she were also in love with me. *That* was what I wanted and what I thought about (most of the time, I'm afraid).

"When I had a sex fantasy she was not the person I thought about. It would have been, well, almost disrespectful to imagine things about her that I didn't know. I didn't know what her breasts were like, for example, so I couldn't imagine them. The female I used in sex fantasies could be almost anyone else— someone I had had sex with and remembered, someone I hardly knew, or even one person's breasts and other parts of someone else's body. But I think that would have changed if I had actually had a physical relationship with Jennifer. The trouble is, I never did."

In 1770, the eighteenth century "natural" philosopher Rousseau wrote about the separation of sex from love in his relationship with his common-law wife, saying that throughout the years with her he felt no love, only a means of satisfying sensual desires. By "love," one must assume he meant limerence, since there appeared to be considerable affection and companionship as well as sex between these two.[53]

That sexual attraction can exist without love has been abundantly documented, although the idea has been more culturally acceptable for males than it has for females.[54] That this is changing is reflected by The Group's reaction to the statement, "I have been sexually attracted without feeling the slightest trace of love": a surprising 53 percent of the females as well as a more expected larger percentage (79 percent) of the males agreed. The converse, love without sex, was not as popular, but still included a substantial proportion of the respondents. More than half of the females (61 percent) and more than a third (35 percent) of the males agreed with the statement, "I have been in love without feeling any need for sex."

There was opposition to this feeling that love and sex could be separated—almost a third (32 percent) of the women and only slightly fewer (29 percent) of the men—said that "in my experience, love and sex cannot be separated." If The Group's responses represent "cultural consensus," the consensus is clearly not a firm one. Additional responses complicate the picture further: 73 percent of the females and 51 percent of the males agreed that "I enjoy sex best when I am in love with my partner." And to top it off, only a tiny 2 percent of The Group (all male) agreed that "sex is best when love is not involved." About a third (slightly more women) indicated that they "think about sex a lot more when ... in love." But a surprising 14 percent of The Group said, "Sex with _____ was disappointing, although I knew we were very much in love."

To summarize this confusing mass of data, The Group seems to feel that love and sex *can* be separated, but would prefer to have them in combination. Very much so, if we are to believe the two-thirds of the women and slightly less than half of the men who maintained that "sex with the one I love is ecstasy"; the 71 percent of the entire Group who said, "Sex with the person I am in love with is intensely pleasurable"; and the wholesale rejection of the statement, "I have enjoyed sex more when it was with someone I was not in love with."

It is useful to distinguish sexual fantasies from limerent ones. Limerent fantasy is rooted in reality—that is, in what the limerent person interprets as reality. Your limerent daydreams may be unlikely, even highly unlikely, but they retain fidelity to the *possible*. The image of the moment of consummation, in which your LO indicates to you by word or gesture that the feelings are returned, is the more blissful—even when only in fantasy—if the events imagined to lead up to it could actually occur. As beautiful as a scene on a Caribbean island may be with you and LO dancing together in the moonlight, the scene brings the glow of bliss only when you are able to fill in the gaps, as it were, between present circumstances and the desired event. In acute phases, limerent fantasies are intrusive rather than voluntary, and they often reach a peak of satisfaction in a situation that may or may not lead to a sexual embrace.

In contrast, sexual fantasies are for most persons under more or less voluntary control. Here, it is necessary to distinguish between fantasy and arousal—the latter being a physiological as well as psychological state accompanied by definite sensations in the genital region. Fantasy is mental activity which creates and or augments those sensations. Sexual fantasies may involve intrusive and involuntary desire, but they differ from limerent imaginings (at least for those whom I interviewed) in that sexual fantasizing may also involve strangers, imaginary individuals, and situations that could not take place—even ones that you would not wish to have take place. Group sex, rape, seduction by a mysterious stranger, intercourse with animals: Such fantasies can be arousing for people who would not actually wish to engage in them in real live. As one young woman said:

"Between you and me, and I would not want it to go any farther because it is pretty embarrassing, I can really get turned on by some pretty disgusting ideas—like gang rape with me as victim, or by the idea of being forced to engage in fellatio with a real brute. Now I don't know why such images titillate me and make [masturbation to orgasm] possible, but sometimes they do. But let me tell you emphatically, I would never want such things actually to transpire! For some crazy and ridiculous reason, such images sometimes 'work,' but I don't enjoy them. In fact sometimes I find the idea of using them so repugnant that I'd just as soon forget the whole thing and often do."

Or a man, in speaking of his wife:

"In my head, I imagine us engaging in lewd acts together, but I haven't the slightest impulse to enact such scenes in actuality. I might conjure them up in a hotel room out of town if I feel that jerking off will help to relax me, but that's as far as it would ever go.

Of course, we know that these activities *are* sometimes actually enacted by some people, but the point here is only that many people can become aroused by the thought of sexual partners, acts, and situations that are not truly desired. The limerent, however, passionately desires that every detail of the limerent fantasy should actually take place. Furthermore, the moment of imagined consummation is often a handclasp, mutual gaze, words of endearment, or even a sigh.

Being limerent sometimes increases sexual interest in other partners when LO is unreceptive or unavailable. Consider Lucy:

"Mitch didn't care. It was obvious and I could no longer convince myself otherwise. He had left me in bed at the hotel to go home to his wife for the night. The plan was that he would call me in the morning. I was delirious with missing him and with wanting to embrace him again, and I awoke after just a few hours sleep to shower and prepare for his return. As I dressed and applied my makeup, I imagined our embrace when he returned to the hotel room. I was ready two hours before his call came.

"The call brought disaster. He said he was very rushed and would just have time to join me for a few minutes for breakfast at the hotel coffee shop. Then he'd have to rush off to a business appointment. My heart sank. I struggled to keep my feelings out of my voice and to sound cheerful and unconcerned, but he knew.

"Breakfast was brief and grim. I could neither eat nor hold back the tears as we discussed trivia.

"After Mitch left, I made a few phone calls. I just couldn't bear the thought of being alone. I wanted to be with a man, to prove to myself that not all men would reject me, that maybe Mitch would yet come to love me. Joe, whom I had met for a few minutes at Sybil's party last week, invited me over when I called. Within two hours of that breakfast, I was in bed with Joe.

"Yet I know that if it had not been for my state of anguish

over Mitch, going to bed with Joe, or even being with Joe, would have had no appeal. It was Mitch I wanted. It was Mitch I pretended to be with during sex with Joe.

Sometimes married people find sex with their spouses more pleasurable when they become limerent over someone else. Some informants said that being in love made them "more sexual" generally. Others seemed to substitute an available sexual partner for the unavailable LO. More often, of course, sex with the previous partner is not desired. As Maureen expressed it,

"It was not a matter of finding it more pleasurable with my husband after I fell in love with Max; it was that it wasn't quite as unpleasant as it had been. I was generally more turned on. I pretended it was Max, sometimes successfully."

Among history's more illustrious love stories is the tragic relationship between French logician and scholastic philosopher, Peter Abelard, and his pupil, later a famous nun, Heloïse. The formidable obstacles to their love included Heloïse's enraged uncle and guardian, Fulbert, as well as the theology with which Abelard was identified.

Abelard was castrated as punishment for his departure from behavior considered appropriate to his calling. But Heloïse's limerence for Abelard, as depicted in her letters over the remaining years of their lives, remained intense. Despite the separation between them, she begged for at least verbal reassurance of his affection. Calling him the "sole cause" of her misery, she implored Abelard to console her.[55] Her emotional well-being depended on his actions. Abelard's letters to her after their separation can be viewed as classics in which a formerly reciprocating LO attempts to establish a limerently and sexually neutral relationship. His attitude can also be read as the psychologically mediated outcome of his neuterdom.

In one letter, she refers to sexuality with remarkable directness considering her day and her position of authority and dignity as the abbess of the convent of the Paraclete. She tells Abelard that she continues to think about him and about the pleasures that they formerly knew together. She complains of insomnia and of being distracted from the Mass by visions of sexual union when she should instead be contrite and ashamed. She recalls everything, she says, and relives their time together in her imagination.

Like Heloïse, the majority of 778 undergraduate college students who answered an anonymous questionnaire eight centuries later reported that love was intensified after a sexual relationship had begun. They also mentioned that the more in love they were, the greater was their desire for sexual intercourse; this was equally true for females and males.[56]

Whether or not sex destroys romantic love or limerence, as moralists have proclaimed vehemently, seems rather to depend on the *meaning* attached to sex by the two people involved, the *limerent* meaning. In former times, sexual surrender of a woman to a man also communicated complete social and emotional surrender. If this occurred prematurely so far as the development of the man's limerence was concerned, the effect was quite different from what it might be among people today for whom sex carries no such connotation of commitment. In other words, sexual surrender once indicated the end of uncertainty in LO's response, uncertainty that was as necessary then as now for limerence to reach its peak. Today it does not. In The Group, only 31 percent (32 percent of the women, 26 percent of the men) accepted the statement, "A man is more likely to fall in love with a woman he has not slept with." Only 30 percent (32 percent of the women and 25 percent of the men) accepted the statement, "A woman is more likely to fall in love with a man she has not slept with."

It must also be emphasized that there is a difference—if not an incompatibility—between sexual competence and limerence. The "missionary" position so denigrated by sexual sophisticates is in fact the position of limerence. Lewdness is out of place in the limerent's fantasy, and female limerents have reported weeping during coitus when it seemed obvious that the partner's feelings consisted primarily or exclusively of "impersonal" lust.

As Jane reported:

"There I was, finally, in Frank's arms and in his bed. His attention was fully on me, and by all rights I ought to have been in the height of ecstasy, but it wasn't like that at all. Every aspect of his sexual performance wounded me deeply. I searched for evidence of love in his actions but found only a kind of animal, automatic, impersonal lust.

"It was *not* that he was behaving badly. He wasn't really. It was just that I wanted his love so badly that I was supersensitive to every move on his part that might possibly indicate love. I kept feeling that I and my love were, really, just a body to him. I kept worrying about it. When he entered me, I felt a terrible pang of simultaneous joy and grief—joy for his presence, grief for the fact that I couldn't feel his love, only his sex drive. And his friendliness. He wasn't being a brute, not in any way. It was me, but I couldn't help it.

"And so I started to cry when he started to come. I knew the closeness would soon be over and I wanted it to go on. At the same time, I was not being a good sex partner. I realized that, and that just made it worse. Really, it was horrible."

In The Group, 95 percent of the women and 91 percent of the men rejected the statement that "the best thing about love is sex." Others told me in interviews that "whether sex occurred or not was irrelevant." As Desmond Morris says:

> ... if two young people are in love today, they will laugh at the desperate athleticism of the copulating nonlovers. For them, as for true lovers at all points in history, a fleeting touch on the cheek from the one they adore will be worth more than six hours in thirty-seven positions with someone they do not.[57]

The anxieties and shyness experienced by the limerent person in the presence of LO may interfere with sexual functioning (which is notably not always identical to sexual desire for either sex).[58] The limerents' continual concern to appear at their very best is not always compatible with the "immodest" behaviors and poses that arise in sexual situations. Male interviewees told

of the difficulties they experienced when interacting sexually
with LO. Sometimes they found themselves unable to achieve or
maintain an erection. Women were frequently caught in the
kind of situation described by Louise:

"I didn't know what to do. I didn't *want* to do the things Lenny
was demanding of me; they seemed immodest, even indecent. I
had no rational objection. I realize sex is freer these days than it
used to be, but I only wanted to be with him and feel he loved
me. I didn't even need sex, although I wanted to be close to him
in every way. I wanted to have him love me and I loved him, so I
tried to give him what he asked for, anything he asked for, but it
didn't come off. I wasn't free. I was embarrassed. It seemed I
couldn't win no matter what I did."

So while the woman is in conflict over trying to be "good in
bed" to attract LO when what she really wants is mutuality, the
man may be experiencing performance failure. Stendhal noted
the problem that arises when a man "at the very instant of
entering [his lover's] bed is struck by the thought of how terrible
is the judge before whom he is about to appear." He recounts a
discussion of such "fiascos" among a group of five young men:

With the exception of one popinjay, who was probably lying, we had
all suffered a fiasco on our first occasion with our most notable
mistresses.

I knew a handsome lieutenant of Hussars, twenty-three years old,
who, from excess of love, as I understand the matter, could do no
more than kiss her and weep for joy throughout the first three nights
he spent with a mistress whom he had adored for six months and who
had treated him very harshly while she grieved over another lover
killed in the war.

The paymaster H. Monday, well known to the whole army, suffered a
fiasco for three nights in succession with the young and seductive
Countess Koller.

But the king of fiasco is the handsome and rational Colonel Horse, who suffered an unbroken succession of fiascos for three months on end with the mischievous and enticing Nina Vigano, and was finally compelled to part from her without ever having possessed her.[59]

Roughly 14 percent of The Group found that sex with LO "was disappointing, although I knew we were very much in love." This was true for both sexes, and it also appeared during several of the interviews—for men, much as depicted by Stendhal (inability to maintain an erection); for women it was not disability but disinclination. As one said:

"Maybe I expected too much. Maybe I couldn't get over my shyness. I thought the situation would change after a while because I was very much in love. I thought love would 'conquer all,' as they say, but unfortunately it didn't. I was very much in love, but couldn't ever 'let myself go.' "

The relationship between limerence and sex remains extremely complicated. Despite virtually unanimous agreement among interviewees that sex with LO under the best circumstances provides the "greatest pleasure" knowable in human existence, it appears that the very nature of limerence and the very nature of sex conspire to undermine the happiness except under the luckiest and most extraordinary of circumstances.

3

The Other Sides of Limerence

The pain in limerence, and perhaps the relative importance of limerence to human beings, can be estimated by considering the words to popular songs and folk ballads. In a 16-hour survey of random radio programming by a local popular music station in Connecticut in 1977, 45 percent of the songs concerned erotic or romantic love. Of this music, 40 percent expressed pleas for return of feeling, and 30 percent contained mournful descriptions of the pain of unreturned love.[1]

UNREQUITED LIMERENCE

As we saw with the fantasies that featured LO being present at the death or illness of the limerent, there can be some enjoyment in this preoccupation with and longing for returned feelings when the limerent recognizes from the outset that the possibility of mutual commitment is low. Cynthia was a teenager whose obsessive fantasizing about her rock star idol, Paul McCartney, took her through all the phases of limerence—from the detailed imagining of incidents and conversations, to the many obstacles, to the magic moment of consummation in which LO gives open and undeniable evidence that the feeling is reciprocated:

"Well, I'd begin by walking home from school just the way I always do, except this time I am alone, and I just happen to see this cute little kitten and it looks like it might have a hurt leg, so I follow it into an alley. I'm just sitting there with the kitty in my arms and holding it, and it's purring away when this huge black automobile comes driving up and a man gets out and asks me if I've seen a cat. Well I have one here I just found, I say, but how do I know it's yours? I had grown fond of it.

" 'Well, miss, why don't you talk to Mr. McCartney. As he spoke, I was struck dumb by the sight of Paul McCartney himself, the man I spent most of my time thinking about and wishing about—for me, the most important person in the world! He lept out of the car and came bouncing toward me with this huge beautiful smile on his face.

" 'Hey, miss,' he said, 'that's Trixie, my kiddie's wee kitty you've got there. Did you know?' "

" 'I think she's a bit hurt,' I said, amazed at how normal my voice sounded, 'because she was limping when I found her.'

"He knelt beside the crate I was sitting on and just looked for a moment or two. Trixie had not moved. She still cuddled in my arms.

" 'Well,' he said, 'I think the old girl is a bit out of sorts or she'd be jumping about. Would you mind very much coming with us to the veterinarian? My chauffeur will see you get home to your door afterward.' "

Cynthia's fantasy continued through nursing the cat back to health, a procedure complicated by the need for daily exercise of a lame front paw. Paul was too busy, the family was away, and Trixie took an instant dislike to the veterinarian. So Cynthia was asked if she might possibly manage to visit the McCartney home for an hour or so each day. Apparently, in Cynthia's fantasy,

Trixie had run off because she had been left with strangers, and this particular breed of cat fares poorly under such circumstances. Mysteriously, she had responded favorably to Cynthia. It was suggested that she help to accustom the cat to Paul since the family might not return for another few weeks. This brought Cynthia into Paul's presence daily, and the sessions with Trixie gradually turned into a friendship between Cynthia and her idol.

"I knew that Paul was very responsible to his family. The magazines said so and showed pictures of them all together having lunch on airplanes and in dressing rooms during rehearsals. This present separation was only because Linda's mother was very ill and Paul was finishing up a new album. Trixie had to be left behind because of the British regulation against letting animals into the country. They had only owned the cat a short time, and Paul had had least contact of all because of his busy schedule, and because he's such a sweet and nice person that he'd always let others play with her even when he was around.

"Anyway, when he heard that I took dictation and typed, knew how to read music, and was not presently employed, he offered me a job as secretary to himself and Linda. That was how I practically became a member of the family."

Her fantasy progressed with her continued employment during which Cynthia was able to demonstrate her capabilities as secretary, nursemaid, and short-order cook, as well as reliable caretaker of the family cat, while never revealing to anyone her total absorption with Paul.

"Then Linda McCartney, Paul's wife, became ill, and after many months, she died. Paul was unconsolable for weeks. I was the only one besides his daughters he allowed into his presence at first. It was months before he was anything like his old cheerful self. I kept in the background as much as possible, except that I did whatever I could to relieve him of responsibilities. I think my heart was breaking almost as much as his during that time, although worse was coming.

"After about a year, he began taking other women out, and I

spent most of my spare time in my room silently weeping. I had never been jealous of Linda, because that was something beautiful, something I had no right to, something I would not have wanted to interfere with. But now the future began to look uncertain, and my love for Paul, the biggest thing in my life before I knew him or ever expected to know him, had now grown even stronger.

"Then one day, as he was dictating a letter, he suddenly stopped short and just stared at me. It was as if he was seeing me for the first time. 'Cynthia,' he said. 'Cynthia, look, I. . . .' He faltered, and my heart began to pound. We looked in each other's eyes for a long moment in which neither of us spoke. Then we both stood up at once and came toward each other, and in the next instant I was in his arms."

Her fantasy contained many details omitted here. At the height of its intensity, she spent hours at a time in her room reading magazine articles about the object of her limerence, listening to his music, and giving herself up to the process of limerence fantasization. This kind of behavior is not unusual in a teenager and is often referred to as "infatuation." Cynthia also had a conviction like that of other interviewees. The possibility exists for you as a limerent that although you may not in actual fact be acquainted with LO—LO may never even have seen your face or heard your name—some element of hopefulness (in a limerent sense) can be constructed from a belief that *if* circumstances enabled the acquaintance to occur, you possess qualities that would not only have appeal, but possibly *unique* appeal, for that person. The quality may indeed be no more than the monumental intensity of your own passion. If so, the difference between infatuation and being in love dissolves. Although Cynthia was too level-headed a young woman to claim that a *bona fide* love affair with Paul McCartney was a possibility in any real sense, her limerence was based in hope born of a certain confidence about her own capability should the unlikely conditions indeed arise.

Note, too, in Cynthia's fantasy, that it begins in the reality of her everyday world with an event that may be improbable, but which is not impossible. It *could* happen. This unlikely, but possible, premise is then pursued more or less realistically in relation to available information. Cynthia *is* studying shorthand and typing. Paul McCartney *is* widely reputed to be a man devoted to his family. People *do* grow ill and die. The limerent fantasy, intricate as it may be, is satisfying only when it retains fidelity to the possible. The more plausible the steps leading up to mutuality, the more thrilling is the image of the moment of consummation.

Externally, Cynthia was what her mother called "a typical adolescent, crazy about that horrible rock music." In general, she was quite normal, kept more or less regular hours, achieved above-average grades in school, and, except for one fan letter which she prepared with great care and showed only to her very best friend (whose own favorite was a different popular musical performer), never engaged in any overt actions that would help her to achieve her limerent goal. I asked her about this.

"Well, it's really my sense of reality. Okay, I'm in love with Paul McCartney. I admit it, to you, anyway. I would not admit it to my mother or my friends, not even my best friend, in just those words. I mean, it's batty. It's impossible. A million other girls probably feel exactly the way I do—or worse. I went to see his show and I got the best seat I could afford, but it took four hours of standing in line! Afterwards, I joined about 2,000 other fans trying to catch a glimpse when he came out the stage door. I mean, really! I've got this crazy kind of hangup, but I'm not *crazy!*"

By the time Cynthia confided her fantasies to me, she had long since progressed to limerence within a quite "normal" relationship.

In contrast to Cynthia, how different it is, and how intensely painful, if your LO is part of the immediate environment. You see no reason why mutuality should not occur. Of all the tales of love told to me during my years of research, none were more poignant than those in which the reaction of LO to the limerent person was consistently one of rejection. Since some degree of hope is essential for limerence to survive, it seemed remarkable that so many such cases turned up.

Many of the individuals said that their situation was not generally known, even to close friends, and in some cases was known to no one before myself. It appears that considerably more of such experiences are endured than is generally assumed. The private journals and diaries that were made available to me were virtually all in this category, and I think that was no accident. Personal record keeping served as the sufferer's only confidant.

The state of unreturned limerence is one of relative (and often self-imposed) isolation. Happy lovers are off somewhere together enjoying the bliss of mutuality. Indeed, whenever an acknowledged relationship exists, even if it is troubled, much time is spent in interaction. Although they may eventually grow bored or annoyed, friends and family are usually around to serve as sounding boards, advice givers, and sometimes sources of sympathy and support. Besides there are *things* to tell them, real events, not just reports of emotional upheaval generated by the subtleties of what limerents imbue with meanings not visible to the listener. To say, "Then he beat me 40 times," makes a more entertaining tale than, "I could see it in the way she looked at me."

The secretly limerent person fixated on an LO who gives little or no positive response more quickly runs out of "material" capable of holding a friend's interest. Furthermore, many interviewees told of passions that required secrecy. Often the reason was sheer embarrassment. So they poured it into their diaries, and some of them, when they learned of my interest, allowed me to read the diaries and tape-record their stories.

In telling the story of one such prolonged limerence, of Fred for a young Frenchwoman named Laura, I have emphasized the situations and reactions that occurred again and again in the accounts to which I was given access. Features such as the duration of Fred's limerence and the amount of contact between him and Laura, his LO, are in the middle range of such stories. Limerences were reported that persisted as long as 15 years without reciprocation. The 17 months of Fred's exclusive attachment to Laura is somewhat shorter than average. Duration generally is dependent on the behavior of LO and on situational factors. Whatever the reason for Laura's actions, there is no doubt that Fred's state would have differed had she behaved differently.

Furthermore, the end of his limerence, when it finally came, seemed possible only because he was able to alter his situation and put both an ocean and a new lover between Laura and himself. In this sense his return to the United States seemed both cause and effect. He left France when he did partly to free himself from the effects of Laura's daily presence, but he was capable of making the decision according to terms allowed by his limerence. Among those whose stories were similar to Fred's were employees who worked in the same office, professor and student at a university, psychotherapist and patient, members of a dance company or other artistic group, students attending the same school, or people living in the same neighborhood. The basic similarity in the situations was that there existed a relationship between the two people during which occurred the neutral and totally nonamatory contacts that perpetuated the limerent reaction. Because Fred saw Laura daily, their neutral contacts were more frequent than most.

Another factor in these cases was that the limerent person was handicapped in trying to end the limerence by transferring the feelings to a more receptive LO, although in most cases, as in Fred's, some attempt along these lines was made. For Fred, it was a combination of the pressures of his work and the foreign environment that made it hard for him to meet someone who would become a new LO. Had he been located in Paris, where it was easier to socialize with English-speaking persons, and had he had more free time, he might have had greater success in finding others to distract him from his obsession with Laura. In other cases, factors that inhibited the transfer of the attachment to another LO included lack of confidence in physical attractiveness, relative isolation from opportunities to attract another person, and social pressures, such as those brought to bear on married people or on the homosexual person in love with a heterosexual member of the same sex.

Situations in which no clear overt act ever takes place between the limerent and the LO can nevertheless provide all the elements for producing the limerent reaction.

For some of the people who experienced a long period of limerence, eventual reciprocation by LO, even marriage, actually did follow the period of secret longing. For others, mutuality was followed by the kind of reversal of feeling that Fred feared would occur if ever Laura truly responded as he longed for her to do.

My sources suggest that the experiences of people involved in actual relationships (as opposed to this condition of secret pining) are essentially similar and sometimes more intensely painful, particularly if you are limerent about an LO who maintains total control over all aspects of your interactions. You wait for the telephone to ring; each time you are together it is at LO's initiation and therefore contains the message that restimulates, renews hope, and prevents recovery. Some LOs are experts at judging just how long an absence of contact can be interposed without destroying the limerent reaction, or so it seems to the sufferer. (The view from LO's vantage point must here be inferred.) I am describing a totally unreturned (by even mildly objective standards) limerence for ease of exposition, and to reflect a condition that especially typified the written records. Limerence insufficiently returned within a love-sex relationship is not different in any basic way from one totally unreturned. A spouse of 30 years who never feels completely certain and whose limerence therefore is sustained at a high level of intensity feels much the same as Fred did. If anything, emotional swings from joy to despair and from anger to gratitude are more violent in the context of a relationship that includes a level of commitment and mutuality.

Finally, before beginning Fred's tale, I want to underscore what many people—particularly those who have never experienced limerence, or who have but have "forgotten," or who distrust their own mental balance—may find hard to believe: Fred and every other person whose situation, and limerence, was similar to Fred's were fully functioning, rational, emotionally stable, normal, nonneurotic, nonpathological members of society. As a group, except with respect to the limerence reaction itself and events that followed as its direct consequence, they could be characterized as responsible and quite sane. For those interviewed following full recovery, there were no remaining traces of the former obsessiveness, or even of the distorted vision of the LO.

I cannot overstress this point. Too often, in fiction and in psychiatry, a limerent reaction blends into or is interpreted as a "mental illness." I can conceive of several reasons for this, none of which include any necessary link between limerence and mental disturbance. First, limerence is basically at variance with rationality and with a conception of human behavior as essentially the visible outcome of logical thought. The limerent's behavior may sometimes reflect the internal stress. It strains credulity that a rational being should reveal this encapsulated bit of "insanity." Second, individuals who *are* mentally ill or under emotional stress for other reasons therefore exhibit their limerent reactions more openly. An existing instability does not cause limerence, but may cause it to show. Finally, some adopt a strategy of overt response to their own limerence that escalates to desperate and obtrusive levels.

Limerence *is* associated with various forms of violence. Consult police records for statistics on accidents, murders and suicides in which a limerent component clearly exists. Such tragedies seem to result not from limerence itself, but from limerence augmented and distorted. Fred's limerence is, in this sense, pure; and pure limerence, while clearly a madness, operates within a more limited domain.

He has no indisposition that I know of, but love, desperate love, the worst of all maladies in my opinion. In short, the Boy is distractedly in love. . . .

—Maurois [2]

Oh Love! Thou bane of the most generous souls!
Thou doubtful pleasure, and thou certain pain.

—George Granville, Baron Lansdowne [3]

Then you reach the final torment: utter despair poisoned still further by a shred of hope.

—Stendhal [4]

Fred Johnson was one of the two university undergraduates who first stimulated my professional interest in what I then called "romantic love" during a long conversation on a winter's afternoon more than 10 years ago. It was he and Bill Golding, you may recall, whose love affairs had unsettled their lives and distracted them from important long-range goals such as pursuit of their academic studies. By the time Fred graduated that June, my professional interest had taken hold, and Fred and I had a number of additional discussions. He had just "gotten over" an unhappy relationship with Carol, a young woman he had known since high school. He talked to me at length about himself and his feelings for her, and the ups and downs of their time together. He was, in retrospect, my first more or less formal interviewee, and he later said that those conversations (which did not seem formal at the time) were at least partly responsible for the manner in which he recorded his limerent reaction to Laura.

Fred was not a psychology student, and it was almost seven years after those conversations before I heard anything further from him. Perhaps he would not have stopped by my office then, except that he had learned of my continued interest in studying romantic attractions.

He had gone on to obtain a doctorate in architectural history, and his dissertation concerned peasant housing of sixteenth-century France. I won't attempt to explain how he got into that field. The important thing is that Fred spent two years in a small city in southwestern France which happened to be located near the only library with resources appropriate to his scholarly enterprise. While there he lived in a men's residence where Laura was employed as receptionist for almost two years, beginning in September 1972 and ending in June 1974.[5] During that time, he traveled to Paris about a dozen times, mostly on weekends, and took a two-week Christmas holiday back home the first year. His initial departure for Europe occurred almost three years after his relationship with Carol had ended. She subsequently married a mutual friend. While quite thoroughly over Carol, no one had taken her place—"which suited me fine," he said. "I'd had enough misery. My idea was to concentrate on my work. Really, once Carol was totally gone, I had a few good years—until Laura."

Fred sketched out the basic facts of his stay at La Grangée as they related to Laura, then asked me about my research findings. Like so many others, Fred listened to my description of the state of limerence with his head involuntarily bobbing up and down in affirmation. He told me about the diaries he had kept while in France and how he had felt that the material was possibly of "scientific usefulness," but that he had almost destroyed them a number of times "out of the humiliation of having been so crazy." We agreed that he would send them to me and that I would so alter the details as to render them untraceable to him. The excerpts, as well as all descriptions of his later comments on the material when he visited me again a few months later, conform to that stipulation.

Although Fred met Laura on the day of his arrival, limerence did not begin for about six months, not until after his return from a Christmas visit to his family. He described the beginnings of his attraction:

"During those first months, Laura was basically part of the scenery, even then, one of the nicer parts. At that time, I was so involved with getting material in the library, taking photos of buildings in the nearby villages, seeing to their proper development, reading and struggling with the almost medieval French, that my social life consisted of a couple of evenings a week at a local café with American or other English-speaking men who also lived in the residence.

"After my visit home, I began to hang around the public rooms. At first it was because the trip had consumed my extra funds. Later it was also because of Laura. It was cold and rainy that January, especially cold for that region. One day they had made a fire but it had gotten somewhat out of control when I wandered down to get warm. Laura was having trouble with a huge log that kept threatening to roll out of the fire and onto the floor. The place was fairly empty at that time—if other people had been around, Laura would have had plenty of assistance since she was, as I said, attractive.

"I guess it was the first time I had actually got physically close to her. There we were struggling together with the fire, touching, and she used this perfume, and, well, it happened. Just like that. The erotic impulse, you might call it.

"Not that I gave it any thought. At least not for a couple of days. It must have been about a week later that I saw Laura in the office when I stopped by to pay my monthly bill. It was the way she looked at me that did it.

"I had been keeping a journal that consisted mostly of lists of things to do, places that I had been to, and an account of my expenses. That notebook gradually turned into the diaries that I will send you. I think it took a couple of weeks before I started writing, but after that I became pretty regular, as you will see."

Although Fred had warned me, I was surprised at the quantity of material that arrived a few weeks later. Even the first entries contained complaints about the state in which he found himself.

29th January, 1973:
Damn it! I have reverted to daydreaming erotic romantic fantasies. The pure joy of work is gone, and I am beset with the process of imagining outlandish circumstances that would find me in Laura's arms from whence would come a passionate amour. It is very strange, I did not expect it, but I could almost enjoy this suspended tension condition I am in, if my work were not the loser. This game with Laura is delicate and not entirely subtle. I do not think it can be played solitaire, and it is an attraction, not a sex need. Not just anyone would do; probably only Laura would do. But so far she has been perfectly aloof, which gives me much to contemplate.

7th February:
Fantasies intrude like flashes of wife and children in the movie *The Pawnbroker*. Almost in full color. For example, Laura is hurt

and I rush to the rescue or she displays affection. Because it is so irrational, I find it embarrassing, to think of and even to write of.

The entries during this period indicate that there had been no interaction between Fred and Laura that he did not initiate or that could not be interpreted simply as Laura doing her job. However, Fred had already passed into the stage in which almost any behavior on Laura's part short of emphatic rejection was able to be interpreted as "positive."

10th February:
I feel it in front, just below the sternum. Pressure, pressing inward. And I can hardly eat. I cannot say that sex has nothing to do with it because my fantasies lead through affection to sex. Always to sex. But sex in an idealist form. Ecstasy of affection expressed sexually. No interest in plain sex. Sex must be embedded, adorned in the fantasy. Maybe being in love begins by liking, but I have taken a giant step to another universe. Can I cure it by forcing myself to see Laura realistically?

Fred took pains to describe what he called Laura's "unsuitability." Yes, she was attractive, but there were the cultural differences, and her personal interests were quite different from his.
Although he referred often to this unsuitability, he had begun to describe what emerged as Laura's admirable qualities. Further, despite her polite aloofness, he had developed a strong belief in reciprocity hidden behind the same feelings of shyness that he experienced.

12th February:
I have taken to looking at myself in the mirror quite often, and it is clear that I am not the best-looking man here, but that has not stopped my certainty that this attraction is not one-sided. Maybe she is struggling with herself because I am not as handsome as other men who are interested in her. I am amazed at the physical sensations. There is a tension slightly to the right of the middle of my chest, deep. Sometimes it extends down to my

stomach. It is more intense when I inhale as if the air constricts the tissues. I can see why they call it disease of the heart; that is more or less where I feel it. A sigh is a drawn-out exhalation relieving the pain. This passion *is* an ache, and it is somewhat relieved by thinking of Laura.

15th February:
Nothing has really changed. It is still difficult to work. Sometimes there is a tightening in my throat, often accompanied by a vivid bit of imagery. The images sometimes come in very small flashes—just a kiss, maybe from an unidentified woman.

By this time Fred had altered his schedule to increase the frequency with which he encountered Laura. He also attempted through subtle means to give her every opportunity to respond to him. One day while he was sitting alone in the lounge with a book, she came in with a magazine in her hand as if about to sit down and read it. It seemed to him that it was when she noticed his presence that she changed her mind and left the room. His initial interpretation of her action was that it was a clear and undeniable indication that she was not interested in him. That night he wrote:

23rd February:
I feel a large impassable gap between us across which I must look ridiculous. Thus it is that my image of her image of me as reflected in her behavior and my own, not a change in her qualities (her attractiveness, for example), has produced this new condition of relative indifference towards Laura. I am afraid that this relief is temporary, however, and I will return to being more intensely stricken, but it shows the dampening effect that clear rejection can have. At least it is giving me an interlude in which I can get some work done.

As predicted, Fred's next encounter with Laura ended the period of respite, and the fantasies soon returned. The diary contained long passages in which Fred described his hopes of establishing the beginnings, at least, of a relationship with Laura.

As Stendhal had done, Fred set himself deadlines by which time he tried to force himself to accomplish some positive steps, but these were invariably ignored when the time came and his apprehension overwhelmed him.[6] The only "progress" was an arrangement whereby he was permitted to use the typewriter in the office for two hours each morning, at the time that Laura worked on bookkeeping. At first it seemed that their relationship would undergo alteration with this new arrangement, and in a sense there was a change.

5th March:
I cannot say that anything has really happened between me and Laura with the exception of certain looks that pass between us, but working in the office makes the current situation enjoyable. Moving to a deeper level of involvement may take away some of the slow minor pleasures that are possible as well as risk jealousy and possessiveness. I feel much more romantic toward Laura than sexually attracted. I mean, I imagine us expressing mutual affection and admiration in romantic settings.

The ultimate moment in my imagining is looking at each other and holding hands. Laura has turned out to be a much finer person than my original impression. She is a very conscientious worker and treats everyone with sweetness and consideration. I cannot follow all that she says when she speaks rapidly, but every day brings improvement. We do not talk to each other very much, since she is busy and my only excuse for being there forces me to type, which is good because I am getting some real work done. But in the few conversations that we have Laura is very considerate and speaks slowly. She is really helping me to speak French better.

Note here the tendency to find value of some kind, despite the suffering. Such "rationalizations" were common among interviewees.

Fred decides that his difficulty with conversational French and the ease with which he is able to understand Laura's speech combine to make it quite logical that he attempt to hire her to give him private lessons. He gives considerable thought to the details of what he will propose, how much money to offer, when the lessons should take place, and particularly how he can frame his request to cushion the blow should she refuse. The plan works, and Laura agrees to stay at the residence for an hour after dinner on Monday evenings. However, although Laura cooperates, her essential aloofness remains.

23rd March:
I would love to be able to imagine Laura burning with passion behind her cool exterior, but I am forced to admit it is unlikely. Even after all these weeks and all the time we are spending together, the only real contact between Laura and me is eye contact.

This would continue to be basically true throughout his stay at La Grangée and the duration of this attraction to Laura.

23rd April:
I am inhibited in writing this diary. I find it frightening to commit so much personal material to paper. I suppose the main reason for doing it is because there is no one else to speak to. It would be very embarrassing to have anyone read how much time and energy I am putting to this thing. I still fear that what I want to happen might in fact happen, and it scares me as much as the possibility that it will not happen. The attraction is my invention. It is ugly because it is impersonal. How can I say that I really like Laura when she so clearly is not the sort of person who could really be part of my life? Last weekend in Paris, I met Nancy, a Sorbonne student in Renaissance literature. Although traveling to Paris is expensive and time consuming, that is not why I failed to really try to initiate a relationship with someone who, by all objective standards, including her obvious interest in me, would make a good friend, maybe even someone who could enter into my life. The reason was Laura and this thing that has happened to me. It makes no sense at all. No wonder they talk about drinking a love potion!

17th July:
Laura really looks great in summer clothes. This morning in the office she was cheerful and friendly and joked with me. I feel like a rag doll thrown about emotionally. I wish that I could say that if she really showed interest I would be the one to resist. This feeling in my head and gut is a continual presence. I cannot seem to get away from it. I sit still and think and feel when I should be working.

3rd August:
It seems to me that being romantically attracted to Laura means that I am bending my image of her until it is distorted. Things that might produce an unpleasant picture, I simply do not see. When she appears by relatively objective standards, beautiful and capable, I look long and hard. But when she is not at her best, when I catch her face in an unflattering angle, I turn my eyes away. If she were in love with me, she would do the same, and we might both be aware of the process in the other because we could feel it in ourselves. If that is true, "loving back" is actually furthering a deception. Only the best angles are allowed to show or be seen. To do anything else is to increase the risk of the dreaded rejection. But it is a disservice to a person not to perceive them the way they really are. I try to find the reality in Laura, but I know that I can look directly at her and perceive only that which excites me.

2nd September:
Last night I entertained myself with light and playful imaginary scenes in which Laura and I enjoyed one another and ourselves thoroughly. We acted like children frolicking around among the hedges in the garden. When suddenly she stopped and said, "Do not look at me like that, it turns me on." We kissed each other; we were affectionate. It was sex and affection.

15th September:
I have become distracted and unfocused. I cannot work. I am afflicted with a stupid infatuation that I refuse to idealize into something else. It is an emotional deception. Laura just hap-

pened to be around at the right time. At any rate, the whole thing is insane. I am not being myself when I am in her presence. She does not even understand my language, so it is quite illogical for me to care how she feels about me. I have tried to talk to her about architecture, and she has shown absolutely no interest in the subject. She does not care about the things that interest me most, and I cannot really want someone around me who would be bored with my work. Yet I find myself twisting the whole thing upside down and convincing myself, at least momentarily, that for Laura to be uninterested in what is most important in my life is somehow an advantage!

Fred has been thinking that being with someone who knows nothing about his work might enable him to get away from it, whereas if he were often in the presence of someone in his field, it would be harder to relax. But after working out this complex rationalization, as he calls it, he rejects it.

15th September [continued]:
In fact Laura *is* interfering with my work and with my life, even if she is not intending to, and even if she is as innocent and neutral as she pretends to be.

It was about this time that Fred first considered leaving France in order to escape his limerence. This theme began to emerge more frequently in his diary entries. Another repeated theme was his berating himself for failing to take more definite and assertive steps.

15th September [continued]:
I am in great distress. I must go over the new set of photographs. I want to lie down. I just want to think of her endlessly.

In his distress Fred writes long passages almost daily describing every little interaction between himself and Laura, complaining about the time spent in fantasy, and intermittently including complimentary descriptions of Laura's behavior and appearance. The lessons in colloquial French had continued but, unexpectedly, they produced more discouragement than pleasure. Laura prepared conscientiously and did not deviate from the task at hand. Fred's behavior in this situation was unlike his usual pattern with women. He was perhaps more shy than some young men of his age, but under other conditions quite capable of flirting and making blatantly sexual advances. It was Laura's unrelieved failure to provide even the smallest degree of encouragement, and Fred's limerence, that paralyzed him.

20th September:
I have just read back over this diary. In March I would never have believed that so much time could go by totally without progress. I have become desperate. My passion has taken over my consciousness. Hours of every day are devoted to Laura, to what has become fastidious concern over every detail of my dress and appearance, to the endless daydreaming, and to the search for ways to interest her in things that we might do together. Her image is everywhere I look. Everything I think of, no matter how remote, leads me back to thinking of her. The first thing I see when I wake up in the morning is her face, and she is in my thoughts whether or not she is in my presence. I have become determined to do something about this, but I do not know what to do. Other things scarcely exist for me anymore. I forgot to pick up the photographs I had ordered, and they were almost sent back to Paris. I am incapacitated. I like Laura, she is nice, but this extraordinary reaction of mine is entirely inappropriate. I have a kind of sinking feeling almost all the time and I welcome problems serious enough to distract me from this idiocy. My major feeling is not wanting to work on my dissertation, despite the approaching deadline. My stomach aches, and I feel sunk, depressed. If I could only be absolutely sure that she is not interested in me, I would have nothing to build hopes on, but when she is at all nice to me, I suffer.

15th November:
I am worse, not better. It is a hideous time-consuming and volcanic subterranean stirring, a whirlpool in my gut that pulls

me down to my bed to daydreams and away from my work. I am hopelessly lovesick. What can I do?

Fred decides that he will leave France in six weeks, but he has sent for certain necessary materials that will not arrive for at least a month, and it will take him several weeks after that to incorporate them. He blames his obsession for not having sent for them sooner. Now he feels trapped and unable to leave. He also finds it extremely painful to consider the prospect of no longer being able to see Laura.

15th December:
I try to stop the thoughts but my body goes crazy. It is concentrated in my pelvis and gut. It is as if there is a demon in there. It is not sexual arousal. It is emotional turmoil.

When Laura's behavior admits the possibility of return, or, rather, when Fred is able to so interpret her behavior, he feels better. He is usually happy when actually in her presence and even happier when he anticipates being with her. For example, despite the discouragement he feels after each of his Monday-evening sessions, he is invariably elated during the day in anticipation of the hour they will have together. From time to time he experiences periods of absolute certainty that Laura is in love with him and spends his days imagining valid and consistent reasons for her aloofness. Sometimes his assumption of her positive reaction becomes so strong that he writes with the plural first person pronoun "we." For example:

7th January, 1974:
Time drags when we are alone together. The mutual attraction is there but we are both conflicted and hesitant about initiating every action. We both recognize that there would be many problems to overcome. Our interests are so diverse. Not that there has been the slightest hint of these things in our conversation. It is just that one sometimes feels so strongly that one *knows*.

When, as occasionally happens, Laura behaves in a more friendly way, the incident confirms for Fred the growing feeling of "intimacy" between them. Yet, when two years later he and I read the diaries together, he marveled at what a fool he must have appeared.

As if referring to a physical illness, some days he would say he was "better." Occasionally he did not even mention Laura but talked of other things, but then some incident would set him off and he would be lost to lovesickness again. He was annoyed at how dependent was his emotional state on what was probably inconsequential, even incidental, behavior on her part. If she were late going to work in the morning, he would worry about her; and if she looked at him or smiled, he became ecstatic and embroiled in fantasies.

15th February:
I feel that there is much similarity between us but that could be part of the blindness. It frightens me that my feelings toward Laura could become more intense, because if they did it would be unbearable. Yesterday I witnessed a conversation she had with a friend by telephone from the office. This has happened many times before, but now that my French has improved it occurred to me that it might be a man to whom she spoke and I tried to follow the conversation. I do not want to become jealous.

Fred decides that he will wait it out. He gives up any thought of leaving France earlier than his original plan. The entries in the diary continue in a similar manner through the spring, sometimes worse, sometimes better.

4th April:
I will be in the middle of reading about a certain architectural structure, and a Laura fantasy will begin—stirred by what? Everything reminds me of her. My eye movements follow the words on the page, but they no longer make sense. I find myself in the middle of the next page and do not remember getting there. I try to keep from thinking of her, but in truth I am

obsessed. I read about a certain type of dwelling popular in Burgundy in the 1780s and begin to wonder what sort of house Laura lives in. It is a continual struggle just to do ordinary things.

As we later read the diary together, Fred kept saying, "She could not have loved me. It is impossible on every count. She tried to have the kind of impersonal friendship that was appropriate to the conditions. That was all that was responsible for my insane feelings of hopefulness. I managed to go all those months in a hopeless situation feeling continual hope."

20th May:
Being with Laura makes it worse. Not seeing her makes it worse. I am scheduled to leave France in less than three months. I look forward to the day; I do not know how I will be able to bring myself to go through with it. Yesterday I fantasized as follows:
Laura leaves the residence for home, but her car breaks down along the way. It happens I have rented a car for the weekend and encounter her. She gets into my car and we begin to drive toward her home on a lonely road. We have only gone a mile or two when my car also fails us. We walk about a mile to the nearest town and have dinner together in the café while the local garage mechanics are sent to retrieve and repair both automobiles. It turns out that to fix Laura's car will require several days, so we set out in mine. By this time it is late. The mechanics did a poor job and the car breaks down again in the middle of a forest. We know the nearest house is miles away, and our only hope is a passing car. We cuddle together as night comes on trying to keep each other warm since we are prepared with neither jackets nor sweaters. Gradually our mutual inhibitions dissolve, and our passion increases to such intensity that we ourselves are shocked by it.

When Fred read that entry in my office he laughed out loud. "That," he said, "could never have happened, but back then I did not realize it. I actually believed there was a chance that Laura might respond to me. I do not believe that now. I have reread the diaries and I have thought carefully over as many of the events as I can remember and I find no trace of evidence that Laura felt anything other than the politeness toward me that was part of her job." He himself was amazed at the ingenuousness with which he was able to interpret disinterest on her part as passion disguised.

His departure for the Unites States in August did not mark the end of his attraction to Laura, although it declined rapidly once he was away from her. By January of the next year he had entered into a relationship with Linda, and by the following summer was quite certain that absolutely nothing remained of the attraction he had formerly felt for Laura. Despite this, it was only partly in order to supply himself with a few additional photographs for his book, that he returned to France the following June. He said he expected that he would see Laura as she had appeared to him before his limerence began, that he would feel neutral about her and see her realistically.

He stayed for a week. During the first two days his expectation appeared to be confirmed. But to his amazement the limerent reaction was restimulated long before the week was up, and he was, as he put it, "almost where I had been the year before." This time, emboldened by the brevity of his stay, he engaged in the kind of assertive behavior that had not been possible earlier and asked Laura if she would have dinner with him. She refused saying she was sorry but she had a previous appointment. "What surprised me more than anything else in the whole business was that even *that* did not end it. I was unable to put the image of Laura's face out of my consciousness throughout the plane trip and, indeed, I thought of her frequently for several weeks afterward."

Limerence can live a long life sustained by crumbs. Indeed, overfeeding is perhaps the best way to end it. It bears a definite resemblance to the condition of the laboratory rats and pigeons who continue to press the bar or peck at the disk even when the probability of food reward is gradually diminished, so that on the average only one in hundreds or even thousands (for pigeons who were very persistent and rapid peckers) of "responses" actually pays off. When the animal is presented with an uncertain relationship between its actions and the behavior of the food-delivery mechanism, quite remarkable results are obtained. Even for laboratory animals, the key elements seem to be doubt and hope. Ordinary gambling resembles this laboratory behavior in its persistence even when chances of winning are slight. Perhaps for both limerent persons and habitual gamblers, the size of the possible prize is also important. Both gamblers and limerents find reason to hope in wild dreams.

As Ruth, one of my earliest interviewees, put it:

"Love is irrational. Whether you call it a mental illness or sublime spirituality, you behave in love in ways that do not represent your own true best interests, ways that deflect from the goals you've built your life around, even if the deflection is slight, even if it is easily rationalized and even when it is disguised as beauty or experienced as ecstasy.

"How can I say that my seemingly interminable passion for Eric, a 15-year obsession, was reasonable? Consider the 30,000 hours—I actually calculated my estimation, and that's a conservative figure—I spent going over every word he said, every gesture, every letter he wrote, when I might have been reading, or learning a foreign language, or enjoying the company of others. Instead, I was caught in a merry-go-round of wondering how he felt, wishing he would call, anticipating our next time together, or endlessly searching in my recollections of his behavior and my convoluted reconstruction of the possible reasons for his actions for the shreds of hope on which my madness fed.

"Long after he no longer bothered to hide from me certain signs of his loss of interest and his vulnerability to the enticements of other women, I could still *see* love in his eyes, even in his ill-treatment of me."

Finally the anguish of limerence is revealed in this diary excerpt from a mature woman whose LO was a coworker in her office. She had known the man for five years, and had been limerent toward him for three with no real evidence that he viewed her in other than a neutral manner. Part of her saw this, but that did not diminish her passion, which she came to see as a disease:

"This passion is a foreign growth. Sometimes it shrinks down to bare perceptability, but contact (even a phone call or seeing him in the corridor from a distance) stimulates it again. I am returned to the state of anguished yearning. It is seductive. Its growth is sometimes unfed. Fantasy brings moments of relief, if not ecstasy. Fantasy only brings the image of ecstasy, a positive moment amid the pain. But that transitory vision, with its small relief, then stabs me with intensified desire. I am worse.

"When I am in his presence each moment hangs separate and disconnected. I try to act 'normally.' I alternate between wild moments of abject limerence and near neutrality. Occasionally, there are flashes of dislike, even hatred of him. But these do nothing to stop or diminish the limerence. They reside in a lonely room in my mind.

"If I had not written in this diary, I would never have believed myself capable of such long-term idiocy. But this volume provides incontrovertible proof. I can't hide my shame from myself."

READINESS AND LONGING FOR LIMERENCE

Before limerence begins and after it is over, you may be in a state not of limerence but of readiness. My interviewee Philip was in such a state after he got over his broken engagement with Harriet and before he met Jane. Some people become limerent at puberty, or earlier, and remain limerent through various relationships, for many years thereafter. Dancer Isadora Duncan wrote in her diary that after her first experience she was continually in love all her life and that at the time she wrote, in her late thirties, she was recovering from the latest attack.[7] The diaries of adolescents often describe longing for "someone," as if limerence gets turned on at a certain age, or hormone level, or stage of "psychosexual" development, regardless of the presence of a suitable LO.[8] Even before a particular potential recipient of limerence appears on the scene, the young person feels an emotional stirring that can be described as wanting to be in love. As Morton Hunt noted, this bursting readiness can erupt in a cloudburst of feeling as soon as an object for it is found.[9] And we have already seen that adolescents do not always wait for suitable peers, but focus their youthful attachment on to some popular figure, such as a musician or film star.

This longing for love or for someone is reflected in the reactions of The Group. Two-thirds said they "need someone to love and to love me," and more than half complained of loneliness. Approximately half accepted the statements, "Sometimes I feel sad when I am with other couples because I am alone"; "I have been very lonely"; "I feel a great need for an intimate relationship with someone"; and "I wish I could find the right person for me."

What is a "potential LO"? The answer appears to be anyone who meets certain rough criteria. Bea was frank about it.

"I love Bruce. I love him more than I have ever loved anyone. I am quite helpless about it. Fully involved. *But* I also know that I would have fallen in love with any fairly decent-looking unmarried man who had happened to move into the apartment next door. Anyone. I know that and yet, now, it could not be anyone else. That's just the way it is."

Perhaps there is some truth in the idea of being "in love with love." And yet, some interviewees did not seem to feel it. In later interviews, during which the invariant characteristics of limerence could be described, those who called themselves nonlimerents said that although they liked companionship, and really enjoyed having a steady relationship, they had never felt a longing of the type described. They wanted companionship, affection, friendship, and sex, they would say, but not the intense and exclusive relationship I described as limerence. The difference between those in the state of limerence, no matter how mildly at the time of the interview, and those who were not—especially those who declared that they had never been—was striking. Limerents said that they "wanted it badly," "thought about it a lot," or "couldn't imagine being happy without it." Those for whom the experience was totally foreign said that it would be "nice," "convenient," or "add to life's pleasures." In other words, virtually all young persons interviewed said that they felt that a relationship was important, but only those who by other criteria were categorized as limerent felt it as an intense need. This may be why psychologist Martin Bloom expressed the view that:

> ... love experiences are cumulative ... a love experience leaves a strong impression which never entirely dies out.[10]

As the courses of both Fred's limerence for Laura and Philip's for Harriet demonstrate, limerence toward a particular LO does indeed persist for what can be a very long period, and even indefinitely, when through misrepresentation of LO's behavior, hope is periodically rekindled.

Then, at very low levels of limerence, the feelings begin to seem not directed at the particular individual any longer, but as a more diffuse searching for someone who will provide the longed for mutuality. Al was an example:

"It's definitely finished with Peg. I don't even think of her. If we happen to meet, it's almost like meeting any acquaintance—no pounding heart, etc. But I have real interest in finding a substitute, well, I don't mean someone who'd be like Peg, but someone else to have that kind of relationship with. I'm doing a lot of dating hoping it will happen."

When I questioned Al more closely, he admitted that as far as his feelings for Peg were concerned, if she showed some sign of real interest, he'd "probably respond." But he felt that that was unlikely, and some of the other women he knew had begun to have as much appeal for him as Peg did at that time. It was just that "it" had not yet happened with anyone. Not since Peg.

Al's low-level, nonexclusive state of limerence should not be confused with being entirely free of the state. His general focus was still a desire for a return of feeling, and he spent a considerable amount of time thinking about that. This transformation is an important change, however, from the unpleasantness of nonmutuality to the pleasant expectation of a new relationship.

How long susceptibility to limerence does last seems to depend on sources of "hopefulness," which may be based on how you feel you look to others (based on their reactions to you) as well as on the actual actions of LO. Perhaps limerence tends to decline as a person grows older, mainly because sources of hope that the feeling could possibly be returned are reduced. After a sufficiently extended and "inactive" period, a person may not only recover from limerence toward a particular individual, but also from the state in which limerence is sought. Frieda was such a person:

"It seems I was in love from about age eight or nine until I married Henry. And I was in love with Henry. Then, with the house to manage, bills to worry over, babies to take care of, gradually, I'd more or less let myself kinda go. I still wore makeup, but it was a hasty once-a-day thing, not the time I use to spend on my appearance. After a couple of years I stopped using curlers unless we were going somewhere. I don't mean I became a slob, I just wasn't doing what I used to do. I'd go days without even looking in a mirror. And I put on weight.

"Then, when it began to look bad for my marriage, I saw the first problems that I didn't know how to take care of. That was about when the idea of someone else first occurred to me. But I assure you it was only thinking, no real interest. No reason to think anyone'd be interested in me. All the men I might have found interesting were married or had gone off somewhere. I really didn't want any complications. I just wanted to concentrate my energies on building a life for me and my children. If I 'thought' of anyone, it was someone rich to help with some of the financial problems that were starting to come up."

Frieda was a formerly limerent person for whom a period of mutuality with her husband was followed by nonlimerence, a nonlimerence sustained by doubts about her ability to attract anyone who would interest her and the relative absence of potential LOs in her social circles.

NONLIMERENCE

In *The Summer Before the Dark*, Doris Lessing's character, Kate, describes "a savage woman," Mary Finchley. In amazement, Kate tells her friend Maureen about Mary's sexual adventures, but it is neither their quantity nor the conditions under which they occurred that is responsible for Kate's incredulity; it is Mary's nonlimerence. It took Kate some time to realize that:

> Mary was quite different. She had never been in love in her life. She couldn't understand what I was talking about. At first I thought—as usual—she was joking. But *she* thought I was inventing it. Yes, really—she really believes that the way everyone goes on about love, being in love, is some sort of a conspiracy, the emperor has no clothes. It was about then I discovered she couldn't read anything or look at a play on television or anything. She says, "It's all about people torturing themselves about nothing". . . . Love—all of it, romantic love, the whole bloody business of it—you know, centuries of our civilization—it's been left out of her. She thinks we are all crazy. You fancy a man, he fancies you, you screw until one or the other is tired, and then goodbye, no hard feelings. . . .[11]

Kate's reaction to Mary reminds me of my own initial reaction to my friend Helen Payne.

"Nonlimerent" refers to a person who is not limerent at the time. Both the limerent and the nonlimerent states tend to be sustained. The most frequently encountered patterns were limerents who had always been in love with someone or wanting love, since early age, and nonlimerents who simply could not remember being any other way. There is no limerent or nonlimerent personality, however, and it can be harmful to attribute other characteristics than those closely associated with limerence to persons referred to as "limerent" or to attribute characteristics of any sort to "nonlimerents" other than that they are not limerent at the time or that they do not know the limerent experience.

It is my impression that either state is able to exist in individuals who differ in virtually all other ways. The same person who is limerent now may someday become nonlimerent, as Frieda was, and vice versa. The terms can refer both to the state of a person at a given time and to the person over a period of time, depending on the context. For example, you might ordinarily be a limerent, but not in this particular relationship. For you, then, it is a nonlimerent relationship. In *Gone with the Wind,* Rhett Butler is a nonlimerent who eventually succumbs. Scarlett O'Hara incited limerence in others but not in Ashley, on whom she was fixated for years. Wagner, about whom Cosima, his mistress (later wife), was wildly limerent, was consciously nonlimerent. He said:

As I have never in my life enjoyed the true felicity of love, I shall erect to this most beautiful of my dreams [the Siegfried drama] a monument in which, from beginning to end, this love shall find fullest gratification [in Tristan and Isolde].[12]

Some few of my interviewees had crossed over from limerence to nonlimerence after an early experience described as "traumatic" and, so far as they could tell in retrospect, very like the limerent pattern. One is tempted to call it "Byronic" nonlimerence, since this appears to be precisely the sequence of events that occurred in Lord Byron's life. But too many things are also called Byronic, and since he represents Romance Itself to many people, they might find it so hard to believe, that the meaning of the expression would be lost. From the reports of his biographers and from his own words, it appears as a distinct possibility that he fought both hard and consciously to maintain his nonlimerence. For example, in a letter to Lady Melbourne, Byron complained that he wanted the affair with Caroline Lamb to end and that he would do nothing himself to renew it. It was not that Lady Caroline had lost to one of her rivals, but that

Byron was "tired of being a fool," tired of wasted time, tired of
what would today be called "game playing," of "compliments,
romance and deceit." [13]

The majority of consistently nonlimerent persons interviewed
appeared to maintain their invulnerability without conscious
effort. Limerence simply didn't happen to them, and they were
completely befuddled by my descriptions. Such persons often
mentioned that they had long been concerned about what was
"missing" in their lives. Clearly, love as described in song,
drama, literature, and by friends, with its ecstatic bliss of mutuality, had never happened to them. They wanted it as one wants
to see a movie all have raved about. Not passionately, but with a
degree of uneasiness about feeling left out. Ella represents this
attitude. I talked with her relatively early, before I recognized
the existence of true nonlimerence as opposed to nonlimerence
within a given relationship. At the time, Ella's tale was as baffling to me as my description of limerence was to her:

"I like people, and I'd like to have a relationship with a special
person, someone you can count on, with things you like to do
together, someone to feel affectionate toward, maybe sexy
toward, maybe not, depending on sexual inclination of the moment. Take Steve, for example. We met at summer camp, and it
was really amazing to me how much fun we had together. We
rode horseback, played tennis (well, we volleyed), discussed and
exchanged science-fiction novels, and tended to like the same
movies. It was great. The next year we wrote to each other, and
our letters were complex and intense. They were fun, like par-
ticipating in the production of 'literature.' He was enrolled in a
training program in Wisconsin and I was still living at home in
Ohio finishing high school.

"I was shocked by his proposal. It was not that I had never
thought of marrying Steve. I actually *assumed* that if I ever
married anybody, it would be Steve. But not this way, not the
sudden way he changed toward me. When he came to Ohio that
Christmas I was really glad to see him. I had looked forward to
the great event and had scheduled the week filled with people to

meet and things to do that I knew he'd enjoy. But as I realized almost immediately, he was no longer the person I had known.

"The first evening of his visit he sat me on the couch and started questioning me about who I had been seeing, especially who I had been sleeping with, while he was gone. Then he said that he had figured it all out and that we could get married right away, during his visit, and I would drive back with him. I couldn't believe my ears, and I was finding it harder and harder to breathe. Here was my old friend Steve, someone who had provided some stability in an upheaving world, suddenly gone mad before my eyes. I know he must have received my letter all about my new job and how I felt it was the best thing that could possibly happen to me right now, at this rung of the ladder. 'Rung of the ladder.' I used that very phrase. He knew I had plans but he had completely overlooked them.

"I assure you I *was* upset now. I was also deeply insulted. Steve didn't seem to be talking to me. He didn't seem to know or to care what my intentions were or what I was interested in doing. On the one hand, he was declaring eternal love, and on the other, he showed no concern for my life, my job, my friends, or what I wished. He was a stranger to me.

"When I tried to explain how I felt, the only thing he seemed to hear was that I wouldn't quit my job to go to Wisconsin, so he *backed down* and decided that then he'd come to Ohio. He said that he couldn't 'live' without me, that his mind was made up, and that he knew from my letters that I felt the same way!"

One wonders whether this is the way Philip appeared to Harriet. On the other hand, what an expert "player" in the game of love (limerence) Ella must have seemed to Steve. The non-limerent person who is fond of, affectionate toward, and sexually attracted to you but who does not succumb and does not understand what you want therefore plays the game ingenuously and without artifice, because it is not a game at all.

Ella's experience was not wholly different from others she had had; it was only the most surprising and most frightening. From her early teens, men had been attracted to her and she had often felt it necessary to discontinue seeing a man because he had become "too serious." One thing she had liked about Steve was that until his wild declarations of love at the time of his visit (when he was probably exposing a long-standing hidden limerence), Ella had felt safe and confortable with him, safe from just that sort of attempted encroachment into her personal life.

"After that, I really watched it. If anyone began to give me those looks, I'd cut it fast. I never wanted to have what happened with Steve happen again. I didn't want to be hassled. I didn't care what they did when they weren't with me. I mean I wasn't jealous and I didn't want their jealousy ruling my life!"

People can be jealous for various reasons, over various things. You may be nonlimerent and still be jealous; you may be limerent and yet not be jealous. Your limerent desire for mutuality and exclusivity may not imply hostility toward a rival as does jealously. Sexual jealousy and limerent jealousy are not identical. It is not so much with whom you sleep but whether you return the feelings that matters to the limerent. But the limerent exclusivity is an alien thing to the nonlimerent mind. Nothing like limerence exists there. There is no other state quite like limerence. Therefore it is difficult for the nonlimerent person to imagine or, probably, for the formerly limerent nonlimerent to remember. The need for exclusivity is therefore seldom distinguished from jealousy.

The feelings you as nonlimerent may have about another person may include sexual attraction, friendship, and affection, without the compulsive and intrusive fantasizing or the exclusivity. You may even be jealous, but the jealousy, if it occurs, is more like the jealousy you might experience if a co-worker were selected for an advancement on the job for which you felt yourself to be more deserving. It is not pleasant to be less preferred on the job or in bed, but that is not the same as the limerent need for exclusivity and reciprocation.

Nonlimerent lovers interviewed also used the word "obsession" to describe their reaction to a new lover, particularly during the early "courting" phase of the relationship. But this obsession seemed more like the kind of intense interest a person might have for a new hobby or possession rather than like true limerent obsession. Nonlimerent lovers do not report *intrusive preoccupation,* but rather that thoughts of the person are frequent and pleasurable. The only disadvantage to this "obsession" is that they might get carried away in conversation with others (much as might the owner of a new racing car).

Many nonlimerents remembered a limerent experience in the past. The retrospective accounts of true limerents are notably subject to alteration in the direction of minimizing the condition, but nonlimerents who feel some social pressure to romanticize the whole thing may find it just as easy to go in the other direction, toward embellishment. The two tendencies would, of course, produce indistinguishable end products.

Joe described himself as a "formerly limerent nonlimerent." When I interviewed him, he was 27 years old, sexually active, and exerting his main efforts toward building his career. He was, as he put it:

"... definitely not interested in marriage at this time. Maybe never. I have been in love, I have been hurt, and as far as I'm concerned you can keep it. I don't have the time or the interest."

Joe had suffered through a very painful limerence, one which kept him from his work and severely damaged his self-esteem. He was determined that he would prevent himself from getting into such a state again.

"I simply won't let it happen. I'll never let myself go like that again. If some woman appeals to me in more than just a friendly or sexy way, if I get any sign that that's what's happening, I'll run. I've already done so a couple of times."

I wonder how many people are like Joe. In the hundreds that I have interviewed, only a very few—maybe four or five all together—have described themselves, as he did, as consciously, deliberately, and successfully, avoiding limerence.

As the characteristics of limerence emerged from the previous morass of vague and conflicting material about love and being in love, the interviews changed, as well. Although the results of earlier questionnaires and interviews remained interesting in some ways, they had often to undergo reinterpretation or re-evaluation in the light of later findings. Obviously, it was not possible to ask people whether or not they were limerent until the state had been clearly defined. Such synonyms as "being in love," "romantic love," "passionate love," and "erotic love" were all used in descriptions of sexual companionate relation-ships by people who were later recognized as nonlimerents through their responses to key questions that referred, for exam-ple, to intrusiveness of thought. The terms they used did not necessarily imply the set of traits that were found to be invariant aspects of limerence.

As one aspect of an altered interview strategy, I began to ask several general questions at the start to give an overall picture of what I was interested in hearing about. Some of the questions were:

Are you in love?
How many times have you been in love?
Describe the most important love experience you have had, emphasizing your feelings and how they changed as time passed.
Do you have a philosophy of love? Tell me about it.
What advice might you give to others?
If you are not in love now, would you like to be?

Once I discovered the state of limerence and its absence and began to describe these specific conditions to my interviewees, most readily applied one label or the other to themselves. In fact, the relative emotional independence from the lover often gave the first indication that the person was not limerent. Some nonlimerents tried to piece together an image of limerence from their feelings of friendliness, sexual attraction, impulses toward bear-hugging, and other forms of affection, and perhaps a bit of philosophy. I jokingly called those who tried to cling to the limerent ideal despite their showing none of the classic signs of the condition, "pseudo-limerent nonlimerents." A limerent person pretending to be nonlimerent would be a "pseudo-non-limerent limerent."

In any case, my interviewees applied the labels to themselves. The wonder of it to me, as observer, was that the labels went on so easily, that they stuck like glue, and that there were so few cases that refused to fall easily into one or the other category despite a bit of "pseudo" this or that used from time to time to handle the rare recalcitrant case. The majority of nonlimerents seemed happy to accept their status once they had been given words in which to describe it. Vera said:

"This is wonderful. Now I know what is happening, and I can tell Barry all about it. Maybe that will make him leave me alone a little more often and not feel so bad about it. I think, from what you say, that he must be limerent."

Or as Sheila confessed:

"I thought that there was something that others were experiencing that I was deprived of and it made me feel terrible. When Tim and I began getting really serious, I was thrilled. I felt that the thing I had been missing had suddenly happened. Looking back, I think it was part the glamour and adventure of the entire situation and part real sexual attraction toward Tim. Mutual. But when you read me that list, that was not the way it was. I thought about Tim a lot, but never when I didn't want to. There was no big desire for what you call 'mutuality.' I really didn't care about his other relationships as long as they didn't bother me in any way. Pardon my crudeness, but I *was* concerned about disease. I mean, that was the limit of my concern. That and the fact that I had become financially dependent on Tim. I didn't look forward to any competition over the dollar.

"Do you know, I think that both Tim and I were nonlimerents and that that's why we got along as well as we did. If we had been able to talk about it in these terms instead of beating around the bush like that, it would have been better, but probably both of us were afraid to come out and say we did not 'love.' There was a possible custody case coming up. Even more important might have been that both of us were trying to hide our limerencelessness from ourselves as well. We both were telling ourselves that maybe it could be like you read about in books next time. And so we parted, and I really liked Tim, really cared about him. We could have had a good life with each other if we hadn't been chasing rainbows.

"So I'm a nonlimerent. Well, it sounds like a nice and healthy thing to be."

Ben was another nonlimerent trying unsuccessfully to fit his feelings and interests into a limerent image of love:

"I am in love at the present time—with several people, but especially with Jane. I think about her very often and I really enjoy being with her. I might even consider marriage. She's got all the qualities I've ever thought about in a wife. She's attractive, intelligent, makes terrific pies, plays chess, and never hassles me. Not so far, anyway.

"Most women I know, the women I take out, after a while they get to a point where they begin to overstep what I call my 'privacy privilege.' They begin to want more than I can possibly give them. I don't really know what it is they do want, but it certainly isn't what I am giving. That's all too clear. I've learned the signs. If it starts, off I go. That's the end. I can't take that."

People like Ben—and I found them among women as well as men, among the mature as well as the young, among the very intelligent, the highly artistic, as well as the duller of those I interviewed—taught me not to form or to express premature conclusions during the interview. We may well learn someday whether there are more limerents or more nonlimerents, and therefore, something about what people can expect of their partners. All I can say now is that there seem to be plenty of each. When I described to Ben the details of the limerent state, he was wide-eyed. No, he had never felt *that* way. But he recognized the validity of the description through the behavior of others. Limerence still made no sense to him, but now, at least, it had a name and it happened to a lot of people. They weren't making it up in all those songs and all those movies.

4

The Social Effects of Limerence

Thus far I have emphasized what it feels like to be limerent. But what does limerence look like to others? What does a limerent person do? How does limerence influence interactions with others, and how does it affect practices and institutions in society? First, of course, limerence exerts profound—although often unrecognized—effects on any relationship in which it exists, whether in one or in both individuals. But because limerence interacts with other aspects of a person's life, its significance extends beyond the relationship with LO. Limerence figures in human tragedies, in the arts, and in historical events that affect the entire society, as well, inevitably, as in the progress of commercial developments.

The goal of the specific state called limerence has confused writers down through the ages. What does "return of feelings" really mean? Some have assumed that the limerent yearns to "possess" LO, but in what sense? A king might own his subject or slave; if he is also in love with her, he might give her her freedom so that she can express mutuality "freely." The consummation of limerent fantasy, that thing the limerent fervently desires, is not mere copulation, not mere cohabitation, not even *mere* marriage, but something so elusive of precise definition it is sometimes deemed "spiritual." We have also seen it called inherently impossible. If I want you to want me as I want you when what I want from you is that very wanting, we end up, if not with a paradox, with a very elusive idea. Sartre's image of a "mirror game" of "infinite reflections" is not so outlandish. No wonder limerence seems to observers a wish to be loved, rather than love itself.

The goal of limerence is not possession, but a kind of merging, a "oneness," the ecstatic bliss of mutual reciprocation. In fully developed limerence, you feel *additionally* what is, in other contexts as well, called love—an extreme degree of feeling that you want LO to be safe, cared for, happy, and all those other positive and noble feelings that you might feel for your children, your parents, and your dearest friends. That's probably why limerence is called love in all languages.[1] It feels like love, at least at the time. Lovers in the bliss of mutuality are affectionate; they are continuously doing things for each other, little (and big) acts of consideration that demand the appellation "love." Surely limerence is love at its highest and most glorious peak.

But love and limerence are clearly distinguishable. Your feeling for LO is inordinate relative to that person's actual value in your life (apart, of course, from the value as LO). As one woman wrote on the back of a questionnaire form:

"I recently reread my diary of 10 years ago, when I was in love with Brad, someone for whom I have no feelings at all anymore. It was very painful to read, not because of Brad, but because he was occupying so much of *me* at a time when there were other things in my life that I no longer have, but didn't appreciate at the time because of my total focus on Brad. My father was still living then, and my children were adorable babies who needed their mother's attention."

... which is why we distinguish love from limerence, this "love" from other loves.

LIMERENT BEHAVIOR

> Every lover grows pale at the sight of the beloved. One trembles at the unexpected sight of the beloved. Those besieged by thoughts of love sleep less and eat less. A lover is always timorous.
>
> —Andreas Capellanus [2]

The limerents I interviewed described both feelings and behavior, but until now I have not focused on the behavior, the external "symptoms" of limerence.

One of the strongest limerent feelings is a wish to hide the condition from LO (and from others) as an inevitable part of the "game," until reciprocation is certain and some commitment has been made. One behavioral change however, that is also likely to be obvious to close friends and family is the limerent's disappearance from customary places.

As limerent you want (1) to be with LO, or (2) to be where LO is likely to be, if the relationship fails to permit actual continual contact. In *Combat in the Erogenous Zone,* Ingrid Bengis speaks about how she would pace back and forth in front of her lover's house without making her presence known to him.[3] Poor substitutes for being in LO's presence are (3) to be alone thinking about LO, and finally (4) to talk about LO. Jim doesn't come around to the old hangout anymore. Bea's friends never see her. Rose is always too busy with something or other to sit down for a relaxed talk with her neighbors the way she used to do. The effect of limerence may be almost anti-social.

One of the values that may come from better understanding of limerence is that you as the observer may become more sympathetic and less likely to take it as an affront when a formerly reliable friend disappears. You can preserve your relationship by not interpreting your friend's sudden and strange disappearance as a rejection. When limerence strikes, your friend's sudden aloofness has nothing to do with you. You are still a friend, and may be much needed during the recovery phase.

Another behavioral counterpart to limerence is extreme emo-

tional lability, or "mood swings." The shift from the elation of
perceived reciprocation—real or not—to the despair of rejection—again real or imagined—can occur with such swiftness as to
seem instantaneous. Most interviewees told of their own experiences, but some also described limerence as it appeared in someone close to them. Harriet Vernon, for example, had come to me
as a client because of the strain between herself and her 20-year-
old daughter Lily. Lily's mood swings had worried her greatly.
She thought that perhaps some form of neurosis was involved.

"For days at a time, she does nothing at all. I can tell she's been
crying, although she won't discuss it with me. I worry and don't
know what to do, and just when *I* am about to go out of my
mind, she gets a call on the phone and *voilà*: metamorphosis!
There's humming and dancing and even an offer to help with the
housework. Of course, that only lasts for a while. She goes out
once or twice, maybe, and then it is back to the old unhappy
mood. It's terrible. It affects the whole family. It's very hard to
be around someone as unhappy as she is when she's down. It's
easier, of course, when the mood turns positive, except that by
now I know it won't last."

The behavioral aspects of limerence, with certain exceptions,
tend to be undesirable. As well as interference with other relationships, they include interference with work, destruction of
peace of mind, and even violence. With these effects it is not
surprising that certain societies have held the general view that
the limerent state is a madness to be avoided if at all possible, or
else simply denied.

Many societies have attempted to prevent love or, more often,
to control it in some way, as Columbia University Sociologist
William J. Goode has pointed out.[4] In traditional China, romantic love was viewed as dangerous.[5] The important decision of
who would marry whom was made with the cooperation of
family and matchmaker. Nietzsche is said to have regarded love
as the enemy of achievement and power.[6] Love has been accused
of disrupting the equanimity of communal life, and one often
hears of decisive action taken by the leaders of collective com-

munities to break up attachments between couples and generally try to control members' love lives.[7] Limerence, however, cannot be controlled by the unhappy limerent who wants to end it, nor does it bow to the dictates of society.

POSITIVE EFFECTS

The greatest of heaven's blessings

—Plato [8]

They say that through its agency everything in life is transformed, everything is illuminated.

—Nelly Ptaschkina [9]

The pleasures of limerence, though they may not be evident to an external and impartial observer, must be counted among limerence's positive attributes. Many interviewed insisted that there were other advantages as well. Although it was not quite a unanimous judgment, the vast majority of limerent informants waxed eloquent in descriptions of the benefits of limerence, even when they had suffered greatly.

One of the signs of limerent behavior that is hardest to hide is the effort at self-improvement, especially in physical appearance. As the intensity of limerence rises, the initial happy conclusion of the limerent that he or she must be admirable to LO to have evoked the first glimmer of positive reaction gives way to doubt. The first hope, a necessary ingredient, may then be lost, and the limerent strives to regain it by more attention to personal details. Fred changed his hairstyle several times and took more care with his dress for the daily casual encounters of his long unrequited limerence. (I once recommended to an unhappy limerent that she find a way to render herself ugly in some way so that she could extinguish the hope that she continued to have for reciprocation. I was not serious, but there was an unfortunate truth to my comment.) Since an attractive appearance has value in the culture apart from that of capturing the interest of

LO, the limerent drive to increase attractiveness can be counted as an advantageous by-product of the state.

Glenda had been a file clerk in a law firm for two years before she met Jack, her first LO. When Jack said he found her "really basically very pretty," she began looking in the mirror almost for the first time. Gradually, she made little changes. A touch of eye makeup, a new scarf, a softer hairstyle, more becoming clothes, and she was transformed. Her co-workers noticed and so did the boss, who gave her a new job in the reception area at a substantial salary increase.

In the movie *Rocky*, Adrienne undergoes a similar transformation. Although many might interpret that as the filmmakers' impatience at having to portray a plain young woman, or simply the increased availability of money for new clothes that came with Rocky's good fortune, it is a very realistic aspect in a basically accurate portrayal of limerence.

The effects of love on physical appearance were also depicted some years ago in a Hollywood film called *The Enchanted Cottage*, in which two homely individuals fall in love and become beautiful, at least in each other's eyes (and to the eye of the camera). In *The Second Sex*, Simone de Beauvoir describes a transformation that was only partly, as with the actors in the movie, the result of cosmetics. Expectation also helped:

> I had left her two hours before, badly made up, carelessly dressed, her eyes dull; but now she was expecting *him*. When she saw me, she resumed her ordinary expression, but for an instant I had time to see her, in readiness for him. . . . Her hair was carefully done, her lips and cheeks had unaccustomed coloring, she was dressed up in a lace blouse of sparkling white.[10]

Desmond Morris finds the physical transformation wrought by love not entirely conscious. He considers a love affair to be "as good as a diet and a corset combined" and suggests that when sexual activity is also included "exercise comes built in." When lovers are "under the influence of their passionate emotions, their stomach muscles ... automatically contract and stay contracted." [11]

One woman was emphatic about the effect of love on appearance. She said:

"During those suburban years, life was husband, children, housework, and the gossip of the morning coffee klatch. Whenever someone in the group was having an affair, it was immediately obvious. She didn't have to say a word. Usually she discontinued attending the daily gossip sessions, because now there were more *interesting* things on her mind as well as the problem of making up for time spent with her lover and lost to household chores. We could tell the moment we looked at her. False eyelashes and loss of weight were dead giveaways, but even if she were wearing an old sack that hid her figure, took the eyelashes off for our benefit, and managed to continue to attend regularly, there was still something about her that we could all agree on, even if we couldn't quite define it.

"Later on, when gossiping became 'consciousness raising,' we talked about it more analytically. A less immediately visible effect was the typical reaction of the husband. Usually he was so delighted with his new pretty wife that instead of analyzing, he just enjoyed! Sometimes marriages improved during affairs, and that may have been one of the reasons. It turned out in my own case that the improvement continued even after the affair was over, but not everyone was that lucky.

"Yes, my appearance changed, too. Just like the others. I think I lost 10 pounds the first week simply because food became unimportant *and* because each pound taken off increased my conviction that I was both lovable and loved.

"But there were also—I had not thought about this before— ways in which I felt inclined to change because I believed they would make me someone *he* might like better, even when he wasn't actually there to observe. I'd have been a fraud if I had been one person for him and someone else as soon as his back was turned. It would have detracted from the experience, spoiled it somehow.

"Maybe it was just guilt over the double life I was leading, but I really think it was more that I tried to fit myself into the sort of person I felt *deserved* to be loved. I think the standards were mine, not his. When I was patient and helpful with Timmy at night when he was complaining about his homework, instead of being my former bored, distracted, and easily angered self, it was because that was what I felt a mother ought to be like. Some of that changed later when things became unsettled, but much of it either remained or returned after my emotions had calmed down again."

This theme of having benefited, even from a love affair that did not last, was frequently expressed.

One of the classic pieces of literature on love, *The Dove's Neck Ring*, was written in the early eleventh century by the Arabian scholar, Ibn Hazm, who noted:

> And how many a stingy one became generous, and a gloomy one became bright faced, and a coward became brave, and a grouchy-dispositioned one became gay, and an ignoramus became clever, and a slovenly one in ... personal appearance 'dolled up,' and an ill-shaped one became handsome.[12]

Stendhal felt that love made him a better person—more moral, more congenial, more generous, and more pleasant to others as well as to himself.[13] And psychiatrist Robert Seidenberg said that someone who is in the hopeful or elated phase of love "generally has a warm feeling toward the world.[14] The goal of the limerent is to inspire a similar reaction in LO. Favorable characteristics are developed and displayed to try to achieve that longed-for objective. The result of this process is that the limerent is more attractive to others as well. More than half of The Group indicated that they "like to be in the company of" people who are in love.

Some people were very specific about what they had gained, others more vague, although just as insistent. Steven, a young university instructor, said of his relationship with Helen, a student:

"I had the usual, and reasonable, I think, hang-ups about having an affair with a student. On top of those, which were bad enough, I had my own personal brand of hang-ups about having any kind of relationship with anyone. To say I was shy is a gross understatement. I was terrified in the presence of women. Of people! Every class session was a trauma. Only Helen could have broken through. She had a kind of unrelenting, yet gentle, persistence. She literally drew me out of myself. Of course I was attracted, but I had almost become accustomed to living with frustrated attractions. She'd come up to the office to see me about a paper she was working on and I'd answer her questions, but unless she took the initiative there were a lot of silences.

"Still, I began to hope she'd come back, and I found excuses to spend a lot of time in my office, something I'd never done before. In the end, despite everything, all the pain and torment and tragedy, when it was all over, I was a different person. In a sense, it was almost worth it. Even though Helen rejected me, and even considering the severe way I reacted to that, if it hadn't been for Helen, I might still be sitting alone in my apartment every night playing those godawful jazzy albums and wondering if life· was ever going to happen. I don't mean to say that I've turned into a flaming extrovert. I'm still likely to hold back more than most people, but not like before. Nothing like before."

The positive effects of a love affair do not necessarily vanish when the relationship ends. Nor do they necessarily vanish when it turns out to have been an unhappy one, as Steven's was.

Another enduring positive effect occurred often enough among my informants to deserve mention: the person in love often developed intense interest in and knowledge about whatever it was that deeply involved LO. The limerent might also adopt some of the attitudes, personality, and behavior of the other person.[15] Whether or not this was an advantage depended on the situation. Steven listened to Baroque music with Helen and found a permanent addition to his aesthetic pleasures; Beatrice picked up Gordon's interest in photography and later became a professional photographer herself. In other cases "transfusions" were not positive. For example, initiation into drug taking by LO was mentioned occasionally by college students on questionaires and in interviews. Drugs were also viewed as relieving some of the distress caused by limerence. Usually these interests were transitory, lasting only as long as the limerence itself. Whether or not an interest persists after passion subsides seems to depend on whether it really fits in with later life. Virginia, whose happiness in her first days with Sid was described earlier also told about a particularly fortunate transfusion:

"I was one of these ordinary people who do ordinary things. Not that I thought about it that way. But I was always too busy wondering what to watch on TV or deciding whether to buy a new coat or planning to take a course to improve my steno to really develop a consistent interest in anything. I had learned to knit and I enjoyed it at times, but it was at a level of a sweater every year or so at most. I went bowling once or twice a month with a group from the office. One year I made my own Christmas cards. That was about it aside from the daily routine.

"With Sid, that really changed. That aspect of his personality was one of the first things that attracted me to him. We met on an airplane, you know. He was attending a professional convention and was loaded down with books and papers and a clipboard. I, of course, had my Agatha Christie. (I *did* read occasionally.) During the first part of the flight, I was deep into my mystery and he was busying writing and shuffling through papers and looking things up in a thick book he kept between his feet. Neither of us was particularly aware of the other until dinner was served and he asked me to hold one of his notebooks while he hastily packed the others away to make room for the food. God, that was like him! He had a way of getting so wrapped up in things that minor social etiquette just didn't enter in. And I never minded. Neither did anyone else. It was so obvious he really needed the assistance. It was a special kind of rare charm, and it only worked because the dedication was real.

"Later, when we began to spend a lot of time together, I got a really close look at that dedication; and not only did I admire it, I emulated it. It wasn't that he made me feel less of a person, and it wasn't to keep me busy when he was busy. He inspired me. He set an example of how to do it and also how much pleasure it brings. He really loved his work, and although I'll never match him in total absorption to the point of asking favors of strangers without even noticing that they *are* strangers, I know what it is to spend an entire weekend working happily away on a story. I also carry materials with me on airplanes, and I sincerely believe that I have found a talent in myself and a joy in life that might never have happened if it had not been for Sid."

MUTUAL LIMERENCE

From the interviews and other sources of information, certain fundamental combinations are apparent in human relationships. First, of course, there is the relationship between two mutually limerent individuals, the reciprocal relationship. Although there may, indeed *must* be obstacles along the way, this is the relationship of the limerent's fervent desires and of the dramatist's happy ending. We have already seen that its intensity depends, for each individual, on the intensity produced by the particular combination of circumstances during its development. Excessive fear on both persons' parts can prevent the establishment of reciprocity, even when each is limerent toward the other. Furthermore, although limerence increases with uncertainty, we have seen that externally imposed obstacles of sufficient magnitude, including those imposed by parents or by society, can delay or prevent limerent consummation.

Even when reciprocity has occurred and commitment to a formal relationship (such as marriage) has been established, reciprocity is usually followed by a decline in limerence, and a blissful period may be followed by later dissension. But before considering the difficulties that intially mutual limerent partners may later run into, there are at least two other types of relationships to be identified.

AFFECTIONAL BONDING

The first of these is an affectional and sexual relationship between two people in the absence of limerence on either person's part, either for each other or for anyone outside the partnership. It is a primary relationship, described frequently enough in the interviews to warrant clear recognition. Informants who described what I came to call "affectional bonding" usually replied affirmatively to my initial question about whether they felt themselves to be in love. But unlike those whose relationship was based on limerence, they did not report continuous and unwanted intrusive thinking, feel intense need for exclusivity, describe their goals in terms of reciprocity, or speak of ecstasy. Instead, they emphasized compatibility of interests, mutual preferences in leisure activities, ability to work together, pleasurable sexual experiences, and, in some cases, a degree of relative contentment that was rare (even impossible) among persons experiencing limerence.

Some of these relationships had begun with limerence; others seemed to have been affectional bonding from the outset. It should be recalled, however, that I was rarely able to interview both members of a partnership.[16] In several cases in which I did speak to both partners, what was described as affectional bonding by one person was matched by hidden limerence in the other.

Affectional bonding, not limerence, often represents the cultural idea. It is rational by comparison with limerence, and loving in what many feel is the "true sense of the term," *i.e.*, having concern about, or caring. It is what is described as the hoped-for relationship between limerents after the honeymoon when the serious business of charting a common and compatible life course begins. Many whose descriptions of their relationships fitted this category were "old marrieds," whose interactions seemed both stable and mutually gratifying, at least from the perspective of the partner who served as my informant. Relationships based on affectional bonding were usually monogamous, although not for the reasons given by limerent persons. "Faithfulness" stemmed from convenience and consideration of the other's feelings, or even from what appeared to be almost purely practical considerations. Zorina, for example, said of her relationship with Carl:

"We're both "clean," and that's something we want to keep. Neither of us would want to sleep with anyone else for the same reason we watch our diet. VD is no joke. We've been together five years now, and will probably get married and have children. We know and like each other, and, really, what else is there?"

Some of those who described affectional bonding appeared to be persons who had never known the state of limerence. But others reported a past history that included limerence. Frances, for example, said:

"I've been what you call limerent. That was me about Richard for three miserable years. When he left me with the twins (who were only six months old at the time) and Ronnie, who was two, I had to spend the next 10 years on pure survival, during which there was no time for me to look around and no one seeking out a not terribly attractive woman in her mid-thirties with three dependents.

"Today, the children are doing fine, and I have managed to get a job that keeps us from constant near poverty. Many times I've thought about how nice it would have been if someone had come along to ease the terrible burden when it was terrible; now I just want an easy life and that's what I have with Henry. I like him, I love him by any reasonable meaning of the word, and we have fun together. Most important, he and the kids have really hit it off. I think that if I started to fall in love again—and I don't say it couldn't happen—I'd run like hell. I don't need that again."

Richard and Marion, who were both interviewed, also claimed never to have felt the fears and emotional need for exclusivity or to have been afflicted by the prepossessiveness and intrusive thinking that are aspects of limerence. As Richard said:

"I have never felt the way you describe about anyone, and from what you say, as well as what I have seen with my own eyes, I would not want to. My feelings for Marion are, well, as strong as the feelings I have ever had for anyone, and as far as I am concerned, I can see no reason to look elsewhere. She and I are friends, companions, and sexual partners, although the last is not as frequent as it used to be. But that's not a problem. It's just that we have been so busy these past few months, me on my work, she on hers."

Marion's description of the relationship, obtained in a separate interview, fit with Richard's very well:

"Richard is the finest and truest friend I ever had, and I believe that we will probably marry. It's just that there isn't that intensity that other people get into. I don't know why not, but that's the way it is. Frankly, I think we both like it better this way."

With the current incidence of couples deciding to live together without being married, the question arises as to whether limerence or nonlimerence is more likely to spur the arrangement. It might be supposed that affectionally bonded pairs, in which neither partner was limerent, would be most inclined to cohabit rather than undertake the deeper commitment of marriage. My findings on this issue are equivocal. According to Bunny's report, she and Lou fit the expected pattern:

"We were serious enough about our relationship to decide that we'd both be better off together rather than apart, but it wasn't a matter of life and death for either of us as it sometimes seemed to be with other people. Living together as roommates and a little more was perfect. If our families had put pressure on us, we would probably have gotten married, but they didn't. If I ever get pregnant, I guess we will, but it's not a big issue with us.

But Marilyn told a very different tale, despite outside appearances that resembled Bunny's:

"I wanted to get married. What I mean is that I was in love and am still in love with Arthur, and that means I want a commitment. The stronger the better. But Arthur didn't want to get married. He was all too clear on that. Living together was all I could get, so I grabbed it. I'm still hoping."

THE LIMERENT AND THE NONLIMERENT

The third, and probably most prevalent, sort of relationship between two people, at least during some stages of their interaction, occurs between a limerent person and an LO who does not reciprocate with limerence. The bulk of those interviewed, whose stories are related in these pages, fall into this category. In a sense, there is some lack of reciprocation in all limerent relationships, since limerence intensity continually wavers. Although I would categorize the following relationship between Bruce and Emma as primarily between two persons limerent about each other, the limerent need for total reciprocity often produces, as it did in their case, intervals of dissatisfaction on one or both parts. As Bruce said:

"Throughout our entire relationship, it was always apparent to me, and I believe equally apparent to Emma, that one or the other of us was more in love. Sometimes she was the one; sometimes it was me. We always seemed to know who it was. It was a very unstable situation, because as soon as she seemed interested in me, my anxiety lessened, and that nervousness that I lost turned out to be a part of the love. Or so it seemed. It was dumb. I know it was dumb, but that's the way it went, just the same, for the whole two years before we finally broke up."

Relationships between two people who are committed to one another but in which only one of them is experiencing limerence should be differentiated from the fully unrequited condition in which no commitment exists (Fred and Laura, for example).

In addition to the three types of relationships—both limerent (mutual reciprocation), neither limerent (affectional bonding), and one limerent, the other not—if the level of each person's sexual activity is considered, there are many more types.[17] In heterosexual relationships we can also pair each of the four possibilities (sexually active limerent; not sexually active, but limerent; sexually active, but not limerent; and not sexually active, not limerent) for the women with each of the four possibilities for the men. One can imagine the bliss of the relationship in which both partners are sexually active and limerent, or the frustration of the relationship in which one partner (of whichever sex) is sexually active and limerent while the other is neither. With both partners sexually active and nonlimerent, the relationship might be affectional bonding. The chaste but limerent woman paired with a sexually active but nonlimerent male is a classic of fiction and of sex-role stereotyping. This situation was described by several female interviewees.

Since the culture evaluates behavior differently depending on the sex of the person, and more specifically, has traditionally favored the expression of sexuality in men over that in women, the relationship in which the woman is limerent but not sexually motivated and the man sexually active but not limerent may be quite different from the relationship in which these roles are reversed.

It should be pointed out that a number of informants felt that their degree of sexual interest was related to their limerence. Some found that the anxiety and fear of rejection that was part of the limerent state interfered with sexual functioning. Others said that their interest in sex was heightened by their limerence.

For this reason, the sexuality classification should not be used to refer to fundamental characteristics of individuals, but to examine a given relationship at a particular time. Martin, in the following example describes a shift in his relationship with Betty:

"In the early days of our marriage, there was no question that both of us were highly interested in sex and both of us were very much in love. It was what you might call a honeymoon. Then it stopped. I don't know why it stopped or even when it stopped, but one day I had to recognize that the honeymoon was over and things were different. Neither of us were as interested in sex as we had been during the early days, and I suppose that is nothing unusual, but the problem was my interest in sex remained higher than Betty's. So there we were. We were commited to each

other, married, with a baby on the way, but I don't think either
of us were in love anymore and we had a sex problem."

At the beginning, Martin and Betty were sexually active limerents, but they had shifted to a relationship in which neither was
limerent and only one retained a marked interest in sex.

With all the possible categories of relationships, can any general statements be made about which are preferable, most likely
to be stable, or in danger of erupting into clearly undesirable
states? Are relationships in which the partners share similar
feelings less troublesome to their participants? The mutually
limerent relationship already mentioned is blissful; the relationship with neither partner sexually active but both limerent might
resemble a fictional ideal of "untainted love"; and the relationship in which neither is limerent but both sexually attracted
might be characteristic of the swinging set. The relationships are
not all equally stable, since limerence itself is an unstable state.
The mutually limerent and highly sexual relationship would not
be expected to remain so for long. Indeed, the differences in
sexual interest in a relationship between two people who are
both limerent might actually serve to sustain limerence longer
than would be the case if both partners had the same sexual
interest. We have already seen cases in which limerence was
sustained for a long period of time within a relationship under
the condition that the partner was not perceived as limerent, for
example, Gregory's marriage to Beatrice, described earlier. In
fact, mixed relationships probably last longer than relationships
in which both members are limerent. The nonlimerence of one
partner may provide the degree of uncertainty and the degree of
hope that may permit the perpetuation of the other person's
limerence and commitment to the relationship.

Whether nonlimerent lovers maintain sexual liaison with more
than one person seems primarily a matter of physical desires and
convenience. As one person put it:

"I could easily have several lovers and would like to, in a way,
but it gets rather sticky when you are living with someone who
objects. I am not jealous but my lover is. Besides, there are only

so many hours in a day, and if it's going to cause an uproar, there isn't much point in it. I don't need it."

In other words, the nonexclusivity that nonlimerents often feel may permit freedom from the discord that the need for exclusiveness can bring about. Especially if not terribly interested in sex, the nonlimerent finds it easy to sustain a comradely relationship that is also intimate in many dimensions and sexually faithful as well.

But nonlimerents often find themselves the unwitting causes of suffering that seems real but that they are at a loss to comprehend. A young woman described her relationship with several men:

"It seemed that I was more in love, at least at first. I would become attracted, want to spend a lot of time with them, enjoyed the process of discovering common interests, and even found myself creatively inspired by the relationship. But after a while, things would suddenly change and I would be asked where I thought the relationship was 'going.' This was a question that always puzzled me, because I was quite happy about where it *was* and didn't feel any need for it to be more than what it was."

In such cases (I found that there were many), the partner seemed stricken with a kind of insatiability; it seemed that no degree of attentiveness was ever sufficient.

"For example, they would call and wonder what I was doing when I really had something to do that was important to me and had nothing to do with them. They acted as if everything I did absolutely had to involve them all the time, at every turn.

"But it is not as bad as it used to be because I have learned to be very clear and definite. I recognize the signs of trouble, and when it starts, I simply leave. After a while, maybe four or five months, I can go back and things will be civil. They simply have to learn that if they want my companionship at all, they must let me breathe."

The word "suffocation" was used repeatedly in reports by interviewees fitting the nonlimerent pattern. As one said about "in love" lovers:

"They are always being 'hurt,' and it's impossible to predict what will hurt them. I'll have a good time at a party only to be hit on the way home with something like, 'Why did you ignore me all evening?' Really, it's exasperating!"

David Norton, writing in *An Epistemology of Romantic Love,* is no different from those I interviewed in his dislike of the role of the nonlimerent LO:

"First, let us inquire whether the state of passion is objectively good or beautiful. The answer will be evident to anyone who has been an object of it [but did] not love in return. Nothing is more tedious and oppressive; for the one who has eyes for none but us has lost the world and, having nothing to talk about, can only repeat a handful of tiresome phrases—tiresome because they are shorn of the medium in which our interests are engaged. From our situation within the spacious world, the other's obsession appears hermetically sealed, a stifling closet. Moreover it debilitates us, making us clumsy; for the eyes forever upon us make us hyperaware of our own simple acts— like walking—which we do best without thought. No, this 'inferior state of mind,' this 'form of transitory imbecility' is neither objectively good nor beautiful."[18]

Quite often, however, it is the limerent, rather than the non-limerent partner who terminates the relationship. Very often the break is accompanied by a "scene," which leaves the non-limerent person saddened, distraught, and lonely. Leonard described his relationship with Marg:

"Marg and I had been seeing each other for maybe about three months, quite regularly, and as far as I was concerned the situation was ideal. We read the same books, enjoyed the same movies, and sex, at least for me, was perfect. One of the main things I liked about our relationship was that Marg was there for companionship and recreation, and I wasn't forced to spend a lot of money and boring time just trying to 'make it' with someone. I am the sort of person who would rather have one dependable relationship than a lot of hassles. Myself, I could have other lovers, and I would not mind if Marg did, but she'd mind even knowing I feel this way, so I went along, which is why it really surprised me when the pressure began anyway.

"No matter how many times I tried to explain to Marg that she was the only person I was interested in, she kept going on about how I was not interested *enough*. I really did not know what she meant. I liked her, we saw each other two, maybe three, times a week, and it was *I* who first brought up the idea of marrying her (at 36, I was more than ready to settle down).

"To this day, I cannot explain what happened. We had spent the day with my family. Dad and I watched the game while Marge talked to my sister and mother. I really didn't notice what she did the whole time. It was a perfectly ordinary day as far as I was concerned. The first hint I had about what was going to happen was on the way home. Marg was very quiet. I thought she was tired and I let her alone. Then, when we got to her house, she lit out of the car slamming the door and didn't even say anything. It was crazy. I had no idea of what was going on. I parked the car and rang the doorbell and she wouldn't answer. It was late, I was tired, I didn't understand, and so after a while I left and tried to telephone when I got home. The phone must have rung about 40 times when she finally answered. All she said was, 'It's over,' and hung up. By this time I was really getting annoyed. I had a heavy schedule lined up for the next day, and it was after two in the morning. I went to bed.

"The next day when I had a moment free, it was dinner time. This time no answer after 10 rings, so I drove over to her house. To my surprise, she let me in. By that time I didn't know what to expect. Obviously, she had been crying, and even though I had no idea what was causing her to act like this, I felt bad and tried to comfort her. But when I put my arm around her, she jerked away and became hysterical. She told me I had not been fair to leave her alone all day, and furthermore that my mother didn't like her and kept telling her about how popular I was with other women.

"Now, I know how Mom is, and she was talking about high school, not about now. Marg was upset. I seemed to be making her more upset. Everything I said that tried to help ended up making it worse. So I left. The next day I got a note saying not to call her again and that she would send certain items by messenger, some of my clothes I had left there and some jewelry I had given her. That was that. I still don't understand it. Mom told me that she liked Marg, but that Marg had seemed strange during their conversation.

"I don't know. Maybe I wasn't able to feel about her the way she wanted me to, but except for insane scenes like that—it wasn't the first, I must admit—I really liked Marg."

Members of The Group had been troubled by the pressures placed on them as the nonlimerent partner in a relationship with a limerent. Both limerents and nonlimerents object to the role of LO, especially when they do not return the feeling. In all, 91 percent of The Group found it unpleasant in some way, 84 percent found it very uncomfortable, or worse, and a full third checked "oppressive." About 40 percent agreed with the statements, "We were not getting along, and I knew we would have to end our relationship, but I did not want to hurt_____"; and "As far as I was concerned we were finished. The only problem was how to break it to_____." Half and more than half of The Group, respectively said, "I tried to break off with_____in the least painful way"; and "Breaking off was very hard because I could see it was hurting_____." Twenty-five percent of The Group also said, "I kept seeing_____much longer than I really wanted to because of_____'s jealousy and dependency on me"; and "I always seem to be the one to have to break off the relationship."

Of course, the acceptance of such statements does not permit the conclusion that the person is always a nonlimerent. They may be descriptions of "nonlimerent relationships" by a person who had been or would be limerent over someone else, or they may refer to the person in a relationship whose limerence is not synchronized with that of the partner, in other words, whose limerence has not fully crystallized or who may be shifting toward a new LO. It must be borne in mind that there are two forms of nonlimerence: the nonlimerence of the person who has never experienced limerence (but who might in the future) and the nonlimerence of a particular partnership, one that might resemble affectional bonding but to the person ready for limerence is never more than a stand-in for the "real thing." As Beryl said:

"I really liked Bill, but I always knew that the lights weren't flashing and the bells were not ringing. It was a good, wholesome, fun, and happy relationship. But after Arthur, I still wanted the other glorious and foolish kind of love. Bill helped fill the time while I waited. I loved him as one loves a friend one cares very much about, but I kept hoping for the magic once again, and I knew it would never come with Bill."

THE DURATION OF LIMERENCE

It is important to remember that both states, limerence and nonlimerence, tend to endure, although the reasons are different. Limerence is sustained because one of its aspects is the desire for limerence itself. This desire transcends the feelings directed toward a particular LO and persists even after preoccupation with that LO has diminished to a low level. This is that state previously discussed under "Readiness and Longing." In the writings of other observers, it seems to appear from time to time as the notion of being "in love with love," a state assumed to come about "naturally" at the time of adolescence.[19] This longing for "someone" should be clearly distinguished from a realistic or practical desire to engage in a mating relationship for economic or procreational purposes, or even for the companionship of affectional bonding. Those inclinations seem largely to lack the involuntarily obsessional quality of the limerent state.

Hubert expressed his desire for a relationship that would meet certain practical needs:

"I am tired of running around. I want someone there when I come home at night. I would like to have children. No, I really don't feel it as an emotional necessity, but I do feel it as something that would make my life more pleasant—more worthwhile. People are social and I am social, and I really get lonely and would like to have someone to talk over the day's events. It is not the feeling that you have described as limerent, but it is a very strong and definite and logical feeling of need."

Interviewees like Hubert expressed the desire for a mate in much the same emotional terms as they might express desire for children, for a home, or for participation in a favorite hobby. I don't mean by that to imply that this interest is insufficient to establish a sound and permanent relationship. It is just that the issue concerns more "rational" goals, not involuntary, passionate yearning. For the limerent, the longing for a partner is so intense as to be experienced as a necessity; for those not in the state of limerence it may be very much desired, but failure of attainment does not produce the type of intense misery that may be unique to limerence.

Many persons, including many of my informants, have commented on the transitory nature of limerence, and various estimates have been given of its average duration. As noted in the previous chapter, the upper limit of intensity appears to be set by perceived reciprocity. This results in some limerences arriving at a more intense state than do others. A limerence nipped in the bud for one reason or another may be of relatively brief duration. Arlene told of a relationship that contained all the elements of limerence as I described them to her but that endured for only a total of three days. The couple had met in Venice, he being an architect from Switzerland and she a social worker from the United States and both long married. From the outset they were aware of the impossibility of a permanent union, a factor which may have permitted a certain short-circuiting of the more usual ploys, plays, and fears. Shipboard romances and other temporary liaisons are widely reported, and it may be that under the weight of the overwhelming obstacle of an impossible situation, these affairs sometimes manage to contain many if not all of the limerent characteristics, albeit in an attenuated fashion.

Leaving aside such extreme, and possibly dubious, romances,

my estimation of average limerent duration is approximately two years. It is based on both questionnaire and interview data. The duration of the experience covers the period from "the moment" of initiation of limerence until a feeling of neutrality is reached for a given LO. The extremes may be as brief as a few weeks or as long as a lifetime. Few full-blown limerences calm down in less than six months. When limerence is really brief, maximum intensity may not have been attained. The most frequent interval, as well as the average, is between approximately 18 months and three years. Lifetime limerences are rare, but they do occur. Some people continue to experience limerence at different times throughout their lives, so that there appears to be no age unaffected. If the state of readiness or longing were also included, the total number of cases would be greater.

I suspect that the duration of relationships in which limerence on the part of one or both partners played a role in its initial formation is much longer than the duration of limerence itself. Although limerence may initiate a relationship, it is not essential to its persistence, especially, when some formal commitment between the two people is made, either privately or publicly. If a relationship does persist after the limerence of one or both partners has ended, it is because some other kind of bonding has taken place or because circumstances make it difficult to disengage.

On the other hand, many relationships are of briefer duration than the limerence of one partner—sometimes the limerence of both partners. Your limerence may begin long before a relationship can be said to exist except in your own feelings (maybe in the feelings of LO as well, but it still takes overtly indicated commitment to make it a "relationship"), long before the first "date," as we have seen in numerous cases, it can persist long after LO has departed. Other relationships continue without limerence on either side.[20]

The danger in otherwise stable relationships is that one of the partners will suddenly become limerent over someone else, a turn of events that may shake the relationship at its foundations. Although nonlimerent lovers do not experience the emotional need for exclusivity that characterizes limerence, this is no safeguard against jealousy. In what may be a stable relationship only by external observation, one partner (especially one who has been previously limerent) may actually be in a state of readiness or longing for some time before finding a new LO. When the ideal is to marry for "love," it is publicly frowned upon to have a series of love affairs, or limerences, outside marriage. Hence, a series of marriages and divorces.

MARRIAGE

Smetena's opera, *The Bartered Bride*, first performed in 1866, is one of many works of fiction in which the plot turns on the issue of marrying for love versus marrying to bring financial advantage to the parent. The nineteenth century saw a romantic revolt against marriages arranged by families, in which the talented and beautiful could be matched with the wealthy, or adjacent lands could be joined by family ties. Indeed, many of the practices which separated the sexes and thus facilitated arranged marriages could be interpreted as aids to the prevention of limerence and, especially, to the prevention of limerence-inspired decisions that disrupt the social order.[21] That divorce should increase, as it has in this century, may be an inevitable consequence of the selection of marriage partners by limerence— not merely because the limerent eye overfocuses on the attractive features of LO, but also because the same logic that says marry where your heart leads also says divorce and remarry where your heart leads. The conflict between the direction in which one is impelled by limerence and the actions dictated by parents and other social forces is still much in evidence. Heads of state experience the traditional pressure to choose according to religious, economic, and political issues, but even when the initial choice is left strictly to personal feelings, as it is in the United States and some countries of Western Europe, freedom to change marriage partners is always at least somewhat restricted. Thus the love affair of the twentieth century is that of the Duke and Duchess of Windsor, which continues to inspire one popular dramatization after another.

The romantic ideal holds that for every person there is on earth the "right" other person, and you know when that person comes along because your feelings tell you. To marry your LO is to experience the ecstasy of ultimate reciprocation. Or so you feel. In fact, not even marriage may constitute sufficient proof that the feelings are returned. Evelyn's experience is an example:

"Okay, so we were married. I still didn't believe Ed loved me. There was something about the way he acted, little things he did, or forgot to do. He walked around the house with an air of distraction, as if I weren't there. It was worse than when we were not married, because then he'd talk to me. Now he just expects things of me. If he gets them, there's silence; if he doesn't, there's still silence plus a look of annoyance."

On the other hand, the greater uncertainty intrinsic to the state of being unmarried, no matter how entangled the pair might be in terms of joint friendships, possessions, and activities, can more often keep alive the limerent state in a way in which marriage cannot. It might well be the decrease in uncertainty that produces the occasional upsets that follow a change to the marital status after a period of cohabitation. Greg spoke of his relationship with Judy before and after they became legally bound in matrimony:

"Something happened to me after we got married. It was a real shock. I had thought that we knew everything about each other and that nothing could possibly break us up. I don't know how to explain the difference, but it was dramatic. We recovered after a while, we didn't actually break up, but we went through a pretty rough period that lasted almost a year. It's over now, I guess, I hope, but what a terrible time we had! It was as if we really didn't know each other before, not even after three years."

In other cases, limerence seems gradually, and less stressfully to be transformed into the genuine love of affectional bonding. Mary and Frank were among the best examples of this pattern. They had been married for 15 years when I interviewed Mary.

"We were completely in love when we married and, the honeymoon was something out of a storybook. The intensity faded of course. After a year or so, we could tolerate brief separations, but Frank still phones me every day from the office just to see how I am, and I would still rather be with him than anyone else in the world. If I don't love him exactly the way I did those first few months and years, I don't love him any less. The love is different and still intense. I can't imagine it ever being less. We are different people now, but we have grown together in ways that have actually brought us closer than when we started."

Descriptions of such happy marriages occurred regularly among older interviewees. They suggest that love can replace limerence given the right circumstances.

But nonlimerent veterans of limerence may take some convincing. Some frown on any connection of limerence and marriage. As one well-known magazine editor was reported to have said:

"I was lucky always to have fallen in love with men who didn't love me. It was tough being rejected, and my torch-carrying years were no picnic, but at least I didn't marry any of them. I shudder to think what I might have had to look at over the breakfast table today if I had gotten one of my wishes."

Nancy, a science reporter in her fifties, told me something similar:

"I loved Nelson for almost 10 years. It had all the earmarks of what you call 'limerence.' I would have given up my job or traveled to the four corners of the earth if he had wanted me to. Fortunately for me today, he insisted on remaining married and I eventually had sense enough to take advantage of an employment opportunity a few thousand miles away."

Recently, some of the discussion about what can be called the nonlimerent ideal of marriage, a union based on mutual compatibility and affection and on a sensible partnership of common interests, has been focused on the idea of sexual nonexclusivity, such as the idea of "open marriage." [22] The major problem seems to be that both people do not feel the same way at the same time. One of my informants told of the concessions she made during a three-year period of limerent involvement with a man who made frequent public reference to the desirability of "free relationships." But in Karen's view:

"There was nothing at all free about it. I was not only not free to leave Saul, but I was not even free to be faithful. He practically made it a condition of continuing to see him that I go out with other men and even sleep with them. He'd then brag about our situation to others in a way that told me I had better conform or he'd find someone else with whom to carry out his fantasy of 'intelligent involvement,' as he called it."

Sociologist Mirra Komarovsky's study of the emotional and sexual life of college youth supports the tendency for the majority to require fidelity and exclusivity in their mates despite the rationality of "free" relationships. She reported that in open relationships, the less-involved partner in fact gained the degree of freedom because the more-involved individual accepted it "as the price of continuing or renewing the relationship." [23] Several interviewees complained about how their partner suggested to them that if they objected to the partner's having other affairs, the best solution was to have other affairs themselves—a solution that to a limerent is clearly not a solution.

NEGATIVE EFFECTS

The ecstatic bliss of mutual love is sometimes carrried to frightening extremes as in the following statement made by a 22-year-old poet.

One glorious sunny morning, Camilla and I went out into the country to study, and while we lay on the grass I gently stroked her hair. I felt so wonderfully happy that I wanted to kill us both, so that there should be no anticlimax! [24]

This particular reaction to love at its zenith was also portrayed in the film *Elvira Madigan*, based on the suicides of two actual European lovers. In Japan, such double suicides are called *shin ju*. In earlier centuries, *shin ju* was considered an act of great beauty and nobility. Today, although it still occasionally occurs, it receives less public favor, and when suicide is involved in a love relationship, it is more likely to be the expression of despair on the part of one person.

Louise, one of my interviewees who was also a member of The Group, described a reaction to rejection much like Marilyn Weber's, one of the students whose tales led me to begin my investigations.

"When I found Danny's letter in the mail box, I actually staggered. I was afraid to read it; my premonition was strong. My hands literally shook as I opened it, and I don't know whether anyone noticed or not because everything except that piece of paper in my hand was a blur. It was just one short sentence saying, 'Let's call it quits because it's really over for me.' It was total, final, the end.

I don't remember how I made it upstairs except that I was in a state of true shock. I don't mean surprise. I had more or less expected it. I mean real, physical shock, it was as if I had been struck on the head with a hammer. I lay down on the bed and for a long time I didn't move. I hardly breathed. It was as if, if I remained absolutely motionless, it would in some magical way not be true. In a sense I didn't believe it. My head whirled for a while (with my body still) considering possible logical ways to keep it from being true. (I couldn't find any, but I tried.) Then I considered actions—really far-out things like going after Barbara (the woman toward whom Danny's interest had shifted) with a knife or throwing myself out the window. Many other things just as bad.

"I don't remember how long that went on, but when my

roommate came in, it was dark and she turned on the light not realizing I was there. That threw me out of the kind of trance I was in, and I must have looked strange because she asked what was the matter. I tried to talk but couldn't. I started to sob and handed her Danny's note. From that moment, I sobbed continuously and near hysterically for about five hours until Mary made me take some aspirin and I went to sleep. But when I woke up a few hours later it began all over.

"By the next day I was a complete mess—my eyes were swollen and I looked like I had been stung by a hive of bees. It went on like that for about three days—sobbing, sleeping, remembering, more sobbing, and not eating. I drank some tea Mary made and later some beer. After about a week, I tried to go back to classes but I couldn't. I didn't want to do anything. I didn't care. I didn't care enough about anything to move from the bed to the chair. I finally just went home. We told everyone I had a severe 'allergic reaction.'

"Well, that took care of one semester. My folks were good about the whole thing. I didn't tell them exactly what happened (it seemed insane), but I think they more or less suspected. I would weep at the drop of an association (to Danny) for months. But the worst thing was the immobility, the not caring about *anything*."

Louise had had a reaction of grief; it was very similar to that described by people who suffer the death of someone close to them. As severe as her reaction was, however, Louise did recover. Later she said,

"I think it was the timing and the shock. Actually, it probably was better that way—bad as it was—than if he had tried to let me down gently. At least I knew it was over and there was nothing I could do. I don't know why it took so long except that I was so completely in love. It was as if I had invested my entire being in the relationship. Then in the weeks before the letter, when I was beginning to see signs of trouble, I just refused to believe—until he did what I guess he had to do. About six months later I heard that he and Barbara were getting married, and I was glad in a way. It meant there would never be a relapse."

Members of The Group showed a surprising, even alarming, willingness to use the term "depressed" in describing their feelings. Apparently normal college students, forty-two percent had been "severely depressed," almost a third were "often depressed," and half reported depression "about a love affair." Thirty-five percent of The Group agreed with the following statement: "It would have been easier for me if _____ had broken off abruptly instead of dragging it out when it was hopeless." Despite her shock, and the severity of the state that followed, Louise agreed.

Prolonged unhappiness following rejection is not rare nor is it confined to college students. Literary critic William Hazlitt suffered despondency, disorganization, and inability to work at his former level of productivity for almost two years after being rejected by the chambermaid he loved (mostly in silence) for a year and a half.[25] Stendhal, during one of his times of grieving over an unrequited limerence, said that had an assassin shot him he'd have thanked his murderer before expiring.[26] In his *Memoirs of Egotism* he reports: "and I often set the book down to think about Métilde. The interior of my solitary room was dreadful to me." He once wrote, "I need, I thirst to see you. I think that I should give the rest of my life to speak to you for a quarter of an hour about the most trivial things." [27]

Suicides and accidents (which often result from a kind of suicidal carelessness) are leading causes of death among those in whom limerence is also most frequent—young persons from the teens to the mid-twenties. Seventeen percent of The Group indicated they had "often thought of committing suicide," and 64 percent *of those* claimed to "have seriously attempted to commit suicide." That figure represents more than one out of every 10 (11 percent) of a set of college students who otherwise appeared perfectly normal!

Furthermore, this figure is consistent with the high suicide and accident rates among American and British students reported at least since the mid-sixties. Explanations by professionals have typically stressed such factors as pressure to succeed, fear of failure, and "identity confusion," but careful reading of the possible causes listed reveals that many of these tragedies might in fact have involved limerence.[28] For example, among other contributory factors listed are crisis, anxiety, "depression, neglect, sense of rejection, "real or imagined loss of the love object," and the ending of a marriage through divorce, separation, or death of the mate.[29] More recently, a number of writers on suicide have conceded unhappy love affairs a more prominent position in their lists of possible causes.[30]

As important as limerence is as an aspect of the circumstances precipitating many suicides, even this aspect of limerence has been neglected except in the arts. Major publications on suicide have either omitted a discussion of romantic love as a factor in suicide, or have buried it under general categories of "loss of a loved one," where "loved one" might also refer to a parent, child, or close friend or relative. One recent work on suicide by psychologists did not include disappointment in love among its 44 chapters.[31]

Some of my interviewees had also thought of suicide, and several made serious attempts. Sometimes the attempt seemed a thinly disguised plea. Sally took a great many pills, then telephoned Irv.

"I was feeling the effects sooner than I thought I would and I could hardly dial the number. Somewhere in the back of the dimness into which my mind was fast sinking was the thought that *he might already have left for lunch* or *be on another line!* When he answered, I could hardly speak. I said, 'Irv, I've taken pills.' He later said he told his secretary to call an ambulance and was with me in minutes. I didn't see that part. I was unconscious still holding the phone when he arrived.

"The procedure was horrible. I'd never have another 'close call' like that again. It was almost two weeks before I was back to normal.

"I know the doctors—one psychiatrist, in particular—said it was a 'manipulation' on my part and I suppose it was, in a way.

Irv proposed in the hospital as soon as I came to. I really scared him, but I didn't feel it as a manipulation. I saw it more as a test. If he loved me he'd save me, and if he didn't, I wanted to die. I really did.

"Well, we were married for four years, and I was the one to insist on the divorce. I shudder to think of what a close call it was."

Unfortunately, others are not "saved in time," and some have been known to endure repeated "close calls," stomach pumping, and other unpleasantness, including commitment to mental institutions.

Attempted suicide may have also been involved in relationships that on the surface appeared to be stable affectional bonding. Pioneer sexologist Havelock Ellis and novelist Edith Lees participated in what seemed at least from Ellis's viewpoint an idealized nonlimerent marriage. They would live together for half the year, apart for the other half, and assuming that she did not mind, he told her of his affairs with other women.

Although sex between them was discontinued after a few years, Edith—according to Ellis—found both love and security in the arrangement. But evidence of Edith's intense suffering appears in her personal journal. She wrote that she realized her love was far greater than his, and that he made her suffer "hideously." Edith made several suicide attempts by swallowing morphine and by trying to jump out a window. Nor was Ellis himself able to live according to his own philosophy. He was surprised at the deep hurt he experienced when later a lover rejected him.[32]

Suicide is only one of many types of self-injury described to me. Informants also told of suicide attempts disguised in the form of accidents. In a questionnaire administered to 65 professional and layperson adults at a scientific conference, 29 percent "considered suicide," 6 percent admitted to a serious attempt, and 26 percent said that although they had not actually tried to kill themselves, they had driven their automobiles with "less caution than usual."[33] Self-maiming is rarely reported as such, but several interviewees' stories incline me to suspect that the phenomenon itself is not rare. William told me about cutting his hand in a moment of limerent agony.

"No one knows how it happened. Why should they? I'm telling you in strictest confidence. It was insane, a moment of insanity I will never be allowed to forget.

"It had been back and forth for two years. She wanted me, she didn't want me. She was finished forever, she just needed time to think. Now I think I understand what was going on. She liked me, but my extreme limerence turned her off. If I had only played it right. . . .

"Anyway, I was going literally crazy, and one note in particular threw me. All I could think of was that I wanted to stop the feelings; I thought that I could distract myself with a bigger pain. I didn't think. It was very sudden. I walked into the kitchen and took the meat cleaver.

"Did I get distraction? Not really. I got a lot of temporary excitement, a tremendous amount of blood in the sink, a brief period of intense pain, and now I have to tell everybody I meet some tale about how a meat cleaver slipped and cut off a finger. I'm only thankful it wasn't my thumb. I was going to cut that off, but at the last moment sheer survival intervened and I settled for the little finger of my left hand."

In light of its effect on the rest of his life, Martin's behavior was even more drastic than William's.

"Sarah was stringing me along. It became clear that she was only using me as an escort when no one else was available. She really didn't care for me the way I needed her to and I began to look elsewhere. But Sarah couldn't leave well enough alone, so she'd come around to the store on a flimsy excuse, roll her eyes at me and hint that she was interested in having me take her out, and there would go all my progress and I was back under her spell. It was a temptation I could never resist. After an evening in which I paid the bills and she flirted with every man she saw, I was left high and dry all over again. I was an emotional slave. I thought about her constantly and lived in hope that she'd start feeling about me the way I felt about her.

"Finally, I couldn't take it any more. You might say I broke. I did break. Another person in my state might have committed murder, but what I did was bad enough. I took a sledge hammer from the back of the shop and stormed outside. I had no plan. I just picked up the hammer and marched out into the street and began hammering the first object I came to, which happened to be a neighbor's car. I smashed the roof in. Then I smashed the window-pane of the shop next door, Harry's Haberdashery. I had broken about 30 store windows before they stopped me, and the funny thing is, I don't think I was crazy. I knew what I was doing. I was trying to stop the pain and I succeeded. I spent six weeks in jail, paid $10,000 in fines, and had to face all those guys whose property I had damaged.

"The one good result was that I never saw Sarah again. I guess she heard about it. Every blow of the hammer was a blow to my insanity. It's funny to have gained sanity from a crazy rampage like that. Not that relief came immediately. At first I was so taken up by the results of my destructiveness—the police, the guys in the neighborhood and all. Then not seeing her anymore helped a lot. Of course, no one knew what was behind it. I made up something about headaches. You're the only one I'm telling the real story to."

This confession, like William's, suggests that the attempt to find relief from the agony of acute unhappy limerence is not uncommon, nor is it confined to persons considered unbalanced in a psychiatric sense. At the moment the act is committed, they are, by their own evaluation, "crazy," but I was repeatedly impressed with the absence of psychological or emotional "symptoms" they displayed after limerence and its agonies had subsided and good sense returned.

Ways of affecting conscious experience through "mind chasing" substances were often associated with limerence, according to both interviews and questionnaire responses. Several spoke of actions toward LO under the influence of alcohol. Dee so embarrassed herself that she strictly limited her drinking ever after:

"During that one night I behaved like a different person. First, I went into the bar by myself. I'm not talking about today's type of singles bar, but a real neighborhood saloon in which if you were there and female you were either with an escort or you were advertising your sexual availability. This was 25 years ago, you must remember.

"Anyway, just going into the place was already not me. Then to add to that, I went right up to Earl and the woman he was with and tried to get him to leave her and go with me. I don't know what happened or what he said, but I do remember that he was really firm when he told me to leave him alone. I felt horrible. When I woke up the next morning I felt thoroughly humiliated. Without the alcohol, I never would have acted that way. It was a lesson I never forgot."

Some evidence exists that after the first experience (s), usually in youth and early adulthood, certain coping strategies may be learned that reduce the risks.

Tess felt that although she was still vulnerable both to limerence and to its potential for inflicting great suffering, she now knew ways of handling herself that would prevent her from committing drastic action.

"I can still suffer, but I know that recovery comes in time. When I was younger, I truly thought it was the end of the world. I've learned not to feel that this one person is the total key to my happiness, even though, in a large sense, he is. It's hard to explain but when I was embroiled in those first romances back in high school, each one was almost a life-or-death matter. Now I can still fall in love hard, but I feel a certain cautiousness about it, as if part of me is waiting for the situation to return to normal and part of me knows that it will someday."

On the other hand, some of the most harrowing tales I heard were those of older persons for whom the experience was not new. Perhaps one learns to interpret the feelings somewhat differently with experience, but experience alone seems no safeguard against vulnerability.

When a limerent person is in an actual relationship with LO, LO may show sexual interest in someone else. The limerent may react intensely, even desperately, because sex seems inextricably tied to the "return of feeling." The exceptions occur when "return of feeling" is shown explicitly by some other means. For example, a pimp may be in love with a prostitute, and while he may not find the image of her sexual interactions with others particularly pleasing, their *meaning* makes them acceptable to him. She might even express her love (limerence) for him by providing others with sexual "favors" and thereby advancing his financial cause.

Thus prostitute and procurer can be in love despite the unsavory (and seemingly incompatible with love) nature of their sexual transactions with others. A prostitute explained how Percy separated her sexual activities with customers from evidence of her returned limerence:

"He didn't care what I did—really, anything that paid was okay so long as I took good physical care of myself—washing up afterward, regular medical treatments, etc., and so long as I did not kiss them on the neck. That was his, he insisted. That was what marked the difference between what brought in the money and what was out of bounds."

Thus those exotic societies in which copulation serves "other" functions—hospitality among Eskimos, for example—and arouses no jealousy, are not so enigmatic after all.

Closer to home is the ability of participants in extramarital love affairs to tolerate continued sexual relations between spouses. I am not speaking here of the nonlimerent lover who is not concerned about mutuality or exclusivity, but about a limerent lover who does not interpret the act as a violation of exclusivity. John told me how he felt about Marie's continuing conjugal relationships with her husband, Bill:

"I had no money and no job. Marie meant everything in the world to me. My only real goal in life was for us to be together. But in order to achieve that goal, I had first to go to school, find a way of supporting myself, and all the rest. If Marie left Bill now, we were doomed and our love with it. As totally in love as I was,

I could not be blind to that. If Marie left Bill then, she would get nothing, well, not enough, no matter how she fought the case. If she came to live with me, he'd really nail her, and, besides, I've only got a room and can scarcely pay for that. I loved her too much to do that to her.

"Bill loved her, too, and was jealous as hell. Fortunately, his sexual demands on her were not extraordinary, and there was no other way, for the time being anyway, except that she sleep with him. I didn't like it. It made my flesh crawl to think of it, except that I knew it meant nothing to her. I even encouraged her after a while to pretend it was me, which she said she did, when it was necessary for her to endure it."

In other cases when both partners were married and unwilling to leave their spouses (for financial reasons or out of consideration for social position or for the ill-effects of divorce on the children) some degree of sexual interaction between spouses was sometimes tolerated.

It is in relation to exclusivity that the limerence madness appears on occasion to transcend the boundaries of silent suffering, such as Fred endured, and find expression in actions of violence and cruelty.[34] What spells the difference between the long suffering diary keeper and the wielder of weapons against a roaming LO may relate to how limerent individuals interpret not only actions of their LO, but limerence itself. I spoke with many trapped in a limerence they would like to end. When tiny, intermittent flickers of hope for reciprocation become chains of enduring bondage to a passion which provides no joy and unmitigated pain, some become enraged. Brad described his feelings to me in a long session which he allowed me to tape.

"It had gone on for three years. I felt victimized, a casualty of her beauty and self-assurance and of a society that encourages the madness. Of course I was angry at myself. Every time I called her and received her combination of feigned concern and cool independence, every time I let myself hope only to have her wave me away from her as if I were an insect whenever something of greater interest came along, or every time I found I had given up a day or a week to that old demon, Revery, I would counterreact with fury.

"Sometimes I savor in my mind's eye the most minute details of committing acts of violence to human flesh. Sometimes the victim was whoever it was I thought she was seeing at the time. Sometimes Barbara was herself the victim.

"Usually it was an instance of what seemed to be her lack of consideration, her deliberate, as I saw it, need to keep me as her willing slave, or some such nonsense, that started me off."

Henry VIII of England, a flagrant limerent both in his reported behavior and in the poetry he left behind, was suspicious of signs of nonlimerence in his LO and furiously jealous. He combined his limerences with self-deprecation (and quite possibly mind-deranging physical ills) that resulted in the famous rages and acts of vengeance for which he will always be remembered. Perhaps his influence extended to the setting of a negative example for his daughter, Elizabeth I, "The Virgin Queen."

The reaction of rage seems to be more frequent in men than in women.[35] There were more anger reactions reported by males on the questionnaires. There are more Othellos than Salomes in the classics of fiction. The number of murders committed each year by men is many-fold greater than the number of murders committed by women.

As it was for Henry VIII's wives, the role of LO can be hazardous to your health and welfare. Open any newspaper for evidence. For example, in 1977, 25 people in the Bronx died because of a "lover's quarrel," in which a rejected lover sought vengeance. The rage of a 40-year-old man whose LO left him alone to attend a dance with her sister led to the death by fire of the two women and 23 other persons—after the man poured gasoline on the stairs to the dance hall and ignited it.

In the opera *Carmen*, the limerent she has rejected (Don Jose) appears in the final act to murder her for her fickleness. Bonnie Joan Garland, a 20-year-old Yale music student from White Plains, New York, became a modern-day Carmen when her rejected lover, 24-year-old Richard Herrin, bludgeoned her to death in her sleep.

Just as the audience to the opera is moved to feel pity for the anguished Don José, according to news accounts, there was a certain discernible attitude of community sympathy for Herrin, who was said to have made certain that Bonnie was asleep before striking her, and to have driven about for several hours (during which she might have been saved) before confessing his crime of passion to a priest in a church a hundred miles away.[36]

Even among my informants, there were some rather vicious incidents—battered wives and children, ugly assaults on property, legal actions taken regarding property, suffering on the part of children whose parents' wish to cause pain to a former mate overcame their concern to spare the feelings of children tormented by conflicting demands and divided loyalties. One woman was forced to stand by while her husband threw three years' work in the form of a book manuscript into the fire because he found the story "proved" her betrayal. Another woman described how she had torn up the only existing, and much treasured picture of her lover's dead mother. A mother told me of the tragic death of her son whose "girlfriend" drove her car into him in a fit of jealous rage. Others followed the example of Alfredo in La Traviata and publicly insulted their LOs. Phil was one:

"I was a friend of the student newspaper editor and I gave him some phony information in which I claimed that Sally was one of the women behind some letters that had been circulating on campus about certain faculty members and certain students. The women were angry because they claimed that women students were being harassed sexually. What I did was a literal crime. I don't know if it is a crime, but it is certainly something I'm not proud of. Sally was one of the women, but what I said wasn't true. The point is I was in such a dumb and blind condition of frustration and anger that in a way it's lucky I could get it out of my system that way. Fortunately, there was no real damage."

Although most homicides are not even indirectly linked to limerence, a little more than a third of them in this country concern sexual partners or rivals. Some of these seem very likely to be associated with limerence. Marvin E. Wolfgang notes that the "area of heterosexual relationships is one exceptionally fraught with potential violence whether within the marriage or outside it." Of homicide victims studied, 34.5 percent were spouses, paramours, mistresses, rivals, or paramours of the offenders' mates or homosexual partners, with sexual infidelity frequently a precipitating factor. In any case limerence is at times implicated in violence to self, to property, or to others, including serious assault and even murder.[37]

Intensity of jealousy is not a measure of limerence, since I talked with people who gave every indication of being limerent and who reported minimal or no jealousy. As grief-stricken as they may have been at LO's inconstancy, they did not respond in anger either at LO, or at LO's LO, but only in sadness over the loss. As Lilly said,

"How could I be angry? Of course I was emotionally upset, as well as wounded and desperate, but still I knew he couldn't help it, and I could even see her good points much as I felt I'd have loved to hate her, if I could let myself. I felt terrible, worse than I had ever felt about anything in my life, but my sense didn't let me take it out on them.

"In other words, I was thinking about all those stories you hear about people taking revenge, murdering or something equally gruesome; and I thought not very friendly things, too, but along the line of 'Some day they'd have a falling out, he'll realize what he lost when he rejected me,' etc. Really, no impulses in the direction of violence. Or even anger—except at myself for wasting so much hopeless time."

Lilly does experience anger, however slight, and somehow it ends up being directed toward herself rather than toward LO or even the rival. She *knows* she has *no reason* to be angry at others who cannot help doing what they're doing, but she feels anger anyway.

Suppose Lilly didn't know they could not "help" reacting as they did? Can we explain Lilly's inaction, compared to the murderous vengeance shown by some people, by differences in what their "intellects" tell them? Is the intellect a source of differences that are not basic to the limerent reaction? Both Lilly and the man who caused the dance hall fire are similar in that both were rejected. Were both limerent? If so, was there any difference between them other than their sex? The violence that seems associated with limerence, and that Lilly's story and those of other interviewees tend to confirm, varies greatly from one person to another. I have not interviewed any I knew to be murderers; those whose tales I was privileged to hear tended toward Lilly's end of the scale—a discernible feeling kept, however, well within bounds.

LIMERENCE IN WRITING AND MUSIC

And to think that I have wasted several years of my life, and that I have wanted to die, that I have had my greatest love, for a woman who was not my kind.

—Marcel Proust [38]

The personal journals which were made available to me, including the story of Fred and Laura, were examples of but one of the major forms of unpublished limerent writing. The other two are poetry and personal correspondence with LO. It appears to be characteristic of the state of limerence that you are inclined to express your feelings in writing. But since the limerent state is unknown to or denied by many, and since it so often involves behavior not in accord with the best interests of the actor, shame prevents public display. The fullest expression of limerence in published writing occurs in fiction and in song. Stendhal hesitated about publishing his diaries with their revealing self-disclosures. Instead he published novels. The statement quoted above was what Proust had his character Swann say about himself, not what Proust said about himself. The impulse, described by many interviewees, to tell all, is often stifled in anticipation of dire social consequence.

What cannot be told as reality may be acceptable as fantasy, as romance, or as adventure. Some years after the breakthrough transatlantic flight with Helen Payne, the first person I had heard confess to lifelong nonlimerence, I asked her why the non-limerent person not only can tolerate but apparently enjoy the portrayal of the limerent state in drama and fiction. Her response was that she had always viewed it as romance, as opposed to reality. She explained that just as a person who has never set foot on an oceangoing vessel may enjoy an imaginative account of high seas' adventure, the person who has never experienced limerence may enjoy what to them is an entirely unreal and imaginary account of enchantment by another person and the "noble suffering" of the romantic lover. The same material, of course, elicits different reactions depending on the reader's state. Limerence has been called "romantic love" as opposed to "real love" because to a vocal and often very articulate segment of the population it is unreal. But even when limerence is not believed in, or believed in only secretly, it still makes a good tale.

Morton Hunt reported that the East Germans attempted for 20 years to rid the society of romantic love, which they called "bourgeois trash." But their attacks proved futile, and they encouraged their writers to produce again the love stories the people appeared to need.[39] Writers who, like Communist officials maintain a culturally determinist position that the experience of being in love results from its ubiquitous portrayal, find it hard to believe that the reverse may in fact be true.[40]

Story writers use a multitude of devices to keep their characters from experiencing premature reciprocity, at which point the story would end and the lovers go off into mutual bliss that might be ecstastic for the participants, but would not hold the interest of the reader for very long. That one or the other of the two individuals is committed to a third person is perhaps the most common device, and Hollywood has erected many a light comedy on various sorts of misunderstanding.

When the factor that inhibits full expression of limerent mutuality is the previous commitment of one or both parties to someone else, the story traditionally ends in tragedy rather than mutual reciprocation. This plot is so frequent that I'm sure every reader can think immediately of several examples, particularly among the more "serious" dramas of grand opera, ballet, and classical literature. A random set of examples include Tolstoy's *Anna Karenina* and Fitzgerald's *The Great Gatsby,* among novels, the ballet *Giselle,* and the opera *Madame Butterfly.*

Limerents have certainly written a lot of poetry, and a lot of it has been published. Sappho's poems or Shakespeare's sonnets or Elizabeth Barrett Browning's come immediately to mind; most of the great poets, such as Yeats, have written poems about love. Some poems give very accurate descriptions of the limerent state. For example, Samuel Daniel's poem expresses in a few lines how hard it is to cure, how it grows with adversity and diminishes with reciprocation, and, generally, the puzzlement it evokes:

Love is a sickness full of woes,
All remedies refusing;
A plant that with most cutting grows,
Most barren with best using.
           Why so?

More we enjoy it, more it dies,
If not enjoy'd, it sighing cries,
           Hey ho. [41]

Literature is not, of course, the only art affected by limerence. There may be a relationship between limerence and music that is more intimate, even physiological, than any that can be produced by words alone. Musical tempo varies, but it does so roughly within the range of the human heartbeat. Is music therefore a means of accentuating and transforming the heartbeat?

Although many poems concern limerence, a larger proportion of songs do. It has been reported that approximately 85 percent of popular music concerns love.[42] Similarly, although many plays concern limerence, a larger proportion of dramas set to music do. The celebration of limerence in opera can be understood as an aspect of the nineteenth century shift from arranged marriage to marriage by inclination. The plots of many operas are tales of limerence. If the lovers are permitted to mate at the end, the opera, is "light," but the best-loved operas are "tragic"; for example,*Madame Butterfly, Carmen, Manon, La Traviata,* and *Rigoletto.*

Limerent interviewees frequently told of their "use of music" during limerent unhappiness. Several said that it "doesn't hurt as much" when accompanied by music. Relief did not seem to depend on the type of music. Some used rock; others used classics. A connection between music and limerence is also suggested by the fact that adolescence is a time when interest both in music and in limerence is greater than what it had been during childhood and, in many cases, what it will be in adulthood.

One thing is clear: The relationship between love and music is strong for many of us. Stendhal went so far as to say that "perfect music has the same effect on the heart as the presence of the beloved." [43] Shakespeare's *Twelfth Night* opens with the Duke's complaint about his attraction for Olivia:

> If music be the food of love, play on;
> Give me excess of it, that, surfeiting,
> The appetite may sicken and so die.[44]

Perhaps the relationship between limerence and the arts is best described as expressive: the feelings of limerence are expressed in the artistic product, and the limerent person seems to achieve a degree of emotional satisfaction from exposure to limerence-inspired artistic productions. But limerents, in their intense drive for relief from limerent yearnings, are also likely to become a sort of prey. The limerent state weakens certain sensibilities much as it strengthens others, since the limerent is particularly vulnerable to anything that may increase hope.

COMMERCIAL EXPLOITATION

Any discussion of the significance of limerence to the culture in general should include its role in commerce. There are many ways in which profits can and have been made from appealing to limerent vulnerability. Although we may think of the arts primarily as a means of self-expression, we cannot ignore the fact that both the commissioning and distribution of artistic products are business enterprises. Money is involved with art whether it be theater, book publishing, the managing of concert tours, ballet companies, or the more flagrant commercialism of popular music and television. To judge from the subject matter of many such productions on the market, limerence sells.

It sells specific products that promise the limerent man or woman a better likelihood of achieving limerent aims. There is an enormous market for items and services that help people beautify themselves, attain general self-improvement, and develop expertise in everything from the preparation of gourmet cuisine to the playing of a musical instrument. Fervent concern for improvement of attractiveness to LO reduces sales resistance to cosmetics, shampoo, and hair coloring, diets, exercise programs, clothing, fancy automobiles, and innumerable other consumer items, including those sold as gifts to LOs—books, jewelry, and, of course, flowers. A wedding, the culmination of romance in some circles, is a business bonanza; there is no end to what can be sold, from insurance and washing machines to bone china and sterling silver.

Commercial establishments and services purport to aid the search for limerent reciprocity. These run the gamut from bars, restaurants, cocktail lounges, and private clubs to cruises and other vacations which appeal primarily to "singles." Other commercial enterprises of particular appeal to people in a state of limerent readiness are personal advertisements in the columns of newsstand and other periodicals. Some are aimed at sexual liaisons, but computer dating services in particular attempt to match people with regard to their potential for more enduring relationships, thereby supplementing the many traditional social functions of civic and church organizations in providing a meeting ground for persons in search of LOs and, of course, marital partners.

Do such cultural phenomena influence the incidence of limerence in the society? It seems financially profitable to hold limerence as the ideal. Such commercial use of limerence may also exert an important influence on people not in a state of limerence themselves, making them inclined to behave in ways that resemble limerence.

It should not be inferred that an interest in more purely sexual liaisons is not also of commercial importance. In recent years the proliferation of pornography and large-circulation periodicals devoted to sexuality containing not the slightest trace of limerence attests to limerence having no exclusive hold on the motivations of those who spend money.

5

The Opinions of Philosophers, Psychologists, and Other Experts

Being in love has three images which seem difficult to reconcile with each other. First, it is considered to be the source of the most intense human pleasure, even the most important thing in life—a transcendent state that has no parallel in human experience unless it be that of the religious mystic. Second, being in love is viewed as a symptom of inferiority and weakness, excessive dependency, and low self-esteem. Interestingly, these two images reflect the emotional reactions of the limerent person to LO's behavior: a seemingly positive sign from LO and you walk on air in ecstatic bliss; an action interpreted as rejection, and you sink to the depths of misery.

The third image is expressed in a quotation from Dryden:

For, heaven be thank'd we live, in such an age
When no man dies for love, but on the stage.[1]

It is the view that love is mere fancy, the product of a cultural climate that encourages it or, according to some writers, induces it. For example, Morton Hunt stated:

> Hopeless passion, one way love, and unrequited suffering belong truly to fiction and the medieval knight's long service of his lady. In our own time they exist generally in the form of the bobby soxer's hopeless adoration of the remote idol, but among maturing young people they are more illusion than related. Believed in but not practiced.[2]

And according to Suzanne Brøgger, not many would fall in love who had not heard about it from others.[3] This denial of limerence, possibly the reaction of a nonlimerent, is reflected with surprising frequency in the writings of social scientists and critics, and even more dramatically, in the absence of the topic where one might reasonably expect it to be found, such as in works on the emotions, on adolescence, on marriage counseling and dating guides, on depression or suicide, on individual psychology, and in general on any topic purporting to deal with significant human experiences and interrelationships.

Pejorative labels for intense romantic attachments include "perverted love," "infatuation," "addiction," "destructive passion," "morbid dependency," "deficiency love," "inferior love," "prepackaged love," "masquerade of love," "puppy love," "soul sickness," "idolatrous love," "adolescent love," "selfish love," and Ortega's term "pseudo-love." These terms have often been placed in contradistinction to the preferred emotion variously termed "genuine love," "real love," "mature love," "successful love," "authentic love," or "true love."

Often, the kind of "love" designated by the term "limerence" is not even disparaged, but simply ignored. For example, in a popular book of advice for teenagers published in the late 1960s, section topics include understanding yourself, increasing self-confidence, getting along with others, sex, and dating. The word "love" in the index was followed by five single-page references. "Sex" had 10 references with five subheadings for a total of 55 pages. "Sexual intercourse" was additionally listed with seven references and three subheadings for a total of 12 pages, none of which overlapped with those of "sex." In other words sex was afforded more than 20 times as much space in this handbook for adolescents as was love.

And what were the comments on love, few as they were? First, the reader was told that getting along with people requires the "ability to love." The implication was that to achieve emotional maturity, "you have to learn to love." Unfortunately, the authors provided no advice on how to secure the requisite information or training. Instead, the reader was exhorted to "make an effort" to change in the desired direction. A hundred pages later, the second reference to love indicated that friendship requires the "capacity to love," defined as ability to feel genuine affection, to identify with others, and to be sympathetic. The next reference was located in a chapter that dealt primarily with sexual intercourse. It (intercourse) was part of a happy marriage when combined with love. That's all. The sentence occurred at the end of a paragraph at the end of the section. There was no explanation of what love is. The fourth reference was essentially a repetition of the third, and the last reference was a paragraph which began by advising that, contrary to its portrayal in such unreliable and misleading places as films and magazines, romantic love does not arrive with a sudden awareness that here is the person made just for you, but instead grows slowly as you become "realistically" acquainted with the person. Furthermore, "true love" is giving to others and being considerate of others' needs. If you "really" love, you do no harm, only good.

Not only does such literature offer no assistance to a limerent reader; but by its confusion of sex and love as well as by its failure to acknowledge the condition of limerence as a separate but normal reaction it is likely to create the impression that the limerent response is aberrant.

That a force of the power of limerent desire should have profound effects on many aspects of society is not surprising; it was its failure to be dealt with in the psychological literature in any remotely satisfactory way that was largely responsible for the initiation of my own investigations. But it was only after several years of work that I began to realize fully the confused and contradictory reactions the subject of romantic love evoked in the writers of scientific literature.

TABOO

[Great persons of history do not include] one that hath been trans-
ported to the mad degree of love.

—Francis Bacon [4]

Love was a madness; on this point all
the troubadours were agreed.

—Maurice Valency [5]

I am sick of love.

—King Solomon [6]

Following delivery of a paper on romantic love at the annual
convention of the American Psychological Association, a middle-
aged man in the audience objected to my treatment of this
subject in a scientific manner.[7] After the talk, a young woman
told me that she, like myself, was interested in conducting scholarly research on the subject and had proposed it as the subject of
her doctoral dissertation but was turned down by her committee
and forced to find another topic. It was then that I first recognized that the term "taboo" could appropriately be used in
connection with the study of romantic love.

In 1975, United States Senator William Proxmire made the
headlines when he ridiculed the idea of using public funds for a
proposed psychological study of romantic attachments.[8] Proxmire's objection was not that the subject was unimportant (the
researchers had protested quite logically that a rising birthrate
among teenagers was a national problem of epidemic proportion
and therefore related). Rather he suggested that love was a subject upon which further clarification is inherently undesirable.
His objections, as far as I have been able to learn, were received
as good-humored "old boy, back room fun," and his comment
("there are things about which we would prefer to remain ignorant") resounded throughout Washington cocktail parties as
something everyone knew to laugh about.[9]

During my own years of research I found myself (despite my

conviction of the danger to society of leaving so important a subject unresearched) assuming a certain lightheartedness when referring to the subject, calling it my "ha-ha" research on "ha-ha" romantic love. I later learned that I was not the first to invent a more "respectable" term for the publicly visible spines of my data files. This kind of embarrassment may also explain some of the peculiar labels used by others, for example, "romantic liking." [10] On the other hand, serious study of love would have been impossible without the previous and highly respectable work of the sex researchers. The study of human sexuality set precedent for examination of romantic love, a development that many might find surprising, since it is sex, not love, that received overt and public disapproval through, for example, organized censorship.[11]

One of my interviewees, Billie Jean, described the reaction to her paper on "love" in a college psychology course.

"After each paper was read, two people from the class would evaluate it in a discussion. I had basically said that since love is beautiful we should enjoy it. I said that even if the ecstasy is shortlived, it is worth it for the experience. I think I said it 'ennobles the spirit.' It was a very corny paper. But I didn't think it would evoke such violent debate.

"It was an evening course, and a man and a woman, both mature people in their thirties, were chosen by the instructor to discuss my paper. I think that both of them were nonlimerents. Smith, the man, said that my paper adopted a selfish viewpoint and that I should realize that what I had described was not love, but a 'desperate bid for emotional security,' a neurotic condition. Brown, the woman, agreed with that and added that these illogical and addictive dependency relationships were ruining the world. They were causing illegitimacy and breaking up homes.

"Then some of the other students who seemed to hold a view similar to mine tried to say how beautiful love was, but Smith and Brown said real love, true love, was quite different from what I had described. Brown said that genuine love was caring and concern for the other person, even for all people. Smith said it had more to do with helping people than with wanting to possess them. Most of the students in the class kept quiet."

Philosophers, social scientists, psychologists are not different from the people in Billie Jean's class. No wonder statements that contradict one another are both accepted. No wonder love seems mysterious! Human beings have had difficulty differentiating among:

1. sexual desire.
2. liking, in the sense of friendship
3. affection, and
4. love, in the sense of concern for the person's welfare.

Those without personal knowledge of limerence explained the strange actions of limerents as the result of romantic (imaginative) fantasy. They called it "storybook-like," "unreal," "romantic," the product of artistic imagination; poetic hyperbole; or vagueness. Sometimes the writings better fit the nonlimerent perspective; sometimes they described limerence.

It is not hard to see why a taboo has surrounded the study and analysis of love. No one feels entirely comfortable with the subject. Both limerents and nonlimerents among my interviewees suspected there was something going on they didn't know about, something they took as a personal failing. The limerent interpreted nonlimerent external behavior as self-composure, self-confidence, individuality, independence, and mind over irrational desire. The nonlimerent was not viewed as a person who does not desire, but as one whose "moral fiber" does not *allow* passion to rule over reason. When nonlimerents told limerents to stop being silly and forget an LO who is not worth it and not interested, the limerents tried to obey. They couldn't, but couldn't believe that they couldn't.

Such reactions are discernible in the love literature. Although. apart from Stendhal, I found nothing that can really be considered a systematic and comprehensive approach to the phenomenon, limerence often lurks within the phrases and between the lines, sometimes making its presence clearly felt.[12]

Most statements in the love literature could be interpreted as applying either to limerence or to affectional bonding. These as well as other types of attractions were not clearly distinguishable from one another but instead were fused and merged by being

called by the same term, "love." Writers have been philosophiz-
ing, moralizing, and eulogizing on the subject of "erotic," "passionate," "romantic" love (*i.e.*, limerence) since Plato (and surely
long before that). And more often than not, what is said is
enough to make a limerent dissolve into the walls in embarrassment. It can be dangerous to stick your neck out on the subject of
love—dangerous to your self-esteem and to your reputation. The
existence of an irrational state that affects thinking, mood, and
action among persons otherwise sane would lead to precisely the
effect observed—a good deal of confusion and of logically incompatible descriptions. It is safer to write as a moralist, as an
observer and evaluator outside personal involvement who may
not know the precise nature of the subject matter, but who can
indicate clearly what others ought and ought not do. Much of the
writing in the literature of love was written by persons, who,
perhaps never having suffered the insanity themselves but having
observed its outward manifestations, are adamantly opposed to
it. Limerent persons, sufferers of an unallowable condition, find
themselves speechless save for the ambiguity of "poetic" expression.

In its involuntariness, limerence conflicts with the fundamental position of the Judeo-Christian philosophy, which holds that
human beings are free, rational, and therefore, responsible creatures.[13] Like the cosmological revolution that forced "God's"
children to concede that their geographical position had not
been located in the center of the universe or the Darwinian
revolution that forced the even more terrible admission, that we
are "descended" from brutes, acceptance of normal "insanity,"
of involuntary irrationality as an inherited pattern of thought
and performance, has an unacceptable flavor.[14] It is an idea so
subversive to traditional belief systems that this may be an important reason why limerence and nonlimerence were not isolated and defined sooner. Visible as both states are in fiction and
poetry, their existence in fiction and poetry does not force resolution of the philosophical problems they pose.

It is when an idea is to be incorporated as part of the body of
culturally accepted knowledge (as opposed to popular belief)
that resistance occurs, because at that point incompatibilities

with other ideas are ferreted out for examination and resolution. To say that limerence as here defined, a complex behavior pattern involving thought, emotion, and action, occurs in a similar form among extraordinarily dissimilar people, is to suggest the existence of a kind of "instinct" at the human level. The taboos, the confusion. and the disparagement of love can be viewed as a response to the very nature of limerence.

Love has been called a madness and an affliction at least since the time of the ancient Greeks and probably earlier than that.[15] Madness implies loss of control and inspires fear. The unpredictability associated with irrationality is the same element that inspires fear of "wild" organisms—spiders, snakes, insects, and strange dogs. Such creatures evoke phobic reactions because we are unable to predict what they will do and are therefore left defenseless. To tame is to develop a way of interacting. We do not "understand" those whose actions are without apparent cause. Despite several decades of propaganda in the "mental health movements," few of us fail to feel apprehension in the presence of anyone designated "crazy." We fear that such persons may be possessed by influences whose aims are unknown to us; we are unable to extrapolate from the present to the future, since we do not perceive connections between now and what went before.

This book is aimed at taming a madness (here called limerence) by learning its habits, identifying its various parts and forms, and hoping thereby to make some predictions about its course. To the degree that these aims meet success, limerence may seem less mad, except, of course for its one most crucial feature, the feature that sets it apart from most other human states: its intrusiveness, its invasion of consciousness against our will.

My initial puzzlement over the relative absence of scientific or scholary investigation of the experience of being in love was gradually resolved. Again and again, prior to our talk, those interviewed had expressed but a vague concept of romantic love. Limerents who had suffered often blamed weaknesses in their own character for their pain. Those who had known ecstasy, and many who had known only its image in fantasy and in intense desire for mutual reciprocation often praised love to the skies and looked with suspicion (frequently expressed as pity) on non-limerent "unfortunates." Those who had not experienced limerence tended not to pity themselves, but to be thankful they had escaped from what appeared to be a condition both irrational and unpleasant. This was especially true when they had been forced into the role of LO or witnessed the effects of limerence in a close friend or relative. If the writers whose words had been so mutually contradictory and puzzling were drawn from the same categories as my interviewees, perhaps the contradictory images in literature could be explained.

FROM CAPELLANUS TO THE HUMANISTS

... from Scripture we know that the Devil is really the author of love and lechery.[16]

Andreas Capellanus was the cleric author of the famous eleventh-century treatise, *The Art of Courtly Love.* Although Andreas accurately—indeed very accurately—described the state of limerence and accepted its existence, he listed virtually all the major points made by love's major critics: the depletion of the lovers' energies, the wasting of precious time, and the disadvantage that accrues when "finer" activities are forgone "for the sake of the foul and shameful acts of Venus!"[17] Love produces estrangements among friends, the person in love "is bound in a hard kind of slavery and fears almost anything will injure this love," and the lover's soul can be "very much upset by a slight suspicion."[18] Friends are neglected and lost, selfishness (except pertaining to the beloved) rules, and a lover would not hesitate to commit any sin if the act were one that aided the lover's cause.[19] Furthermore, "love brings intolerable torment," and even the "delight of the flesh must necessarily be reckoned among the vices."[20] In matters other than those pertaining to love, the lover is slow, lazy, inattentive to important affairs, uninterested in the grief of friends and even driven to commit crime. Love "wickedly breaks up marriage and without reason turns a husband from his wife ... indeed we have known many lovers who have been driven by love to think of killing their wives, and they have even put them to a very cruel death."[21]

Andreas also cites jealousy, "bad digestion," and "loss of sleep which also causes frequent alterations in the brain and in the mind," causing madness. The continual brooding "which all lovers indulge in, also brings on a certain weakness of the brain, and from this come many illnesses of the body."[22]

Concluding, Andreas deplored the unfairness of unrequited love. A "just ruler" would not allow people to fall in love with those who did not return the affection "either at once or after a proper amount of suffering."[23]

Those who idealize nonlimerence for its reasonableness and consider the manifestations of limerence to be signs of psychopathology usually also hold that romantic love is a cultural invention.[24] There is no question but that the courtly love of the eleventh century brought certain cultural changes related to romantic attractions. Surely the culture influences the phenomenon, even if only in the language used to describe it. But that you must hear of love in order to experience it seems a dubious proposition. What is more likely is that the culture may exert some influence on the LO, especially the nonlimerent LO, who, not under the limerent spell, is more amenable to such influence. If the culture is one in which limerence is idealized, LOs will not only be more tolerant of limerent insistence on exclusivity, but will be inclined to imitate limerent actions.

If, on the other hand, the culture is hostile to limerence, there will be an increased tendency to deny it, or at least to hide its outward manifestations. What such a climate does to its incidence can only be guessed at this point, my own conjecture being that it might increase initial suppression.

Once limerence takes hold, its course is determined by LO's behavior and how that behavior is interpreted by the limerent person. The major result of a social environment that discourages the expression of limerence might simply be more clandestine assignations in woods, gardens, and parking lots.

In 1956, psychoanalyst Erich Fromm published *The Art of Loving,* a work that has since been, like its author, highly praised and extremely popular. To Fromm, sex must be understood as not only the desire for physical release and pleasure, but also, and more importantly, as the desire for union. This type of love is contrasted with mother love, which is love given unselfishly, at least so long as the child is helpless and dependent. It is "erotic love" that most resembles limerence in Fromm's schema because of the exclusivity of its objective. He notes that a mother may love all her children, but erotic love involves "craving for complete fusion, for union with the other person."

Although it is apparent that Fromm speaks from experience, (whether personal or not) with the phenomenon of what is here called limerence, his descriptions, like those of most writers on love, stress moralism and evaluation. When he asserts, for example, that "sudden intimacy is by its very nature shortlived," he may be referring to the diminishing effect of "premature" reciprocation on the intensity of the reaction. But the crux of his discussion appears to be the denial of involuntariness. In his attempt to redeem "erotic love" from "possessive attachment," with implications of selfishness, separateness, and sexual union of a merely physical type (what he terms the easily satisfied "itch"), he states that "love should be essentially an act of will, a decision to commit" one's life to another. Not merely an intense "feeling," it is "a judgment" and "a promise." Fromm's commitment to human "transcendence" leads him to inconsistency. Although much of the book consists of wise advice to those who might otherwise be foolishly self-centered in their social interactions, his concluding remarks on the only section in which the reaction discussed resembles limerence are as follows:

> Both views then, that of erotic love as completely individual attraction, unique between two specific persons, as well as the other view that erotic love is nothing but an act of will, are true—or, as it may be put more aptly, the truth is neither this nor that. Hence the idea of a relationship which can easily be dissolved if one is not successful with it, is as erroneous as the idea that under no circumstances must the relationship be dissolved.[25]

Obviously, Fromm's aim is to provide the reader with guidance. That he is judged to have done so is clear from the book's success over the years, but on the subject of limerence, a state that affects a countless number of his readers, he, like so many other writers, founders helplessly.

Poets and novelists aside, the reaction to romantic love as expressed in serious literature is often almost entirely negative.

The soul of a man in love smells of the closed-up room of a sick man—its confined atmosphere is filled with stale breath.

When we emerge from a period of falling in love, we feel an impression similar to awakening from a narrow passage crammed with dreams.

Ortega Y Gasset [26]

Stendhal is virtually alone in failing to criticize the lover, the beloved, *or* the experience. Spanish philosopher, Ortega Y Gasset, in his book *On Love*, published in 1957, ridicules Stendhal, calling him both idealistic and pessimistic. Ortega accuses Stendhal of idealizing an abnormality or mistake.[27]

For Stendhal, the lover is not blind; crystallization is a matter of emphasis, or, rather, overemphasis. Ortega analyzes crystallization for its *logical* fallacies. He concludes that if the person loved does not indeed display truly admirable characteristics, then the love is not "genuine."[28] He declares that some purported cases of love are not really love and that Stendhal's conception in particular was designed to compensate for his own inherent unlovableness. According to Ortega, loneliness caused Stendhal to imagine non-existent love affairs; if love were real, it would not end. Since love does die, even when the loved person remains unaltered, it must have been an error.[29] In disparaging Stendhal, Ortega refers to Don Juan. Unlike the "pathetic" Stendhal, Don Juan is one of a class of men with whom women fall in love with admirable "intensity and frequency." In contrast Stendhal spent four futile decades attempting to win in the game of love, but attained only "pseudoloves."[30]

In the 1970s, trends that were discernible decades earlier culminated in what became known within the profession as humanistic psychology and generally as the "movement." The basic tenets of the human potential movement are that human beings are corrupted by the artificialities and restrictions of the societies in which they live. Society prevents realization of our potentials; we are generally "unfulfilled" creatures whose capacities have been blunted by the trials and tribulations we are forced to undergo.

Abraham Maslow, one of the founders of this largely California based movement and the psychologist who introduced the term "self-actualization" into the psychological vocabulary, was also a spokesperson for an ideal form of love that is clearly nonlimerent. Maslow wrote of "D-love," which he said was not love at all but a state of dependency.[31] "B-love," in contrast, should be welcomed into consciousness; it is never a problem but can be enjoyed endlessly. It has beneficial effects on the persons involved since it is associated with individual autonomy and independence. B-lovers are not unreasonably jealous and they are not blind. It is the other, damaging D-love which blinds you. In true love (B-love) you are able to perceive your lover clearly and penetratingly.

This view has very recently been seconded by humanist philosopher Robert Solomon, who upholds the values of intimacy, sincerity, and egalitarianism when he claims that a love that does not allow freedom from possessiveness is not love but a "masquerade," even though it may be described in the flowery language of romanticism and even though it may be "passionate."[32] Self-confidence and self-esteem, according to Solomon, are essential prerequisites for true love. When the object of the emotion remains inaccessible, it is not love, for only the strong can really love and to suffer unrequited longing is not a sign of strength. Love's aim is a kind of unfolding of self through an intimate relationship with another.

Another writer who denied that "secret love" is in fact love is sociologist Paul Bohannan, to whom "romantic love" is a condition in which your "love fantasies become ends in themselves." You are blinded to LO's "real" personality because you *refuse* to look at the facts. Clearly, Bohannan speaks of limerence, but like Solomon he classified this state as other than "true love" and considers it:

a sort of psychological love potion that some people either administer to themselves or else use as an excuse when they *want to be
irresponsible.* (italics added) 33

The humanist position is also represented by George R. Bach
and Ronald M. Deutsch, according to whom, in a "dehumanized
society," love is increasingly sought, not as a "romantic luxury"
or even as "security," but in hopes of achieving "authentic intimacy" in which the individual comes to feel personally relevant
and validated.34 Their book is intended as a handbook for attainment of this condition through departure from the traditional
courtship system. Thus comes the "intimate revolution," guided
by "a new, free, and realistic rule of love." 35 The old rules cheat
us of intimacy because they require us to disguise ourselves in
distorting roles.

That Bach and Deutsch are mainly disparaging limerence and,
like so many before them, trying to set up a more rational
system, is apparent from their discussion of one of the primary
aspects of limerence, fear of rejection. Indeed, they describe
some aspects of limerence much as my informants have done.
Feelings of lovesickness are as follows:

> I am tense and uneasy, because I am trying hard to guess what you
> want me to be, so that you will love me. Once I psyche out what you
> find lovable, I will bend myself out of shape to conform to your idea
> of lovability for fear you may stop loving me. I dare not show you my
> real self, because I feel inadequate. . . .36

But Bach and Deutsch do not view these feelings as an integral
aspect of a complex involuntary human reaction pattern. Instead, they label the feeling "destructive" and propose a form of
psychotherapy aimed at helping people achieve "authentic" intimacy that would not be hindered by the shyness and fear of
lovesickness. Their basic message is that it is not good to be
lovesick, so don't be lovesick, a message readily accepted by
nonlimerents. Limerents reading Bach and Deutsch, on the other
hand, can only end up looking "neurotic" in their own eyes.
Robert Rimmer is another spokesperson for a "genuine hu-

manist" (and nonlimerent) ideal. Rimmer is committed to not
playing games with people, to being open, self-disclosing, defenseless.[37] He, Bach, and other advocates of healthy uninhibited
sexual pleasure and "genuine" relationships between people who
perceive each other realistically, disparage being in love and
recommend that their readers adopt a more rational, sane, and
reasonable approach. The problem is their assumption that
choice is possible and that the only reason people get into such a
silly state as limerence is willful wrongheadedness.[38]

It cannot be concluded that none of these writers has ever
experienced limerence; only that they view it as both illogical
and pathological. What my studies suggest is that while it is
illogical, it is also normal, and therefore normal human beings
can be illogical. For some this seems a difficult idea to accept.

Premature announcements of the demise of romantic love
occur with regularity. A recent one is "The Demythologizing of
Romantic Love" by William Kilpatrick, in which he calls the
romantic lover "incurably future oriented" and unable to enjoy
the present. But fortunately, according to Kilpatrick, today's
now generation (with more casual relationships) is replacing the
traditional elaborate fantasizing of eternal bliss (in marriage).
Kilpatrick, like others, assumes that romantic love requires focusing on differences between the sexes. Unlike some writers, Kilpatrick applauds the change. He notes the problems that
limerence poses to communal living, to the growth groups of the
human potential movement, and, generally, to the community
spirit of the "global village." The obstacle is limerence's jealousy
and possessiveness. Kilpatrick feels that these disruptive elements do not constitute necessary elements of love, but only of
"romanticized, individual love." Furthermore, this undesirable
form has begun to appear "as selfish and possessive to a growing
number of people," Kilpatrick asserts, citing the words to popular songs as evidence of a change and blaming unfortunate "con-
ditioning." He hopes that the new trends signify changes that
will result in an increase in "nonjealous, nonpossessive" (nonlimerent) love.[39]

In a book titled *Love and Addiction,* Stanton Peele sets out
criteria by which "love" can be distinguished from "addiction"

(another disparaging term for the limerent reaction).[40] These include holding a "secure belief" in one's own value, improving as the result of the relationship, keeping up interest in things and in people outside of the relationship, having common interests that transcend the love aspect of the relationship, and letting each other "grow" in an atmosphere free of jealousy and possessiveness. In the very *social* humanist and human potential movement ideology, which is largely a group movement, limerence's greatest sin is the exclusivity which causes lovers to close their door to the rest of the world. It is possible to view this movement and its attitude toward love itself as one of society's current means of attempting to control limerence. Its message is phrased in nontechnical language in general public media such as magazines, books, and TV interviews and is therefore among the more visible expressions of a contemporary cultural attitude.

Quantitative information about romantic love is not totally absent in the scientific literature. For example, an attempt to obtain systematic data was reported in 1945 by University of Minnesota sociologists Clifford Kirkpatrick and Theodore Caplow. About 400 college students either selected, prepared graphs, or drew their own graphs to describe the course of approximately 900 love affairs (2.2 per student). Unfortunately, the results of the study do not differentiate between old and new relationships, and certainly not between limerent and non-limerent relationships. It is therefore difficult to assess the authors' conclusion that "at least half of the students' love affairs do not involve serious emotional traumas." [41] The statement also implies that *almost* half of them did involve serious emotional traumas, and it permits the speculation that all breakups involve emotional trauma, a "trauma" later termed "not serious" in almost half of the cases.

Twelve percent of the love affairs were followed by feelings of hostility, and 30 percent by intensification of feelings, both of which fit the limerent pattern as described in my interviews better than does the simple and gradual decline in attraction which characterized more than half of reported past breakup periods. Although Kirkpatrick and Caplow give no information about the details of the relationships, it might be further speculated that the half of the reported affairs that did not involve "serious trauma" were nonlimerent relationships for the persons describing them.

Other than this study, sociologists' work on romantic love has mainly focused on mate selection. They have found that "free choice" does not produce random selection with respect to such basic factors as race, religion, socioeconomic status, age, and relative physical attractiveness, but that like chooses like more often than not, even without explicit parental direction.[42] Furthermore, "selection" appears to occur only in the very first stage of limerence, in which potential LOs are identified. You are less likely to find yourself having that essential feeling of admiration for the "wrong type." Once limerence is established, LO's religious, racial, or other categorical "unsuitability" is insufficient to terminate the emotion, although it may well influence outward behavior (such as who gets brought home to dinner). LO's very unsuitability might in fact provide the needed "obstacle" without which limerence seems unable to blossom fully.

At any rate, while society influences the expression of limerence, external control appears to be limited, and may even produce effects opposite from what is intended. Certainly, society did not invent limerence in the eleventh century, since tales of the madness of love occur in the most ancient of written literature as well as in folklore. If anthropologists today fail to detect signs of it in "primitive" communities, that seems not because "those people" are less civilized and therefore less capable of experiencing so refined, sophisticated, and rapturous a state, but because the anthropologists have not known how to look for it. That limerence does exist in nonindustrial societies is suggested by the fact that many cultures have developed "love magic" with which to induce the reaction.[43]

> At the very core of modern romance is a tightrope tautly stretched between, and uneasily dividing as well as soldering, gratified and ungratified, over- and under-evaluated sexuality ... Where romance is the rule, sex is virtually never enjoyed for itself.
>
> —Albert Ellis [44]

One of limerence's deadliest opponents is psychotherapist and psychology popularizer Albert Ellis, for whom "passionate love" is in fact an idealized "sex tease" pattern of courtship in which the modern woman tries to attract the male into marriage. Ellis rails against limerence mainly because of its adverse effects on free and enjoyable sexuality. He views romantic love as a pagan reaction against Christianity, which ultimately adopted the anti-sexual values of the institution it had set out to replace. Primary among undesirable characteristics of romantic love are its intense exclusivity; its emphasis on physical attractiveness, and, above all, its insistence that sex without love is undesirable. The romantic lover thus declares a *monopoly* on sex, one which in fact leaves the nonlimerent high and dry. Ellis, probably because he is self-confident enough to be arrogant, yet honest enough to maintain his good humor, talks a somewhat convincing line of highly sexed nonlimerence.

He provides an excellent and documented listing of assertions about romantic love that permeate the mass media, assertions which he obviously finds dismaying. Yet they largely reflect the state of limerence as it was described by my interviewees, including love's ability to "catch one unaware," its occurrence across a wide range of ages, the intense agony of nonmutuality, its irrationality, its exclusivity, and the longing for "love without which life is dull, pitiful, and meaningless."[45] He clearly implies that the media, and therefore society, are somewhat at fault for producing this madness. Since he equates neurosis with failure to recognize reality, romance stands in the way of mental health. Parents who train their children to be romantic are training them to be "at least semi-neurotic."[46]

Ellis sees as his basic mission the attempt to persuade others to accept what appears correct to his "reality-oriented" perception. Perhaps it is this that leads him to make unwarranted assertions of causality. For example, according to Ellis, romantic love "thrives on" the existence of obstacles *because* it is "an idealized, perfectionist emotion." If lovers saw each other more frequently and under stress conditions, instead of only when well fed, well rested, and dressed to the hilt for their dates, they would not be able to "live up to perfectionist ideals."[47] Ellis does not view romantic love as involuntary. Indeed, he recommends that lovers find better ways of ending it than the typical "heartbreak." His specific suggestions are changing partners, being non-monogamous, and engaging in sexual activities to break up a pattern that depends for its viability on sexual inhibition. Ellis cites psychoanalysts Alfred Adler, Karen Horney, and Sandor Ferenci among other psychological and sociological authorities who attest to the psychological harm wrought by the romantic demon.[48] His own form of psychotherapy is consistent with his perspective on romantic love. He argues (browbeats?) his clients into recognition of the "illogical philosophy" that dominates their lives.[49]

I once commented innocently to a close associate of Dr. Ellis' that his writings suggest to me that he does not fall in love. His friend did not argue with that, but said that he *loves,* telling about the closeness of their own relationship. I'm sure he does, and his crusade *for* enjoyable sex and *against* romantic love is humane in its objectives. His writing reminds me of the befuddlement so often expressed by never-limerent interviewees. If his clients do not inform him of the precise nature of their condition, it is not surprising, for Dr. Ellis is right; limerence *is* a "madness," after all.

When I began my investigations, articles on the subject of romantic love by psychologists tended to begin with a statement such as the following:

It is amazing how little the empirical sciences have to offer on the subject of love.[50]

But in the early 1970s, the pace quickened and several books on love were published.[51] Research reports appeared in the social and behavioral science journals. A favorite topic was the issue of what sort of person falls in love. Some found love more frequent among those of low self-esteem,[52] among persons holding more traditional views,[53] those of lower economic status,[54] or among those whose lives appear to be guided more by "external" than by "internal" sources of motivation.[55] Of course, such studies suffered in indeterminable ways from the problem of terminology and from the possibility that it was readiness to admit romantic attachments rather than actual incidence that was measured by the interviews and questionnaires used in collecting the data.[56]

PSYCHOTHERAPY

In most of the literature on psychotherapy, and especially in the work of Karen Horney, romantic love is viewed as the sign of a dependent personality who is lacking in self-esteem, and even basically masochistic.[57] The prepossessiveness of limerent thinking is a *pathological obsession*; the emotional response to signs of hope for mutuality or of rejection by LO is *emotional dependency*; exclusivity of focus becomes possessiveness, and so forth. There is also a strong current of "blaming the victim." For example, limerents are accused of allowing themselves to get into this "self-destructive" state.[58] On the other hand, if they say they are not in love, their "capacity for love" (and therefore, for "maturity," "growth," "happiness," and other nice things) is suspect.[59]

I spoke with a number of never-limerents who consulted therapists partly to find out what all the fuss was about and what was the matter with them that they could not seem to will the experience into existence. Most often the therapist agreed that here was a real symptom of "emotional trouble." [60] The therapist expected that long-term therapy might well help. "Inability" to form normal love relationships often finds its way into case records as a serious symptom.

Psychoanalytic writer Theodore Reik contends that falling in love results from the perception of a deficiency in yourself.[61] In other words, it is the result of the pathological needs of your personality and therefore itself a sign of difficulty. Imagine how Fred would have been received by a psychotherapist who held such attitudes had he taken himself to be "psychologically treated" for his obsession with Laura.

Lately, Stendhal's view that passionate love is not pathological has been supported by a number of studies, but the results did not seem to have filtered into the therapies experienced by my informants, a number of whom sought help from psychiatrists or psychologists.[62] Others read books by psychoanalysts who contended that their state resulted from a general condition of "dependency," "emotional immaturity," or even "masochism."

The worst happened to a woman I will call Jennifer.

The pattern of interaction described in her story was given to me in highly similar detail by at least a dozen different women. I have taken great care to conceal any possible means of identifying Jennifer or the other real people behind her tale, because one of the many similarities among them was extreme concern that their confessions to me not be made public in a way that could possibly be traceable to them. I think that this reaction is itself of interest and I have included it as a feature of Jennifer's story. Their concern may be related to the lack of credibility that surrounds a person designated as a "psychiatric patient," including lack of *self*-credibility.

I began my book on psychotherapy when I discovered that few people appear to be aware of psychotherapy's shaky scientific foundation. As that research proceeded, I discovered from the professional literature, as well as from my own more direct investigation, that there was considerable evidence that "psychodynamic psychotherapy"—the kind in which you talk "freely" about yourself and the "therapist" mostly listens, can be not only unhelpful but actually harmful. Even under the best of circumstances, even when you receive a certain degree of support, and may even gain increased understanding of aspects of yourself and your situation that help you to cope, that helpfulness must overcome possible harmfulness involved in the image of yourself as a "mental patient." I think this image may explain some of the extreme concern for privacy showed by those represented in Jennifer's tale, but as you will see, the label "mentally sick" is not the worst danger. I never interviewed any of the therapists that the real Jennifers consulted so I admit to giving the story entirely from the "patient's" point of view. I am, however, familiar with the psychotherapy literature and am therefore aware of how therapists write of limerent reactions in their clients.

The *reason* my informants consulted psychotherapists was not, except perhaps for one woman, true "mental" illness. Situations of stress—the need to make painful and difficult life decisions, loss of a loved one and ensuing depression, unreturned limerence, marital difficulties, problems with their children (including many cases in which it was the child and not the mother who exhibited behavioral aberrations)—these were the kinds of problems that brought the women to the doctor's dimly lit chamber. They were psychologically normal people who without treatment-produced damage might have suffered only transient disturbances of customary well-being.

One other ingredient was needed (I don't mean money—that, too, of course): a culturally induced expectation that going to see a psychiatrist or other type of psychotherapist was the appropriate thing to do. In general, the women had been exposed to a kind of pro-therapy propaganda promulgated by television sitcoms, advice columnists, and various kinds of popular reading material. They presented themselves to their psychotherapists with faith that here was a person professionally trained to help, someone who surely knew much more than they about emotional reactions and other "psychological" matters.

Jennifer Waller was not a client of mine. She had read my book on psychotherapy and had also heard that I was studying romantic love. She telephoned me and volunteered to tell her story, provided I assure her of confidentiality.

"I'm terribly sorry. I know it sounds as if I don't trust you and that's not true. Really, I do trust you or I would not be here at all. It's just that I must have your assurance that under no condition will you ever reveal my story to the person involved or to anyone else."

Jennifer had married Mark a year after she graduated from Smith College. Mark was about six years older than she and had completed engineering school the year before. They met at a ski resort. Fifteen years later, he had advanced satisfactorily in his career; Pam, their five-year-old daughter was getting along fine; but the older child, Jimmy, was having "behavioral problems" in school. According to psychological theories popular at the time, some deficiency in the home environment was suspected to be involved, and Jennifer found herself seeing a psychiatrist, whom I will call Dr. Bennett.

"At first I was apprehensive and even a little resentful. The school psychologist clearly implied that Jimmy's problems at school were the result of some mental problems of mine. I don't mean to say that I thought I had no problems. It was just that I had never considered them to be more severe than other people's. I certainly didn't consider myself crazy or unbalanced or disturbed or anything like that.

"My husband and I had a terrible row because I didn't feel that I should be the only one to see a psychiatrist. I even considered looking for another school for Jimmy, but we really couldn't afford a private school. Mark calmed me down by saying that it was not because I was crazy that I had to be the one to go but because I was the one at home with Jimmy. That was not the impression I had during the conference with the school psychologist. I gave in finally when Mark explained that the treatment I would get was covered by his company health insurance policy, but that it would be better for me than for him (Mark) to have 'psychiatric referral and treatment' on the company record.[63]

"Looking back, I feel that Mark was really shaken up by the implication that there was something wrong with me. His faith was undermined, and I don't think he ever recovered from that. He had always seen me as a kind of Rock of Gibraltar. I was always the one who didn't get upset at things. Yet the experts were saying that Jimmy's problems were due to *my* emotional state. Really, from the day of that conference with the psychologist, neither Mark nor I was ever the same. I couldn't even talk to my friend Sally about it. How do you say to a friend that you've been told that you are emotionally disturbed? The fact is that I had been undercut as a mother, a wife, and a person. What else could I do but comply with the recommendation?

"The first few sessions with Dr. Bennett were uneventful. He asked me to tell him about myself beginning with my earliest childhood recollections and to cover everything I could think of. For one thing, this took the focus off my present situation and, I must admit, there was something pleasant about spending a quiet and uninterrupted hour each week talking about myself to a wise and kindly doctor. Sometimes I'd forget *why* I was there and almost enjoy myself.

"Dr. Bennett was in his early forties. I can't say I liked him instantly, but as time went on I began to feel 'comfortable' with him. I remember thinking that he was someone I'd like to have on my guest list at a dinner party. I think I didn't feel attracted mainly because the very idea was absurd.

"It was probably around the sixth or seventh session that I really took a good look at him. He usually said very little and although my chair faced his, the lights were dim and his face was in the shadow. I had been talking about how Mark and I used to go to concerts and museums during our dating days. I felt a kind of positive response from Dr. Bennett. Not that he actually commented, but I had the distinct feeling that he approved.

"At the beginning, he had explained that the therapy required that we be concerned only with my situation, never himself personally. That seemed reasonable but as time went on, I became curious. I never came right out and asked him anything about himself, but I could not help wondering. I once found an item in a newspaper that said he had given a paper at a convention and I was surprised at my own reaction. I clipped it out, read it over and over, and imagined him giving the paper, walking around at the convention, talking to people, and so forth. It seemed silly for me to have reacted so strongly even at the time.

"Anyway, when I made the remark about museums, it seemed that he had slightly forgot his role and his 'um-hummm' showed a trace of enthusiasm that came from his situation, not mine. Or it might have been my imagination. The reason I mention it is that it seemed to mark the beginning of seeing him as a man, not just as this wise expert who would help Jimmy. I would say it all began at that moment. From then on, I thought about him more often, and differently.

"About a month later, I had finished the story of my childhood and was now spending most of the sessions telling about my dreams and just saying whatever I thought of, as he had instructed me to do. He called it 'free associating.' I would also tell about things that had happened between sessions, such as the time Pamela burned her fingers playing with matches that Mark had left around or the time Mark wrecked his car on the way home from an office party.

"He would listen to these things, then ask me for my feelings about them. When I had finished, he'd usually give me an 'uh-huh' and ask what dreams I'd had. I got the impression that he felt that to dwell on such things was a relatively inefficient use of time. He preferred to focus on dreams and associations. Anyway, this one day, I was wearing an especially attractive blue outfit that I knew looked really good on me. Just before the session I had attended a luncheon with some former college classmates. It was our yearly reunion. I had had two martinis.

"Now this is hard to tell because there is nothing that I can say actually happened that day. It was a certain boldness on my part because of the drinks and the way he looked at me. It really started then.

"I went into that session feeling quite normal and mainly hoping that the drinks would not interfere. I began by apologizing, but couldn't help giggling in the middle. Just a little, but, well, I'm not accustomed to having two drinks in the middle of the day. What can I say? I don't know how to explain it. But when I walked out of that office that day, everything had changed. I can't even remember that he said anything in particular. I do remember his eyes. It may have been nothing more than that the drinks made me look at him and see what was there all along. I don't know to this day."

Jennifer reported that after that day the sessions with Dr. Bennett became the major events in her life. As she put it, she "lived for them." No longer did she think of them as "therapy," but as opportunities to be in the presence of the man she loved. She progressed rapidly to 100 percent preoccupation; that is, she spent virtually all possible time thinking of Dr. Bennett. She continued:

"I thought of what he had worn at the last session and what I might say at the next. Over and over again, I imagined that he would indicate through some clear action that he felt the same way about me.

"The weeks went by and I continued to talk about dreams, but I no longer felt that I was in therapy. My associations were no longer free, and even my dreams were edited to avoid anything I felt would put me in an unfavorable image or show my true feelings about 'Chris,' as I had begun to call him to myself. Because so much of my mental life was devoted to him, I invented things to fill in the gaps and give me something to talk about during the sessions. Between sessions, I spent hours planning what I would wear and how I would behave during the next session. I expected that the very next time we were together some marvelous incident would transpire that would bring about the reaction from him that had become the focus of my fantasies.

"At first, it was fun having this titillating 'interest' in my life. Everyone remarked on the improvement in my appearance. Mark became more interested in sex and I did, too, except that I would imagine it was Chris in bed with me. But I began to neglect other aspects of my life. I felt that I was not giving the children the proper attention. I *did* what had to be done, but my attention was elsewhere. I hadn't read a book for months. When I tried to read, I'd see his face on the page and give myself up to reverie instead. I had fallen in love.

"When I began seeing Dr. Bennett I had felt strong and comfortable. My life, except for Jimmy's troubles, was unclouded and, if not thrilling, quite satisfying on the whole. The school psychologists decided that I was the cause of Jimmy's problems. Maybe I was, but now my marriage and my whole life were in jeopardy. This lovesickness was driving out all other considerations. All I thought about was how much I wanted a real relationship with the man I had come to love.

"When there was no change in anything except that my feelings for Chris increased in intensity, I decided that I had to take some kind of action. If Chris was attracted to me—and my obsession thrived on small signs that told me he did—it was time to do something. It was not fair to anyone to go on this way. I had become miserable, and it seemed ironical that the person who was supposed to help me was instead responsible, however innocently. I didn't blame him in any way, and I *still* consider him to be one of the finest human beings I have ever known. I decided it was not fair to him to let what had become a charade continue.

"One day, after much preparation and many losses of nerve at the last minute, I uttered a carefully rehearsed speech: 'Dr. Bennett, I have something that I must say to you before we go any further. For some time now, I have been struggling with a growing feeling for you as a person, as a man, which I feel is undermining the therapy. I do not wish to continue this way. If you do not reciprocate and do not wish us to establish a different kind of relationship, then I would appreciate it if you would refer me to another therapist.'

"When I prepared that speech, I didn't see how I could lose. It was, I felt, a clear and dignified opener. If he did feel the way I felt he did, he had only to admit it and we could work out the details. If he didn't, well, I felt I could take it. It was better to know where I stood. But of all possible reactions I had considered, I never expected the reaction I received. He was quiet for a little while, and then he said, 'Jennifer, what you are experiencing is actually a part of successful psychotherapy. Your emotional focus on me is essentially symbolic. Actually, it is not a reaction to me. You hardly know me, since although you have been coming for treatment for several months, we have not talked about me, but about you.

This, in fact, is the reason why we psychotherapists deliberately avoid giving patients information about our personal lives. Actually, you are reacting to other persons in your life, and I am a kind of substitute for them. Furthermore, this is as it should be. It is *part of therapy* for you to transfer your feelings about significant people in your life, your father, for example, to me. And it is good because it brings the feelings into the present where they can be dealt with.'

"I felt as if I had been hit with a sledge hammer. He was telling me that I was not feeling what I was feeling and he even had a technical name for it, 'transference.' The only thing he said that had a positive impact was that he felt the sessions should be increased to three times a week in order to, in his words, 'work through the transference neurosis.' I left the office in a daze. I had told the man I love of my feelings and he had responded by suggesting that we see each other three times a week instead of just once! The rest seemed unimportant. How wonderful the prospects seemed now!

"When I told Mark about the proposed change, he was furious. To him it meant that I was even more sick than had originally been suggested. It also meant that he'd have to face his company insurance representative again. At my suggestion he telephoned Chris who explained that the change was a perfectly ordinary one when a patient shows a capacity for more intensive treatment. It was actually a positive sign, not a sign that I was sicker, and that he would draft an explanatory statement for the insurance company.

"Although Mark and the insurance company were reassured, I had two incompatible reactions. If I saw the change as an indication of returned feelings, which I did sometimes, I was happy. But I could also see it as a rejection, which, of course, it really was. Part of me even noted that the change was financially beneficial to him. The problem was that if he were attracted to me then he was being dishonest to pretend that the treatment required additional sessions. If he was honest, then he was not interested in me except as a patient. Either way, I lost. But these thoughts were in the background. More immediately was the fact that I would see him more often. Maybe he was sincere but had not yet realized himself that he was attracted to me. Surely with the additional time we would have available everything would be worked out.

"But six months later I was a basket case. I cried after every session and sometimes during sessions. I would live for the sessions and then be crushed by a reaction from him that seemed ambiguous, but, I realize now, was really neutral. If I had been a different kind of person I might have forced the issue, but I had become even more afraid of rejection than before my admission. Once when I cried during the session, he came over to my chair and placed his hand on my shoulder. I felt that I had been struck by electricity. For weeks afterward, I relived that moment in my mind."

Jennifer felt trapped. If she broke off therapy, then she would suffer the total loss of what she had come to want most in all the world. In all situations in which limerent persons come into regular contact with their LO, a similar condition exists. As limerent, you grasp the smallest act or word that might be interpreted as a sign of hope, and it is virtually impossible for any LO with whom you engage in even the most ordinary type of social intercourse to keep from—out of the most ordinary politeness—giving off signals interpretable in your limerent mentality as a possible sign of positive reaction. Nor is politeness always necessary; some informants described rude, even brutal, actions by LOs in which they were able to find cause for fleeting and transitory rejoicing. As one woman said about a husband who had on more than one occasion inflicted wounds serious enough to require hospitalization:

"I know it sounds crazy. It was crazy, but when he beat me, my main reaction was that if he cared nothing at all, he wouldn't beat me. If his feelings were neutral, I wouldn't even be worth beating. Also, later on when he calmed down, he usually became especially nice, at least for a day or so, and sometimes the love I felt from him after the storm seemed almost worth the storm. It was a kind of cycle.

"I only broke out of it when I realized that I was mainly a place to get food and clean shirts—as well as a convenient and compliant punching bag—because his real interest was in Rita Morgan, his secretary. The minute he persuaded her to live with him, I got my walking papers."

And, it should be added, as soon as she was no longer regularly in his presence, her limerence began its slow decline.

In some ways, a woman's limerence for a male psychotherapist is as difficult to escape from as is limerence for a brutal husband. It is an aspect of his socially agreed-on role that he be not only polite, but warm, understanding, compassionate, concerned, etc., and that he focus his attention on his "patients" in a very intimate and personal way. Furthermore, the very nature of the situation provides both obstacles and a rationalization for his reluctance to admit any positive feeling he may have for a "patient." As one of the other Jennifers put it, "I was a sitting duck, a sitting duck."

Jennifer remained "in therapy" for a total of three miserable years, during which her situation only worsened. Dr. Bennett is portrayed here as the most responsible among the real therapists. In several cases, my informants' limerence was compounded by sexual seduction by the therapist, which succeeded easily since it was initially interpreted by the woman as limerent reciprocation. During the period of Jennifer's therapy, Mark, her husband, became increasingly limerent toward her, a condition which made married life even more difficult to cope with. Although Mark never actually voiced suspicions about her feelings for Dr. Bennett, he never liked his rival and repeatedly tried to get Jennifer to discontinue seeing him. In fact, it might have been easier for her to break off the therapy had Mark reacted differently. As it was, his "smothering" attentions and her "frigidity" became frequent topics during her "therapy" sessions. The limerent person does everything conceivable to win the attraction of LO. By telling about her husband's renewed interest in her, she was calling attention to her capacity for arousing male interest. Her comments describing her disinclination to have sex with her husband were a way of informing LO of her availablity, also a way of increasing his interest, or so she hoped.

Before making the final break, Jennifer took several actions in her vain attempt to attain her limerent objective, and then, as hope diminished, to end her agony. Like other limerents, she selected the content of the sessions to conform to what appeared to her to present an image of herself more likely to arouse his interest. She also underwent the physical transformation that was partly due to increased attention to appearance and partly to subtle alterations in posture and facial expression, some deliberate, others unconscious. In addition to these changes, she attempted on two other occasions to challenge him directly. I say challenge because her limerence fed on her belief, despite Dr. Bennett's essentially neutral behavior, that he really did care, but in her words:

"... he was too fine a human being and too conscientious a doctor to exploit his patients by giving in to his own feelings, no matter how strong. In other words, instead of seeing that he wasn't interested, his lack of overt action only created greater respect for him in my feverish mind. Today, I feel wasted and humiliated, but then I think I could have interpreted any action on his part in my favor. Within his role of therapist, he was honest and decent. But now I believe that there is something not quite honest in the role, something he didn't create or invent."

Dr. Bennett's reaction to a second, and stronger, declaration of love by Jennifer was to attempt repeatedly to explain that her feelings were not what they seemed, and that they heralded a breakthrough in the process of reconstruction of her personality along less neurotic lines. But Jennifer could not believe this.

"Therapy had been a farce for a long time. There was no way he could be right because he didn't know that most of what I had been telling him for the last year and a half did not represent my true feelings. When I fell in love with him everything changed. Before, I had been self-critical in an honest way; now everything was geared to the futile hope that we were—even in the absence of signs that would be visible to an observer—lovers."

She employed two final last-ditch strategies, one almost fatal, both intensely serious. She left Mark during the second year of her limerence for Dr. Bennett.

"I had to. I just had to. We had been married for 10 years and he was the father of my children. I loved him in the real sense. But I could not respond the way he wanted me to, and it semed only to hurt him more if I tried to pretend. I did try. As smitten as I was, what I really wanted more than anything in the world was to go back to where we were before that school psychologist decided that Jimmy needed me to go into 'treatment.' The upshot of that probably sincere professional decision cost Jimmy a good deal of his mother's attention and almost his mother's life, as well as a father.

"The really horrid part of it is that the real reason I had to leave Mark was so that Chris, who as far as I concerned, was a shining white knight on a beautiful snow white steed, could declare himself without blaming himself for destroying my marriage. In other words, I had to check out the possibility—remote even to my crazy mixed-up brain—that if I were free, he would be also.

"Well, I did and he didn't, and if anything I think he began then to show the first signs of really rejecting me in ways that not even I was able to deny. If he had only done that sooner, I might still be married, and, frankly, I wish I were except that now Mark has found someone else. . . ."

It was not long after the divorce that Jennifer committed what was almost the final act of her life. One Sunday while the children were with Mark, she got out her father's World War II "souvenir" pistol.

"I had heard enough about failed suicide attempts and stomach pumps. Dad had given the gun to me when I moved into my first apartment. He had been very careful about teaching me how to use it safely.

"I guess my hand must have jerked aside at the last split second. How can I explain that I pointed a gun supposedly at my head which is a pretty large and nearby target and yet miss? I remember thinking that I wanted to keep my face from getting all messed up. What if the children came running in before Mark had a chance to read the note. Anyway, it was still a miracle I survived, according to the doctors.

"The worst part was that even that didn't end my obsession with Chris. He visited me in the hospital while I was still very doped up, and I felt that he had come to me as a lover. It's all very hazy, but after he left I felt that my dreams had finally come true, except the next day there was no word from him. Or the day after or all the next week.

"Finally I called him from the hospital in a state that was worse than the one that had put me there in the first place. I was terribly afraid of what I might do if I let myself get doped up again—I don't mean try to kill myself; I do mean telephone Chris and say something that would undermine his image of me. When

I called I was totally undrugged and shaking like a leaf, but I tried to be calm and businesslike. I called because I had to know for certain where things stood between us.

"I found out all right. There was a certain distinct distance in his voice that had never been there before. And he didn't call me by my name. He was very formal, and I was . . . I guess you'd call it pride, although it seems ridiculous to have pride when a few days before I was ready to give up on everything. I said that I would be discharged from the hospital in a few days and just wanted him to know that everything was fine and that I'd call if I felt that I wanted an appointment. He said he was glad to hear that I was feeling better. That's all. It was the end. It was very clear.

"I think I sat absolutely still in that bed for 10 minutes after I hung up. Gradually, I began to feel lightheaded, almost dizzy. It was really over and I was relieved. Of course, the full recovery period had its ups and downs, but in another two months I was really ready to try to put my life back together. Mark was gone, and I am now trying to make a new life in many ways, and to recover some of the lost time with my children."

None of my other informants who told about developing a limerent reaction to their psychotherapists had so close a brush with death as did Jennifer, although two others mentioned suicide attempts. Four of them engaged in some form of overt relationship with their psychotherapist LO, and in two, or possibly three of those cases, sexual intercourse occurred in the consultation chamber. An additional source of despair was the difficulty they had in finding support—either from family or from professionals. They complained of not being believed. As one said, "When I told a second therapist about my experiences, I could read doubt all over his face."

In the spring of 1971 I was asked to function as a resource person in a workshop on "psychological rape," at a conference of women concerned about rape, an issue which had before then received very little public attention. The event has had profound effects on my own life and on the lives of many others. It was in that workshop that I first heard reports of women psychotherapy patients who had engaged in sexual activities with their therapists. Among the 30 or so women who participated in the session, at least a third reported overt sexual activities, and an even larger number seemed to feel that "psychological rape" described the events of their psychotherapy, even though explicit sexual acts had not occurred.[64]

One of the women, Julie Roy, became the limerent sexual partner of her therapist and eventually sued him successfully. The tragedy of her situation as she told it in the workshop was the lack of credibility afforded psychiatric clients, especially the effect of the damaging label "schizophrenia" which produced crippling self-doubt as well as disrespectful reactions from others. In her case as well as in those of many others from whom I later received testimony, a major obstacle was the difficulty she experienced in getting the lawyers from whom she sought assistance to believe her. They finally did believe her; but without the support of several other women willing to appear in court and describe behavior toward them—especially sexual advances—by the same psychiatrist, Julie Roy might never have won her case.

Psychotherapy, the primarily verbal interaction of "doctor" and "patient" with the aim of "treating" the patient's "neurosis," "mental disturbance," or "emotional abnormality" has now been widely discredited.[65] But when, at the Rape Conference, I casually mentioned my astonishment at the tenacious faith in the procedure demonstrated by the women in the workshop who complained about individual experiences that they assumed were unusual, not about the fundamental principles on which the process is based, *my* remarks were greeted with disbelief. Despite the ill-effects they had suffered, therapy was still *believed in.* Four years later, both Julie Roy's story of the result of her successful litigation against psychiatrist Renatus Hartogs and my book, *Psychotherapy: The Hazardous Cure,* were published; by coincidence, at just about the same time.

It was quite common, even among feminists in those days, to have the word of the woman doubted. I'll never forget the reaction of a woman I'll call Dee, who at a meeting of a local chapter of the National Organization for Women after one of my early talks on the scientifically dubious nature of psychotherapy as a treatment, said,

"I think you were taken in. Those women were just spouting their personal fantasies. You can't believe a psychiatric patient who says that a professional man would do such a thing. That's part of their sickness to say and to sometimes believe that they had had sex with a therapist. It's very foolish to believe them and I'd be careful if I were you about mistaking a woman's wishful thinking with reality."

Dee's comment and other similar ones were as unanswerable as psychodynamic conceptions themselves were untestable. All one could do was argue, and that was futile. Today the evidence that sex takes place in psychotherapy is abundant, much of it coming from therapists themselves in questionnaire responses. The professions have responded to consumer pressure—mostly from women's groups—by tightening ethical codes. My own surveys through anonymous questionnaires turned up about one in a hundred cases of sex in therapy admissions, which seemed, on the basis of other published information, to represent an underestimation.

The incidence of women's limerence for their therapists may also be increased by situational factors such as the relative paucity of other potential LOs for many of the women who contacted me, living as many of them were, in suburbia and spending their days concerned with home and children in relative social isolation.

As Vivian expressed it,

"Dr. Cornbourg was the only person in my life whom I considered my intellectual equal, even superior. Sometimes I just couldn't resist taking some time during the session to talk a little about a book I was reading, or about a current event. Those times were high points in my life. To be in the presence of a highly educated, sensitive person who was ready to devote his attention to my little world and my feelings, was, I guess, very impressive. I really enjoyed it."

This reaction highlights the isolated situation of many women (at home with children) in which any desirable man who pays regular attention to them may become a potential LO.

It took me a long time to recognize the full implication of the natures of (1) psychotherapy practice and (2) limerence and, especially (3) how these must of necessity often combine. Only the psychotherapists, of all the social scientists, deal at any length with the phenomenon of falling in love, but they do not refer to it as such; they call it "transference." It was only when I felt I understood what limerence was through the interviews that I could begin to understand the implications of limerence to the psychotherapy patient, especially the woman patient. We have seen that limerence is ignited by a set of conditions that include:

1. A person who meets your criteria for an LO. (The basic requisites appear to vary, and not always represent what you might consciously define as your criteria. On the other hand, the similarity between limerents and LOs with respect to broad categories of gender, age, socioeconomic status, educational level, ethnicity, etc., suggests that criteria exist.)
2. A sign of hope that the person might reciprocate.
3. Uncertainty.

For the women who told me of their limerence for their therapists, all three conditions were more than admirably met. The therapists were "kindly," "warm," "humane," "caring," which are all things that therapists are supposed to be, according to their own manuals.[66] They were, however, also "attractive," "confused," "irritable," "cold," and other negatives; and most of them behaved in a way that caused the woman to experience far more pain than would have been the case had their behavior been more in keeping with the realities of her experience. Overt sex among those who spoke to me was confined to a small minority who were "swept off their feet" by the attentions of so magnificent a being as the therapist. Ruth was a woman in her mid-fifties, a mother of five who had completed one year of college and had never worked for a salary. Her entrance into therapy was, like Jennifer's, by the most well-worn route for women in her circumstances: a report by the school authorities concerning the "disruptive behavior" of her 12-year-old son, Phil.

"I worried about the money, at least until the insurance came through, but otherwise, I was flattered to be receiving the attention of so busy and important a person. It was really something new for me to have someone like that get to know me and be interested in my problems. I would never have thought about him 'that way,' though. I mean that I never did, although I thought about him a lot. I would always do everything more or less wondering whether he approved and thinking about being able to tell him about it. Life had become more interesting, and it was because of him.

"I thought I was getting better, that it really was a treatment, although I couldn't see how it was happening. In the sessions I would go over my feelings about things, and he always seemed interested in every detail. It was after about eight months that one day he moved his chair over to the side of the desk near where I was sitting and said that he felt I could benefit from some 'muscle relaxation,' that he was pleased at the progress I was making but that even greater benefits would come from a 'loosening up of physical tensions.' He asked me if I would be willing to have him explore my sources of tension, beginning with my hands.

"That was the moment. He took my hand and I looked at him. He was looking directly into my eyes. I don't know whether it was the touch or the look, but my whole body quivered. I felt weak and started to sway. I could hardly hold my head up. It all happened within about a minute. That's all it took. I had been struck, hit by Cupid's arrow, hypnotized, whatever you want to call it. From then on, I never stopped thinking of him and hoping desperately that he would love me. That was why I was putty in his hands.

"In the next sessions he went from holding my hands to hugging me (feeling my back muscles and 'overall tone'), to fondling my breasts to testing for 'vaginal response,' to 'I'm going to show you what loving can be.' It took about six weeks, but it could have been immediate. I'd have given in. Slow like that, I went crazy. I loved him. I didn't know what he was doing. I can't remember when we made the transition from what could still be viewed as professional behavior on his part and when I could no longer pretend to myself that what was happening was not happening."

The trauma might have lasted longer and been more severe had she not finally received the support of her family physician, who encouraged her to terminate her "therapy." I have come to believe that psychotherapy would be dangerous to the limerently inclined woman even if there were no couch (Freudian analysts prefer patients supine during treatment), and the lights were not dimmed (which they often are) and the conversation did not concern intimate and quite often erotic material (according to Freud, sexual frustrations play a large part in the production of a neurosis; to cure the illness, the unconscious sexual processes must be brought to conscious attention).

From the outset, with his first female patients, Freud was thrust into the role of LO. As we have seen, this is a position with certain special characteristics. Unfortunately, Freud did not see limerence as a normally "crazy" and very specific pattern of response. Instead, he decided that it confirmed certain aspects of his theory and that it was a process brought about by the powers of his invented therapy. Recognizing his patients' tendency to misperceive his true qualities, he decided that their reactions were in fact not to him at all but to other persons in their lives. What a patient really felt for her father was *projected* onto the innocent and anonymous therapist. Surely nothing that he was or that he had done was an adequate stimulus for the extreme (limerent) reactions he observed in his patients.

What finally penetrated my own understanding in crystal-clear form was the way in which the existence of this concept in psychoanalysis is a kind of external verification of the state of limerence as it had been revealed in interviews. *Of course*, limerence would be rampant in patients under the conditions imposed by psychotherapy! And Freud, quite probably initially distressed at himself in the role of LO, could hardly have failed to notice its frequency. Unfortunately, what seemed to be true in his patients became a description of what always happens to everyone. Then, if it didn't seem to be happening, it was *still* happening, but, to use a favorite expression, so "deeply repressed" that there was no sign in overt behavior. The "repression," incidentally, was un-conscious, so there was no point trying to argue against the pronouncement. Thus falling in love with your therapist was not falling in love with your therapist, but a part of the treatment.[67]

To Freud's credit, he noticed the state, but he evaded its implications by maintaining that whatever attribute the theory says the patient has, is, if unobservable, still existing, but in unobservable form (where, analysts usually contended, it is likely to be even more troublesome, even the causative factor in the patient's neurosis). Having a transference with your analyst was at one time considered so important that you risked being con-sidered "untreatable" if you didn't have one.

Some of the former patients I spoke with while *Psychotherapy: The Hazardous Cure* was in preparation told me that their thera-pists had accused them of being seductive toward them. Ginny's therapist would not accept a denial.

"That was when my faith began to crumble. I admired Dr. Bean greatly, I respected him, I even felt sure he was helping me, but I had no interest in him as a lover or sexual partner. I could never figure out where he got that idea that I was in love with him."

The conduciveness of psychotherapy to limerence doesn't make it a sure thing; it merely increases the number of people who succumb. But according to Freud, analysis without transference was a pale shadow of what it might have been. Psychoanalysts (like Dr. Bean) who failed to elicit transference must have had secret doubts about their own competence.

Another woman told of the problem she was having conform-ing to the fashion at the time of slim and short skirts. She had a weight problem and was especially heavy in her thighs, which caused her skirt to ride up to a height she herself found unac-ceptable. The therapist, she reported, used this as proof of her sexual designs on him, whereas in reality her interest in him was entirely nonsexual and nonlimerent. The large number of women who came to me after publication of my book can only be interpreted as the tip of an iceberg whose actual size is fearful to contemplate, but I do not want to give the impression that all those who consulted me to complain about previous therapists had suffered limerence. The limerent reaction is not the only way in which psychotherapy can be harmful.[68]

Transference has received increasingly bad press within the professional journals. Even C. G. Jung found it a "nuisance";[69] and Albert Ellis said that it was not necessary.[70] William Glasser prefers to try to "shatter illusions" his patients develop about himself.[71] Increasingly, therapy manuals began to indicate techniques for reducing it. Therapists have been advised to warn the patient in advance that such feelings might occur to generate a realistic image of themselves, and to terminate the therapy.

Not surprisingly, these recommendations fit limerence theory: A patient who had been warned might interpret any limerent reaction as only a side effect of therapy and such an interpretation might inhibit the further development of the condition. A patient who did not see the therapist as all-wise and powerful might not adopt the "idealized" view that limerents so characteristically have of their LOs. Finally, termination of therapy would extinguish all hope. In view of limerence theory, such recommendations should be included in the psychotherapists' ethical code.[72] Some political opposition might occur because transference constitutes an important aid to carrying out a procedure essential to therapy's financial base: prolonged treatment. As Chessick said, transference is the glue that binds the patient to the treatment process.[73] Indeed it does. Unfortunately, what the psychotherapists of my limerent informants tended to do was to allow the women to continue to come for sessions—like any sympathetic and well-meaning nonlimerent LO.

Now that the haze is being lifted from both these phenomena, it is evident that limerence and psychotherapy have combined to produce untold human suffering. The crucial element seems to have been the readiness with which interpretations and judgments masked the true nature of both.

It is *essential* that the profession be called to task for irresponsibility.[74] For the most part, however, I believe that therapists have also suffered along with their patients. LO is not an easy role, and it must be especially difficult for those therapists who do not exploit the situation for sexual services and who do not need limerent adoration to buttress their self-esteem. Dr. Bennett, whose actions were modeled on the most responsible of the therapists that my informants had seen, seemed genuinely concerned for Jennifer's welfare as well as for his own therapeutic success. He was undoubtedly troubled by what he probably labeled Jennifer's "seductiveness." That term appears frequently in the psychiatric and psychological literature on psychotherapy, nor is it an entirely inaccurate depiction of the outward signs of limerence. But its motivational base is quite different from that connotatively associated with "seduction," which is usually thought of as trying to achieve sexual arousal for some ulterior, or at least *purely* sexual motive. In contrast, as an interviewee described feelings toward the therapist during transference:

"He was a god, really, I know that sounds silly, but he was a final authority, especially on me. But more than that, he appeared to me as a person of absolute integrity and moral character. Even after I realized that I had fallen in love with him, I was mainly concerned about living up to what I believed were his standards.

"I assumed that I would never reveal my feelings because I assumed that whatever his feelings for me, his behavior would be as my doctor. I wanted to make his life easier in whatever way was in my power. Although I never actually did it, I wanted to buy him gifts and would stand looking at expensive items in Bloomingdale's imagining the pleasure he would get from the various items I saw. The point is that I loved him. It was not really sexual; it was almost spiritual."

When that woman's therapist, not understanding the nature of limerence, and trying vainly to deal with the situation in terms of the theories of his profession, ran out of patience with her, he said in a quiet tone, one surely intended to convey the full dignity of his profession, "I am not a sex therapist; I do not have physical contact with patients. If you wish, I could refer you elsewhere." In a sense, that response was better than Dr. Bennett's because it permitted less hope of reciprocation.

6

Limerence Among
the Sexes

There is wide consensus as to which sex is more concerned with
love:

> For the Greeks in classic times, love was normally a female ailment
> ... it was not a disease appropriate to men.
>
> —Maurice Valency [1]

> The single word, love, in fact signifies two different things for man
> and woman. What woman understands by love is clear enough: it is
> not only devotion, it is a total gift of body and soul ... unconditional
> ... a *faith,* the only one she has. As for man, if he loves a woman,
> what he *wants* is that love from her; he is in consequence far from
> postulating the same sentiment for himself as for woman; if there
> should be men who also felt that desire for complete abandonment,
> upon my word, they would not be men.
>
> —Nietzsche in *The Gay Science* [2]

> [Love is] a woman's whole existence.
>
> —Lord Byron [3]

Among the first-rate, man's life is fame, woman's life is love. Woman is man's equal only when she makes her life a perpetual offering, as that of man is perpetual action.

—Balzac [4]

Léonore used to say that this sort of behavior in a man was feminine love.

—Stendhal [5]

Love is the delusion that one woman differs from another.

—H. L. Mencken [6]

The woman's need is not loving, but being loved.

—Humberto Nagera [7]
Department of Psychiatry
University of Michigan

To be in love can be a full-time job for a woman, like that of a profession for a man.

—Shulamith Firestone [8]

In *The Second Sex,* French writer Simone de Beauvoir described limerent behavior, but her "woman in love" seemed to be tottering on the brink of more generalized psychopathology. Beauvoir's memoirs strongly suggest that she herself has known the limerent state, from her pre-Sartrian youth, from her affair with American novelist Nelson Algren, and also, probably, from her feelings for Sartre during the first few years of their partnership. In the following passage, the woman is the fearful and uncertain limerent; the man is "sensible."

A lover who has confidence in his mistress feels no displeasure if she absents herself, is occupied at a distance from him; sure that she is his, he prefers to possess a free being than to own a thing. For a woman, on the contrary, the absence of her lover is always torture; ... away from him she is dispossessed ... even when seated at her reading or writing ... he is abandoning her, betraying her.

Beauvoir describes the woman's frantic attempt to allay her fear of rejection and to sustain belief in reciprocation.

> Most often, she clutches at the straw of falsehood. She fancies that the man's love is the exact counterpart of the love she brings to him; ... she takes desire for love, erection for desire, love for a religion. She compels the man to lie to her: "Do you love me? As much as yesterday? Will you always love me?"

The woman finds grounds for hope under every leaf and on grounds invisible to the observer.

> She makes trophies of the extorted replies; and if there are no replies, she takes silence to mean what she wishes; every woman in love is more or less a paranoiac.

The woman tells herself,

> X adores me but is so strange a creature and is so much on his guard against love that when I ring his doorbell, he meets me on the landing and won't even let me in.[9]

But haven't we seen ample evidence that neither limerence nor its more extreme manifestations are unknown to men? Beauvoir, an astute observer of human behavior, appears to accept the generalizations of her culture in which, as Ingrid Bengis put it, one is taught that love is "more encompassing for a woman than for a man." [10]

Approximately half of the females and a third of the males in The Group accepted the following statements: "Women react to love very differently from the way men do" and "Love is very different for women and for men." More than a third of the females and slightly less than a third of the males believed that "Women suffer more when a love affair does not go well," as compared with only 10 percent of each sex when "men" was substituted for "women" in the same sentence.

It was consistent with Beauvoir's viewpoint that half of the females in The Group were "terribly afraid that _____ would stop loving me." Since fear of rejection is a main component of limerence, response to this statement may be used as one basis for estimating the incidence of limerence. It is not consistent with Beauvoir's impressions that the statement was also accepted by more than a third of the males (35 percent). There is a certain pressure on males not to admit any of the symptoms of limerence. The Group's responses are, therefore, consistent with the idea that both sexes experience limerence in roughly equal proportions. The difference in the proportion of each sex's accepting such statements can be attributed to the sex roles of the culture, in which it is, for example, more acceptable for a woman to admit to emotional dependency than it is for a man.

SOCIAL CONSTRAINTS

Throughout *The Second Sex,* Beauvoir insists that women's experiences of anguish and conflict are the result of women's social *situation.* In her view, it is nothing inherent or inborn about the female but rather the social condition of "alterity," of living a life of limited options outside the main cultural stream, that produces stronger, and sometimes more tragic, reactions to love. Forced to depend on men for status, security, and survival itself, women have been and are still *subordinate* to men in society. To the degree that social options can mitigate limerent distress, it follows that women are disadvantaged.[11]

Recent researchers have been surprised to find that when the general happiness and psychoemotional well-being of the sexes are related to marital status, the unmarried woman turns out to be best off, the married woman most unhappy, with the males falling in between, and married males distinctly better off than bachelors.[12]

The *image* of woman as being in greater need of love could well result from a cultural upending of the actual inherent tendency. The *social* forces operating on her—and it cannot be denied that throughout modern history they have operated quite harshly—permitted no other role than one in which she required the protection of a male.[13] If love were not a major concern, she might find herself literally left out in the cold. This is what Simone de Beauvoir emphasizes. To say simply that "love is [a woman's] whole happiness" omits the fact that other sources of gratification have generally been denied her; it need not, therefore, imply anything about what women and men might be like under altered conditions of social and economic power.

Or the term "love" may refer to the seemingly greater inclination of women to react with sympathy and compassion to the plights of other persons in distress. For example, maternal love probably differs from paternal love in ways that transcend cultural influence.

Differences in the way the two sexes behave in psychology experiments and in answering questionnaires seem particularly subject to the influence of current societal fashions and standards, since the behavior frequently changes as those factors change.[14] Furthermore, reported studies on "romantic love" are difficult to interpret because the word "love" has varying meanings, and, as noted repeatedly, even the phrase "in love" may be used to refer to sexual and affectionate, but nonlimerent feelings for another person. So despite rampant unfounded opinion, studies that, for example, find men to be more "romantic" or to "fall in love more (or less) easily" are difficult to interpret.[15]

Interpreting the responses of The Group is subject to the same problems. For example, Table I gives four statements that were accepted by a substantial proportion of The Group, but by a much higher percentage of female than male respondents.

TABLE I

Statement	Percentage of The Group who accepted the statements		
	Female	*Male*	*Both Sexes*
I often lie awake at night thinking about being with _____.	66	45	59
I have spent many hours imagining romantic episodes.	57	40	51

Statement	Female	Male	Both Sexes
When I am in love I spend a lot of time daydreaming about love, romance, and sex.	51	31	45
I like to read novels about love.	52	8	39

Do women really spend more time reading and thinking about love, or do women find it more acceptable—even on an anonymous questionnaire—to *say* that they do?

TABLE II

Statement	Percentage of The Group who accepted the statements		
	Female	Male	Both Sexes
I have been very depressed about a love affair.	60	48	50
I was (am) terribly afraid that _____ would stop loving me.	50	35	45
When _____ broke off our relationship I thought I would never get over it.	41	16	33
I *knew* _____ no longer cared but I couldn't accept it.	34	18	29
I was (am) very jealous and insecure, unable really to believe in _____'s love for me.	34	14	28

Again, these five questions show that female members of The Group admitted to more fear of rejection and heartbreak, but the substantial proportions of males who also accepted the statements—48 percent of males said they had been "very depressed about a love affair," for example—make it clear that distress over love is not a female monopoly. Again, the admission of weakness is itself less acceptable for men than for women. Taking that into account, the differences seem less significant. Women are expected and allowed to be "shattered" by love; for a man, however, it is unmasculine. That 14 percent of the men admitted to being shattered supports the conclusion from the interviews that men are also susceptible to limerence with all its agonies as well as its bliss, and that sexes differ mainly in how they see and describe themselves, not necessarily in the feelings they experience.

Consistent with the contention that both sexes experience limerence similarly are the rates of acceptance of the following statements:

I have been deeply in love with someone who did not love me or know of my feelings.
When I was younger I was infatuated with a celebrity (*e.g.*, movie star, rock star).

Both were accepted by about 40 percent of the total. The first was accepted by both sexes in roughly equal proportions. More women (51 percent) than men (30 percent) accepted the second, which is hardly surprising since the press and films have recently made much of female fans of rock stars but seldom mentioned male fans. During World War II, the "pinup girl" was popular. The star was usually garbed in a bathing suit and posed to encourage the belief that interest in her was purely sexual, not romantic. This face-saver permitted public display of a movie star, on the door of a young man's locker, for whom the attraction could have been limerence disguised as sex.

With respect to other differences in questionnaire responses, the influence of the respective "situations" is clear. For example, traditionally, males are given the responsibility of initiating contact. They, not the females, do the phoning, the asking—for a date, for sex, for marriage—and the female replies. Although there has been some effort to alter this pattern, it remains strong.

Therefore, it is not surprising that the response to the following item showed one of the largest differences between the sexes, acceptance by 55 percent of the women, but only 21 percent of the men: For hours, days, even weeks, I waited for _____ to call.

This does not mean that men do not suffer unrequited limerence. The man, however, would usually not be waiting for the woman to telephone. He might be trying to decide whether or not he is ready to risk rejection by calling, or wish he were not burdened with the responsibility, but cultural expectations are hard to shake off. Limerences stalemated by inaction on both sides were sometimes rekindled when the woman made the calls, as Caroline did:

"I waited and waited and waited. Then it occurred to me that if Barry felt about me the way I wanted him to feel and the way I felt about him, he could be paralyzed, afraid to call for fear he'd bother me and be rejected. I, therefore, had to call but with a good excuse so that I could not appear to be pressuring him if he was not interested."

Caroline called Barry supposedly to obtain the telephone number of a mutual friend. The call resulted in a date, the date in a renewal of the relationship. When she talked with Barry about it after they were married, he said that he had indeed been trying to work up enough courage to call. Would he have succeeded? Might they have ended up married to people other than each other, or not married at all, had she not made that call?

Perhaps social constraints and reactions account for the seeming differences between the sexes. Yet it is hard to believe that limerence is really the same for both men and women, differing at most in incidence, and not importantly. The sexes also differ in sexuality and in reproduction functions.

SEX DIFFERENCES AND SEX ROLES

From the descriptions of experiences given me, I detected no difference in limerence based on gender. All interviewees found themselves preoccupied. All yearned for reciprocation. All felt the ache in the chest during periods of despair. Those differences that did appear in questionnaire reactions seem better explained by reference to differences in socially imposed roles and values, or by differences in sexuality. It was hard to separate these factors on the various questionnaires. I found only one difference that will surprise no one, and even that one had its exception (in "Homolimerence," to be discussed later in this chapter). The only sex difference that appeared consistently was the gender of LO.

Consider the characteristics of all those toward whom you might conceivably react with limerence. The inviolable criterion is, for heterosexuals, that LO be of the "opposite" sex, a more stringent criterion for limerence than even for sex itself. And this difference is considered so important that it defines your "sexual identification." Even those interviewees who described themselves as "bisexual" defined the pool of those who are their potential LOs in terms of gender. Gary, for example, told of early heterosexual experiences:

"I had my first sexual experiences as practically a baby, with little girls on the block. I was a six-year-old Don Juan. We used to 'play' in an old school bus in the backyard of the kids' houses. But it was strictly sex play. I never had a crush on any of the girls. It was mainly a matter of playing with each other's private parts, and, frankly, the big deal was mainly that it was something forbidden. We did a lot of other forbidden things as well, like putting fake notes in milk boxes. We were really predelinquent when I think about it.

"Anyway, it wasn't until I was in high school that I fell in love for the first time—with a male. Since then, I have continued to enjoy sex with females, but I have never loved a woman. I have liked them, been friends with them, and had them as 'lovers' in a sexual sense, but only that. If I could change it, I would, but so far it has never happened. I call myself bisexual because I have sexual relations with both sexes."

I do not, of course, conclude that all those who call themselves bisexual are in fact capable of becoming limerent only toward members of one sex, although they may enjoy sex with members of both sexes, but this is what all of my bisexual informants said.

There was also an occasional tale of a limerent-like reaction toward an older woman by a younger woman who otherwise considered herself heterosexual. Do these cases really represent limerence? Can the potential gender of LO, which is generally so fixed among mature persons, waver between genders during youth? There were too few cases, and those occurred early in the investigations. It may be that these instances of "hero worship" differed from limerence in important respects that I could not then identify.

It might also be that while the experience of limerence is the same for all, there are differences in how easily limerence is stimulated in men and women, how frequently it occurs, and in aspects of the experience that were lost in the process of interviewees searching their memories.

Other researchers have explored sex differences and described them in the psychological, sociological, anthropological, and sexuality literatures. But since limerence has not previously been distinguished either from other forms of love or from sexuality, it is quite possible that the differences described in scientific studies are the result of differences in sexuality per se or differences rooted in the social milieu.[16]

Sex differences that are found in all normal members of each sex (anatomical features and related functions such as giving birth and infant feeding), should be distinguished from "differences" that are statistical (women weigh less than men, or men earn almost twice what women do in comparable jobs). There are exceptions to these generalizations. (Some women are taller than some men.) I found no universal sex differences in the way limerence is experienced so far as it is described in Chapter II. Not even gender of LO can be considered a universal difference. But there may be differences of the second statistical type, differences that hold in general, but with exceptions.

Some statistical differences may be guessed at by considering known aspects of the limerent experience. For example, it is known that limerence comes about when (1) you are in a state of readiness (which means at least that you are not intensely limerent about someone else at the moment), and (2) you encounter a member of your personal LO pool (that subcategory of all humans with the potential of exciting that response in you) who through look, word, or deed suggests that spark of interest in you that sets off the limerent reaction.

Even if the full-blown experience of limerence does not differ depending on the gender of the person undergoing it, there may exist differences in how easily and how often it occurs. For example, the presence of members of the LO pool in your daily life might well increase the chances of your becoming limerent. Gwen described years on an isolated farm in Maine in which there were no potential LOs.

"When I say there was no one, I mean no one. There wasn't a single man anywhere in my life. I went to town only once or twice a month, but even there the only people I'd run into were old Mr. Evans at the drugstore and the young boys who tended the grocery store. Other than that, it was mainly me and the kids and once in a while the mother of one of their friends. It went on like that for almost five years. The last thing I thought about in those days was falling in love or getting married."

Overwhelming "sex difference" still exists, even in the most "advanced" Western countries, in the degree to which a person is out in the world versus staying at home with or without children. Although attractions between women at home and neighbors or milkmen are notorious, they may not be nearly as frequent as is the office affair.

Perhaps limerence lurks in the minds of those who fear for themselves and society should women be accorded the right to move about in the world. Wives fear (often rightly) that their husbands will become limerent toward female peers. Bosses fear the disruptive effects of limerence.[17] With more women in the army, recent government regulations restrict dating to those of equal military rank. Deification is the real problem. If you understand the condition well enough to predict its course, you are less likely to make damaging life decisions based on its emotional imperatives.

Since physical attractiveness seems to be to some degree culturally defined, it might be that in this society at least, men remain potential LOs longer than women, since men are considered attractive longer in life than are women.[18] Whether men are subject to experiencing limerence for a longer period than women is open to question. Limerence requires both hope and uncertainty. Does this mean that there are broad classifications of people for whom limerence is not likely, because either the probability of reciprocation is very low (in which case hope is insufficient) or very high (in which case uncertainty is insufficient)? This is not to say that limerence cannot occur at any age. It clearly can. It is merely more likely to occur at some ages than at others.

One informant described abrupt termination of a limerent reaction as the result of feelings of diminished hope owing to changes in her appearance. Lucille's limerence for Harold had weathered marriage, divorce, and remarriage, but it ended when she felt changes in her appearance had eliminated all hope. As she told it:

"Up to that point I had always kept my weight down. It took work, however, and after a while I simply got tired of it. Maybe worrying about where Harold was during those many evenings in which he was not with me had something to do with it. Maybe it was just boredom. Although he had said he loved me, I think he remarried me mainly because of our twin sons, and because he felt it was the only economical thing to do. It was cheaper to maintain one home. That way he had more money to play around with. Maybe also he didn't want any of his playmates getting serious.

"Anyway, I gained about 40 pounds and I passed my 40th birthday. It was around that time that one day I took a hard look in the mirror and got a pretty unpleasant message. That afternoon I happened to see Harold with one of his 'recreational companions.' The comparison between what she looked like and what I looked like had a great effect: I was suddenly no longer in love with Harold. The idea of his feeling that way about me was so ridiculous (especially knowing how important appearance is to him) that it did something to me, something that turned out to be permanent.

"We're still married, and he still fools around, and I still don't like it, but the old anguish is over. Just like that. I became what you call nonlimerent and I've been that way ever since, over five years now. If anything, it has improved our relationship."

As their mirrors reflect little basis for hope of reciprocation, do people arrive at a stage of life in which limerence no longer occurs? Are the homely and aged generally spared unrequitable passions? The development of limerence seems to require some sign that reciprocation is at least a theoretical possibility. Lucille's confrontation with the attractiveness of a rival reduced hope of Harold's reciprocation to the point that her own limerence ended. (Harold on the other hand, may also have ceased to be limerent because female companionship was easy for him to obtain.)

There is evidence that persons in the state of limerence are inclined to exaggerate or intensify their "sex roles." Mildred pursued a successful business career while also raising her three children. She was, in her words, "a fully independent woman, and proud of it."

"When I met Gregory that changed. Instead of flaunting my knowledge and business sense, and instead of talking about my work, we always seemed to get on to topics that he knew something about, like how to wire a lamp or build a fire. Actually, in both those cases, it was not that I was ignorant. I suppressed my knowledge and played the role of learning from him.

"Around that time I also acquired a taste for those stupidly frilly blouses that always get in your way when you're trying to cook or write or do anything except look at him wiltingly. I really fell right into femininity when I fell in love with Gregory. In department stores I was drawn to cosmetics, jewelry, hats, and other trivia that had the single advantage of fitting in with my fantasy of how attracted to me Gregory would be under the influence of, for example, a rare and exotic (and expensive) perfume. I 'touched up' my hair, I went for more fluttery attire, I became functionally feebleminded about certain things toward which I had formerly shown good sense, if not expertise, and it was all a matter of trying to increase my attractiveness in what I believed were Gregory's eyes.

"In fact, he probably thought I was acting like a damned fool! After 'it' was over, I realized that I really didn't know him very well. So why did I assume that he would be more interested in me if I behaved that way? I can't really say why being in love makes me feel inclined to assume a more passive and feminine attitude, but it wasn't just Gregory. It's happened with others, too."

But strong feelings can be wrong. Consider superstition. Your fear inclines you to acts unlikely to help avoid the thing you fear, but undertaken anyway, just in case. You cross your fingers. It might be that LO could accept less femininity or masculinity in the limerent person, but the limerent person is unwilling to risk failure.[19]

It would be revealing to analyze limerence fantasies. Do they differ consistently according to the gender of the fantasizer? How large a role does physical attractiveness play? Perhaps an even larger role than can be deduced from my interviews, since that was not a topic of particular focus.

Some data came my way, incidentally, which bears on the issue of sex differences. Following the publication of my book on psychotherapy, a number of patients and former patients came forward to tell their stories to me. Mostly these were women. Of 40 persons who contacted me, only three were men, a finding unsurprising in view of the far greater number of women in therapy than men. Perhaps, I then thought, women are less inhibited than men about revealing personal information.

Not so. I received a number of letters and telephone calls following publication of a newspaper and a magazine article in which were summarized some of the main aspects of limerence theory.[20] Here the situation was reversed. For every woman who contacted me concerning limerence, I received messages from two or three men.

I don't feel inclined to conclude from this that men are more often limerent. Most of my interviewees were women and The Group reactions are in keeping with the more traditional view of women being more involved with love. Can they be totally wrong? Perhaps so many men got in touch with me because men do not usually have anyone with whom they can speak about their limerence. If inclination toward limerence is equal, and also equally embarrassing, men may be more often forced into a "closet" situation. It was still later that I considered the possibility that middle-aged men—and most of the callers were mature professionals—might be especially susceptible. Several of them were psychotherapists. With one therapist to many clients, the limerence problems in psychotherapy might be greater in total numbers for women but still exist for therapists, most of whom are men. (Imagine a male therapist limerent about one client, but a half-dozen women clients limerent about him.)

It is difficult to determine whether a difference between the sexes that is not universal is culturally induced or inherited. Although "peculiar," unusual, or "perverted" sexual behaviors are more frequently found in males than in females, whether they are based in "biological" or "learned" differences is not known.[21] The double standard by which sexual activities are judged has been relaxed in certain ways, but is still with us. Sexual molestation of children by adults, for example, is almost entirely a matter of molestation by males of children of both sexes, yet cases of a mature woman "romantically" and sexually attracted to a youth, rare as they are, have more than once been the occasion of glaring tabloid headlines, a major scandal, and the ruin of a woman's reputation. For example, an English schoolteacher, aged 26, was accused of "sexual involvement" with a pupil in her school. The story was front page news for weeks. Although the case was eventually dismissed, the judge refused to award her legal costs because she had "brought the case upon herself."[22] More tragic was the story of Gabrielle Russier, who fell passionately in love with one of her 16-year-old students. When his parents, both university professors and colleagues of hers, could not separate the lovers, they charged her with "corruption of a minor." She lost her job and was jailed for six months awaiting a trial, which was finally held in a closed court. A half hour after she was given a suspended sentence, the government pressed for a retrial and a harsh penalty. One month later she committed suicide.[23] Females are punished for acts which are overlooked, or even condoned, when engaged in by males, in this case a sexual liaison with a younger person.

It is often assumed that men have more "sex drive" than women.[24] Men report more overt activity to researchers, and appear to be more readily aroused by a wider range of persons and situations. One psychological theory holds that physiological arousal can intensify any emotion, especially when the arousal is of indeterminate origin.[25] If men are more accustomed to sexual arousal they might be better able to distinguish feelings of limerence from feelings of sexual attraction, while women might be more inclined to interpret their sexual arousal as an aspect of falling in love, *i.e.*, limerence.

Men

Limerence + Sexual Arousal = Limerence + Sexual Arousal

Women

Limerence + Sexual Arousal = Total Feeling

Only 30 percent of the women and 20 percent of the men in The Group felt that "men need sex more than women do," which means that 70 percent of the women and 80 percent of the men did *not* agree that men need sex more. I wonder what a similar group 50 years ago, or 100 years ago, would have answered had they been presented with the questionnaire.

Table III gives a set of statements chosen more often by men of The Group than by women.

These statements indicate a male assertion of independence from love as well as confirming a stronger inclination to separate love from sex. Women's responses, however, especially to the first statement, were also fairly strong. Surprisingly, to the question of who can get along "better" without "a lover," 22 percent of the women and 19 percent of the men felt that men need a lover more. Only 14 percent of the women and 9 percent of the men thought men needed a lover less than women. The consen-

TABLE III

Statement	Percentage of The Group who accepted the statements		
	Female	*Male*	*Both Sexes*
I have been sexually attracted without feeling the slightest trace of love.	53	79	62
It was ego deflating to want someone so much when they were not in the least interested in me. Naturally, I didn't talk about it.	36	48	38
There are more important things in life than love.	28	37	31
When _____ told me the affair was over, I felt angry and humiliated.	16	22	18
Sometimes I tell my friends about my sexual experiences, but not about being in love.	8	30	16
If _____ lost interest in me, it wouldn't bother me, even though I am in love. I'd simply find someone else.	8	19	12
I have enjoyed sex more when it was with someone I was not in love with.	4	11	6

sus, therefore, was *not* consistent with the opinion so frequently expressed (as in the quotations at the beginning of this chapter) that women are in greater need of love. The explanation might be that to The Group "lover" implies sex not love. In that case, this finding is consistent with the idea of supposedly greater sexual needs of the male.

It is clear from responses to many statements on the questionnaire that the women of The Group tied sex with love more
closely than did the men. Sixty-one percent of the women in
comparison with 35 percent of the men (still a substantial proportion) claimed they had at some time "been in love without
feeling any need for sex." Of course, it is likely that various
people in The Group meant different feelings by the term, "in
love," in that questionnaire item. Or in the next, in which more
women (half) than men (20 percent) stated that they "think
about sex a lot more when ... in love." Sex differences were
pronounced for the statement, "I can only enjoy sex if I am in
love with my partner." Two-thirds of the women in the sample,
but only 20 percent of the men, agreed with that one.

Were the members of The Group who answered the questionnaire merely passing on the culturally given images of what
people are like, and even what they themselves were like? Are
such differences really the result of socialization, and do such
differences in what people say on a questionnaire reflect real
differences in feelings and actions? More important, if differences
are so readily attainable on questionnaires, why did the interview
data suggest so much similarity between the sexes in the experience of limerence? Why are some other investigators also report-
ing evidence that there is no great difference between the sexes
in romantic love? [26]

Putting it simply, if limerence is the same for both sexes, but
both cultural expectation and sexuality differ in some ways, limerence seems a formidable reaction indeed! Although clearly
related both to sex and to culture, limerence seems to enjoy a
certain immunity to influence. People have been trying to control limerence without much success for as far back as records go,
but it is remarkably tenacious, involuntary, and resistant to external influence once it takes hold. We have repeatedly seen evidence of, for example, its imperviousness in the face of logical
reasons for choosing someone more suitable than LO as a mate.

Love magic appears in various cultures and in the literature of
our civilization. But the love potion's ingredients remain secret.
Limerence is unaffected by the intensity of our desire to call it
into or out of existence at our wills. By evidence from history and

from art, as well as from the stories of my informants, limerence can be the ruling passion of a life. It can override self-welfare, and its power over life seems neither diminished with age nor less for one sex than for the other.

HOMOLIMERENCE

Why some people feel limerence and/or sexual attraction for members of their own sex and why others do not are mysteries thus far unsolved by scientific analysis. But it would appear that at least some homosexuals, maybe the majority, might more accurately be called "homolimerents," tending to find an LO among one's own sex since it appears to be limerence rather than mere sexuality that is primarily involved. All of the seven male homosexuals interviewed and all but two of the 23 lesbians had engaged in heterosexual activities. In most cases, same-sex physical interactions were preferred, but as Sorena said:

"Sex with a man is tolerable. Sometimes more than tolerable. Sometimes I'm even in the mood for it. If I'm repelled, it's more by their attitudes toward women than by their physical maleness. But no relationship with a man could begin to hold the positive value in my life that is possible with a woman. As far as I can see, that's what it means to be lesbian. I don't know why it's that way; it just is."

There were variations in the pattern for both sexes. Some did claim to be repelled physically by the opposite sex. Others were neutral. Some were homosexual by unqualified self-description, but had not experienced limerence. Of all "love's mysteries," I find this one of the most intriguing: We know that LOs tend to be selected in relation to overall characteristics of ethnic, racial, and socioeconomic similarity. Age and physical attractiveness are other important variables. All seem to be at least partly affected by cultural influences, including current fashion. LO's gender seems most immutable, *the* primary criterion. So far as I can see through whatever readings have come to my attention, no one has even a moderately interesting theory on what makes a person "heterosexual" or "homosexual," or even "bisexual." Everyone I questioned about it seemed to give the same basic answer: I don't know why I can only become limerent about women (or men). *It's simply the way I am.*

Leon was typical of the males:

"I had always been suspicious: that something about me was different. I just wasn't having the feelings you were supposed to have about girls. Then in an all-male prep school, I fell in love with one of my classmates and went through the tortures of the damned between guilt, humiliation (in my own mind), and desire. I held it in for almost two years. Then one day he and I were camping out, sleeping side by side in our sleeping bags. I could scarcely contain myself, I wanted so badly to tell him of my feelings and to embrace him.

"It wasn't totally sexual. I wasn't thinking of sex with him but of mutual love. I wanted to hold him in my arms and tell him how I felt and have him respond with the same degree of affection I was feeling.

"I put my hand out and touched him on the back. He practically leapt up into the air. He whirled around and asked me what I wanted, whether something was wrong. His reaction was so quick, it was almost violent.

"I got the message. I said I must have moved in my sleep, that I was dreaming of making love to a woman. That was that. Now I think he must have suspected something all along, probably from my actions. How can you keep something like that completely hidden? Anyway, our little bit of playacting communicated that he wasn't available and I wasn't going to insist. I was devastated. I hardly ever saw him after that, and in the fall I fell in love with another boy. But it was about six tormented years before I ever made even the slightest advance."

Although fully homosexual so far as he himself was concerned, Leon dated and had sex with a series of young women. He described his feelings:

"I know that they say that gay guys are supposed to hate women, but I never have. I have good friends who are female and I actually like to have sex with women, in some ways more than I do with men. But I have never, and don't think I ever could, fall in love with a woman. I wish I could. I've tried to talk myself into it, but I can't."

Another homosexual male, Charles, had been married and fathered several children when he felt that, as he put it, his life was "a lie," and he had to make a "clean break." He was in his late fifties when he volunteered to be interviewed.

"I loved my wife and children, but it just didn't work. I kept getting involved with men and I mean really involved. A one-night stand, even a regular pattern of sexual liaisons with men could have been tolerated. After all, I work in the city, and it wasn't hard to keep that aspect of my life entirely separate from my family life. The trouble was that I would get emotionally involved.

"I was in love with Gilbert, one of the messenger boys who worked for the company in the building next door. He delivered items to me a few times, then we'd meet sometimes in the park, at first 'accidentally,' later by design. There was nothing that I had not heard about the way women feel about men or men about women that I didn't feel about Gil. I thought about him constantly, bought him little gifts, and even risked writing love notes and verses. I wanted to marry him."

One of the most famous homosexual limerents was Oscar Wilde, whose affair with Lord Alfred Douglas cost him his fortune, his freedom, his career, his reputation, and probably his life.[27] The recent publication of the private life of Tennessee Williams reveals a similar pattern.[28] Although both men engaged in nonlimerent sexual affairs additionally, it was clearly the limerent attractions that involved them in the most overwhelming emotional reactions of their lives. Williams lives in a more tolerant society, but both men appear to have suffered from extreme and total limerent responses to their male LOs. From their reports, it cannot be determined whether their homosexuality produced more intense reactions or whether it contributed to their ability to tell about it. In the main, their autobiographical tales of limerence differ little from those described by limerent writers such as Thomas Mann, whose story *Death in Venice* is a classic of pure and acute limerence, or the author of the story of love and sacrifice that became the film *Dog Day Afternoon*.

Mason was a 25-year-old music student who came to me both as a client and as a research informant, having heard through friends of my interest in love. His tragic tale rivaled the plot of any fictional piece. Like other interviewees who had assumed themselves to be heterosexual and attempted to quiet the disturbing voices within which beckoned them to unacceptable attractions, Mason had had sexual experiences only with female partners until his sophomore year in college, when he was approached by one of his instructors after a late-night social at one of the fraternity houses. Mason had long admired Mr. Daley, but could recall no other type of feeling, either limerent or sexual. He said:

"I thought nothing of it when Mr. Daley offered to drive me home except that I welcomed the opportunity to discuss with him some of the issues that had come up during the evening concerning changes that were planned for the music curriculum. Was I ever innocent! So we started to talk, and although I realized it was late I was so wrapped up in the subject that I assumed he was, too. When we hesitated outside my house it seemed natural enough to suggest we have coffee, although, frankly, I was a little surprised when he accepted. Then when we got upstairs and he saw the bottle of booze on my dresser, he asked for that and I knew something was going on.

"Still, I thought that he might have been upset about something and just needed to talk. When I finally realized that he was making some kind of more than just friendly advance, I was surprised at my own reaction. I wasn't drunk. I had had almost nothing at the party and had hardly begun the drink I had poured. But it was as if my whole life suddenly made sense and I understood the part of me I had always been fighting and that I wouldn't have to fight it anymore. He sat down beside me and said, 'Look, Mason, you've got to know this. I am very attracted to you,' and I fell in love with him in that instant."

After that night they had a warm relationship that continued for seven months and included lovemaking sessions four or five times a week. Then, when the spring semester had about another week to go, he called to say that he was leaving for France and did not plan to return to the college.

"He thought it best, less painful for both of us, if we said good-bye then and there. He hadn't meant to break it to me like this, but his plans had changed suddenly due to the serious illness of one of his children. Children! He had never mentioned his family, much less that they were waiting for him to join them in Paris.

"I don't remember what I said exactly. I asked for his address, but he said it would be easier if we just remembered the good times we had had. He said he would always remember me with 'great love'—I remember that phrase—and that he did not have that kind of feeling for anyone else but that his responsibilities could not be overlooked. I guess I pleaded with him to see me one more time and became angry when he flatly refused. He said he was leaving in a few minutes, that his bags were all packed, and when I insisted that he let me go to the airport with him, he hung up. He said his sister was taking him and it was impossible.

"I flew out of the house without even getting a coat and ran the mile and a half to the highway where I managed to get a ride with a truck driver who took me within a half mile of the airport. There was a flight to Paris leaving in a half hour. I raced to the gate but the passengers had already boarded. His name was not on the list anyway. I spent the next four hours wandering around the terminal checking flights to New York, London, and to his hometown. Several times I thought I saw him but when I got up close enough for a good look found it was someone else. Later I found out from a friend who saw him off that he had left even before I arrived."

Mason spent the next three days wandering around. He walked many miles without proper clothing. He missed his college examinations, and when his family received notices from the school registrar and from his landlord, they hired a detective who located him living in an apartment in a rundown section of the city.

"I guess you could say they rescued me, although at first I didn't see it that way. It wasn't just losing my lover. That was the main thing, but it was also that I had become a low thing in my own mind as well as in society's.

"I guess it was about a year before I was near normal, but of course I wasn't normal, I was gay. It was like a disease I had to hide. It wasn't until I moved to New York that I began to accept myself. I got into a crowd of gay guys who were also serious musicians. Then it happened again. I fell in love with one of them, and when the affair ended, when he ended it, my world collapsed all over again."

An equally sad, but quite different story of homosexuality was told by several women who, like Mason, discovered their "homo-limerence" only after years of trying to fit the heterolimerent pattern. Their situations are represented in the story told by a 35-year-old woman I will call Becky. When I interviewed her, she had become limerent for the first time in her life. LO was a woman, a friend of many years.

"We had always enjoyed each other's company, but we didn't move in the same crowd because our husbands were not friends. But our children attended the same schools, and from time to time we'd meet and sometimes have lunch together or take the kids somewhere.

"Then, in 1972, we found ourselves in the same consciousness-raising group and from there we both became activists in the

Women's Movement. It was after a Woman's Center dance that our relationship took a new turn. Those were days in which women who were lesbians had begun to admit it publicly. In our rap sessions, we found that many of us had had crushes on women teachers, or on schoolmates as adolescents. I had had, and so had Toby.

"We talked about it that evening as we watched some of the younger women dance. Then Toby said, 'Hey, we aren't exactly senile ourselves. Do you want to try?'

"We did, and the best description I can give of it is that it was just like the descriptions of how being in love begins in fiction. The only difference was that we were both women."

Neither Becky nor Toby (whom I was also able to interview) had even been "in love with" their husbands or with any other man, although they were both "happily married," or in relationships of nonlimerent affectional bonding.

"I was happily married. I still have fond feelings for Gary even after all that has happened between us. I realize how hard it must have been for him to take when I announced not only was I leaving, but that I was leaving him for a woman.

"When I first said it, he laughed. Then when he realized that I was serious, he suggested that my 'affair,' as he called it, continue. He even offered to go away one weekend a month so that Toby and I could be together. I think the fact that he didn't offer to let us go away or to take the children off our hands was another aspect of really not believing. But it was true all right. I was in love with Toby, and we were both willing to let our husbands know about it.

"But Toby balked at the idea of a divorce. She's still married today and living with Norman. I was a purist and an idealist so I left. Gary's good nature also left him when he was forced to face the possibility of a real break. I don't mean this as unkindly as it might sound, but I think that a large part of his anger was not so much because he loved me, but because of all the problems the whole thing caused just at a time when his career was at a turning point. He needed a wife who could take care of the things I took care of, and the idea of having to worry about things like whether the children got to the dentist or had winter coats absolutely threw him.

"It was because of money that he decided to keep the children with him. And, frankly, I was leery of moving them into the city and upsetting their lives that way."

Gary remarried and was promoted to a high executive position. In the meantime, Becky lost her job and found herself living from hand to mouth, even sleeping in friends' apartments when she could no longer afford rent. Her visits to her children became less frequent, because she didn't have train fare for them or anyplace to entertain them. Eventually, Becky turned out a best-selling novel based largely on her own experiences for which she received high literary praise from the critics. Unfortunately, some of the other women whose lives were so altered by their discovery of homolimerence in themselves were less fortunate.

The reports of lesbians included poignant descriptions of secret loves as well as open relationships that were marriages in every way but in the eyes and under the laws of society. Other researchers have reported less sexual promiscuity among female than among male homosexuals, and my interviews were consistent with this. For example, Janice and Rhoda had been living together for 12 years when I interviewed them in their Manhattan apartment, a sunny, plant-filled walkup on the West Side in the mid-sixties.

Janice. Well, here it is, our little heavenly escape from the world.
Rhoda. Yes, we call it Shangri-la. I don't know if it will keep us young, but it has certainly made us happy. We both adore plants, as you can see, and are lucky to have an excellent southern exposure.
Janice. Some people have babies; we have plants. It's cheaper and they don't require sitters.
Rhoda. I don't want to give the impression, however, that everything about our existence is as cheerful as our window gardens. We've had our ups and downs over the years. At first, the main problem was society. Later it was jealousy and personal con-

flict—including sexual difficulties. If sex therapy had existed at that time, we'd have gone. Now we're a pair; we fit together like hand and glove. The kinks have been ironed out, and we're mainly involved with our work. Each with her own work, I mean. We were in business together for a time, but that seemed to place too great a strain on the relationship.

Janice. I guess our roughest period was when I had an affair with another woman about three years ago. I was in love, or thought I was, but fortunately she wasn't in love with me. Anyway, I think we are both pretty satisfied with our lives at the moment. Who knows what the future will bring?

Janice and Rhoda were obviously enjoying an affectionate bonding of some duration. In the beginning, they had both been limerent, but by the time of the interview they had settled into a relationship that much resembles a happy marriage.

It should be emphasized that although the Women's Movement may have made homosexuality among some feminists more visible, it did not, judging by the experience of my interviewees, create it. Most of the feminists whom I interviewed were not lesbians, although they tended, as a group, to be less likely to condemn homosexuality in others, women or men, than nonfeminists or antifeminists as a group.

Olga was proud of her love affairs with women. They seemed to her to be more "politically right" as well as more emotionally satisfying. "Sex," she said, "was beautiful because we understood each other's bodies." But close questioning revealed that Olga had never experienced limerence. Her relationships with women were similar to those she had formerly had with men: sexually satisfying, emotionally close, and nonlimerent.

Indeed, a common pattern among feminist activists interviewed was heterolimerence combined with a disinclination to engage in sexual relationships with other women, even though they generally preferred the company of women to that of men. As Wilma described it:

"If I could will it, I'd be a lesbian. I envy them their emotional independence from men. The trouble is that I can't will it. I'm sure I could go to bed with a woman if I got drunk enough, but I have never come close to falling in love with one. You know those homosexual schoolgirl crushes on women that are supposed to be normal? I never even had that sort of experience. Despite my feminist independence, I'm a totally heterosexual woman."

As the interviews progressed, I noticed that I spoke to no one who could be described as "bilimerent," although a significant minority of both sexes reported sexual affairs and attractions for members of both sexes at one time or another. Twenty-eight homosexual persons were interviewed at length. Of the ten questioned after the characteristics of limerence had been specified, seven indicated that they were, or had been limerent, and all of the seven said that their LOs were of the same sex as themselves, i.e., they experienced homolimerence, instead of hetero-limerence. As one put it, "I fall in love with men, not women. Period. That's what makes me gay." My sample of homosexual informants was small, but there seems a definite possibility that it is limerence, not sexual attraction, which tends to be confined to one or the other sex in a given individual.

MISOGYNY

Writer Julius Lester gave a poignant and humorous description of the difficulties besetting him who would "make it as a boy." It was not so easy, he pointed out. One thing that really upset him was the power that the little girl had if he found himself in love with her. "Who was she," he asked, "to create joy by her consent or destruction by her denial? It wasn't fair," he complained.[29]

I am astonished and disconcerted by the blatant misogyny I have so often found in literature, even in recent essays and research reports. Not only is love woman's province, but she is blamed for it mightily. If limerence is a biologically determined human reaction, then it has been with us as long as we have existed as the species we are today. It is therefore of interest to consider the effect, if any, that limerence may have had on courtship, mating, and the status of women throughout the course of human history.

Prior to the present patriarchal civilization, the codified roots of which began to be formulated between 5,000 and 10,000 years ago, peoples of the part of the world in which Iran, Syria, Egypt, Turkey, Greece, and Southern Russia are located today are believed to have worshipped female deities and reckoned descent through the mother, according to ancient religions overthrown by the Hebrews and later by the Christians and Moslems during thousands of years of often violent struggle. Historians are now including the Holy Inquisition and the persecution of "witches" that raged throughout Europe and even into the United States as battles in the war against remnants of the older system. Although the archaeological evidence is subject to varying interpretations, it is beginning to point strongly to a former civilization characterized by matrilineal descent, goddesses, and a higher social status for women.[30]

Merlin Stone's thesis in *When God Was a Woman* is that the forces of patriarchy waged a savage campaign lasting millennia, during which the ancient "heresy" was expunged from all written works.[31] Statues and temples were reduced to rubble, and anyone suspected of practicing the goddess religions was killed. That the task was not an easy one is attested to by the length of the oppression. It began prior to the writing of the earliest books of the Old Testament and continued through the relatively recent centuries, during which hundreds of thousands (millions by recent estimates) of witches, the vast majority women, were executed, usually by being burned at the stake.[32]

Basic to the victory of the patriarchal forces was the accusation that women are subservient to the devil and therefore the cause of defilement in men, a view promulgated in the myth of Eve's original sin in the garden of Eden, Eve being man's original LO.[33] This view is clearly present in the writings of medieval clergyman Andreas Capellanus, even though he was writing four centuries after the synod of A.D. 785 that declared *belief* in witches to be heathen and therefore the burning of witches to be a crime. Then, as the result of the 1484 papal bull of Innocent VIII, witches were not only officially believed in again, but

hunted down and roasted alive. The infamous *Malleus Maleficarum*, a handbook for the hunter of witches, was prepared at
the Pope's request by two clergymen named Heinrich Kramer
and Jakob Sprenger. Although the Pope's edict clearly indicated
that men as well as women were to be suspected, Kramer and
Spranger "found" men to be more often "bewitched" or "enchanted," and women to be the actual perpetrators of the evil of
witchcraft. The Bible is liberally quoted in the *Malleus:*

> Now the wickedness of women is spoken of in Ecclesiastes XXV. . . .
> All wickedness is but little to the wickedness of a woman. . . . What
> else is woman but a foe to friendship, an inescapable punishment, a
> necessary evil, a natural temptation, a desirable calamity, a domestic
> danger, a delectable detriment, an evil nature, painted with fair
> colours! [34]

Not only are women more vulnerable to false beliefs and
generally more gullible and weak, but they are also more
"carnal."

> . . . the sin which arose from woman destroys the soul by depriving it
> of grace, and delivers the body up to the punishment for sin.[35]
> More bitter than death, again, because bodily death is an open and
> terrible enemy, but woman is a wheedling and secret enemy.[36]

And, finally, there is the famous statement: "All witchcraft
comes from carnal lust, which is in woman insatiable."[37] Thus
the *Malleus Maleficarum* is not merely a guide to finding witches
but an explicit statement that woman as man's LO is the cause of
all evil. She bewitches him and thus gains power over his actions.

The way was paved for this kind of idea by even such a writer
on love as Andreas Capellanus. The fact that there still exist a
dozen virtually complete manuscripts of his twelfth century
work, *The Art of Courtly Love,* indicates its popularity. In Books
One and Two, Andreas describes the practices of the famous
Courts of Love in a style that combines etiquette, advice to the
lovelorn, and detailed analyses of ethical problems related to the
behavior of lovers. Book Three is entitled "The Rejection of
Love." Taking an intense anti-female stand, Andreas strongly

urges men "to avoid all deeds of love and to oppose all its mandates." The man in the grip of amorous passion lives "only for himself and his beloved," neglecting others. Andreas recommends that such a man should be dropped by friends and avoided by all.

When Andreas turns to women it is clear that the double standard essential to patrilinearity has not been forgotten. Undesirable as love is for men, it is excusable: "In men an excess of love or of lechery is tolerated on account of the boldness of the sex." In women, however, it is a "damnable offensive." The woman's reputation is rightly tarnished, and she deserves to be held "in utter contempt."

One might assume that Andreas is speaking not of limerence, or of love, but of sexuality. If so, since sexuality has been traditionally condemned in both sexes by Christianity, at least since the time of Paul, the remark can hardly be considered surprising, especially in a member of the clergy.

But Andreas is not talking about sexuality, at least not about "pure" sexuality. He goes on with remarks that are clearly concerned with limerence:

> The man who is in love is bound in a hard kind of slavery and . . . his soul is very much upset by a slight suspicion. . . . He does not dare to do or to think anything that is in the least contrary to what his beloved wants, because a lover is always afraid that his beloved may change her desire for him. . . .

Andreas argues that the male in the throes of love is inclined to the commission of such criminal acts as adultery, incest, wrath, theft, and especially lying.

Consistent with recent interpretations of archaeological evidence as favoring the existence of an ancient, nonpatriarchal, civilization, later disparaged as "heathen," "heretical," and "idolatrous," is Andreas' finding of a religious basis for rejecting "love of woman."

> Idolatry, too, very clearly comes from love, as is shown by the case of Solomon, the wisest of men, who from love of women did not fear to go after strange gods and like a beast make sacrifice to dumb idols.

... from Scripture we know that the Devil is really the author of love and lechery.[38]

If the wisest and most revered of men—Solomon and David the Prophet—succumb, he asks, then what lesser man can be expected to resist?

> The mutual love which you seek in women you cannot find, for no woman ever loved a man or could bind herself to a lover in the mutual bonds of love. For a woman's desire is to get rich through love, but not to give her lover the solaces that please him ... But even though you have given a woman innumerable presents, if she discovers that you are less attentive about giving things than you used to be, or if she learns that you have lost your money, she will treat you as a perfect stranger. ... You cannot find a woman who will love you so much or be so constant to you that if somebody else comes to her and offers her presents she will be faithful to her love. Women have so much avarice that generous gifts break down all the barriers of their virtue.[39]

While to the modern reader, Andreas may, by sheer hyperbole, have spoiled his case and revealed himself either to be jesting or to be an angry and frustrated limerent who tomorrow might fall again into the state of mutual bliss should things work out in his favor, the fact remains that his writings were taken seriously during subsequent centuries. The misogynist rhetoric that was used to destroy ancient non-patriarchal civilizations can be found not only in Andreas' guide to courtly love and in Kramer and Sprenger's blueprint for witch-hunting, but in the words of contemporary writers as well.[40]

Andreas maintained that "no woman is really wise,"[41] but Ortega y Gasset goes even further in On Love. A woman's mind is "irrational" whatever may be her intelligence, he writes, and her psyche is characterized by a "poverty of imagination."[42] Those who assume that such blatant misogyny is a thing of the past may be surprised to learn that this much-praised book on love was written less than a generation ago.

Ortega's highly male supremacist approach leads him to cite some aspects of limerence as characteristic only of males.

A man feels love primarily as a violent desire to be loved, whereas for a woman the primary experience is to feel love itself.[43]

Like Andreas, Ortega is also disgruntled over the "foolishness" women sometimes show in the choice of a mate, and he actually accuses "her" of deliberately overlooking the superior male (Ortega, for example?).

After insisting that his conclusion is reached through a lifetime of careful observation, he speculates:

> Perhaps her role in the mechanics of history is to be a retrogressive force in the face of the turbulent restlessness and desire for change and advance that springs from the masculine soul. ... the general tendency of feminine zeal seems resolved to keep the species within mediocre limits, to avoid selection in the sense of choosing what is superior, to endeavor never to allow the man to become a semi-god or archangel.[44]

With which Ortega is forced to a conclusion chillingly reminiscent of that reached by the patriarchs of the Old Testament: Woman is responsible for the problems of humanity; man is responsible for progress.

What is the reason for such vehemently anti-female attitudes in the love literature? The misogny of Andreas, Ortega and others added another mystery to the many mysteries of limerence. For a time, I wondered whether (as seems so likely in the cases of Ortega and Andreas) the writers were angry over their own personal situation or the situation of men they had observed under the limerent spell and, as people often do, took it out on a whole group, in this case the female sex. I have already noted the dissonance between the image of the fear-ridden, emotionally dependent limerent and the masculine ideal of strength and domination. Although there is reference in male literature to the image of an avaricious vagina, I think it may really be limerence that is feared by these male writers and their supporters.[45]

The effects of limerence are far greater and endure much longer than the flaccidity of the penis after intercourse. We have seen that limerence can be credited with inducing at least a temporary impotence. It is also associated with a variety of physiological and behavioral changes and can, as Andreas warns, lead to extreme suffering and the commission of fearsome acts, including theft, suicide, and murder. Furthermore, being in love is often referred to not as something one *does*, but as the result of an alien force, a shot from Cupid's dart, a love potion, or *an enchantment*. It is easy to imagine the male limerent, enslaved by his passion to an "inferior" being, attributing his condition to her deliberate machinations, to her sorcery.

Although witchcraft is most correctly considered a religion, one of Webster's definitions of "witch" is "a charming or alluring woman." Valency notes that clerical writers in the Middle Ages admonished: "To love a woman for her own sake was to be faithless to the Father."[46] This seems the crux of the matter. For man, a noble, superior being, to love a woman, an inferior being who, like an animal, lacked a soul, and was reputed by clerical authority to be *essentially* sinful and an easy tool for accomplishment of satanic aims, was to have "fallen" against his will into the hands of evil. From Valency's next passage, it is apparent that it is this state of enchantment, not sex, that is feared. He reminds the reader of the dictum of Thomas Aquinas:

> Paradise would include in its joys an endless renewal of the carnal relation, rationally motivated, intensely enjoyable, but passionless— that is to say, carnal pleasure without love.[47]

The reaction of the church to limerence was so extreme that for a time it was considered *adulterous* to love one's spouse with "excessive" passion.[48]

It seems that limerence may have been a persistent thorn in the movement to control women's reproductive capacities. In the eyes of misogynist males, woman the enchantress was blamed for but continued to cast the limerent spell.

7

Limerence and Biology

... love, is nothing but a blind instinct ... an appetite which directs us toward one object rather than another without our being able to account for our taste.

—Ninon de L'Enclos (Seventeenth Century) [1]

Love is like a fever that comes and goes quite independently of the will.

—Stendhal [2]

The disease that is love brings into conflict our conscious intelligence and our basic will.

—André Maurois [3]

Another aspect of the pattern is that one falls in love not by design and conscious choice, but according to some accident of fate over which the victim has no control.

—Sidney M. Greenfield (1965) [4]

241

The idea that human beings are unique among creatures is so fully accepted that most of us, and throughout most of our history, have spoken of either people or animals, not people and other animals. The absence of "missing links," either in the anthropological record or in existence at present, is increasingly explained as resulting from a human tendency to destroy closely related species. With a logic and persistence similar to that which finds human beings special and superior, we have also tended to view ourselves as free of such constraints as are imposed on animals through genetic influence on behavior. In contrast with the beast moved by "blind instinct," human beings are rational and free, acting through our individual inclinations, not because of a wired-in animal necessity uninfluenceable by experience.

But if it were experience alone that makes us what we are— experience and reason—then even the extended time available for human development after birth seems insufficient to produce the effect of the complex emotional and behavioral repertoires shared by humans whatever their culture.

Granting that we do not operate through full-blown instincts in the old-fashioned sense of a complex pattern fully prewired, it is still hard to believe that we do not at least have built-in reactions in our basic natures that make the learning of significant strategies for biological survival (evolutionary development) easier than if culture operated on the proverbial blank slate. Furthermore, if any of our behaviors are under direct influence of the genes, surely those related to reproduction are most likely candidates. Consider, for example, the unthinking, involuntary components in our "purely" sexual behavior and reactions. They are sometimes stronger than we are!

GENETIC THEORIES

Similarity of experience among diverse persons as well as involuntariness suggests that limerence is well rooted—whatever our cultures and lifestyles—in the very nature of our humanness. Consider what possible advantage limerence might bestow on the human who houses its gene.

In many species, mates form attachments that aid survival of resulting offspring. Some mechanism is needed to guide individuals toward potential partners who are suitable. Inclinations must fit biological necessities. In other words, ancestors with the more effective inclinations reproduced themselves and also avoided inbreeding (mating with very close relatives), by overlooking those nearest and dearest both through reason and learned preference. As a response to the immediately invisible but large and transcending inevitabilities that control who gets to live on and who perishes, limerence answers nature's imperative. Cupid's arrow bends us to a stronger will.

I have not forgotten that the onset of limerence has a voluntary feel about it. We go readily and willfully toward its promises of joy. It is only later that images of LO intrude unbidden and the mind suddenly cannot be set elsewhere the way a wayward volume might be returned to the bookshelf. Then the long hours of sustained and lovesick reverie can only be relieved by imagining some moment of consummation with LO. Surely even these thoughts emanate from a foolish will, but nevertheless a will. Except that then there comes the time when you have had enough and want to finish it. Rational bases for hopefulness have been exhausted. The intrusions and literal aches of unfulfilled desire and precious wasted moments of life force the recognition that control may not be total. You even wonder about the past when control seemed possible, if not assured. Uncertainty increases. You wonder if you had the control you thought you had and whether you ever will again.

As we have seen, most writers on love talk of madness, and a part of the madness is the victim's lack of control. Not all call it illogical or abnormal, it must be admitted, but even so strong an advocate as Stendhal spoke of it as a disease. Recovered former limerents tend to agree. Those whose limerence was replaced by affectional bonding *with the same partner* might say, "We were very much in love when we were married; today we love each other very much."

When I began my investigations, the multitudinous contradictions in what was said about love suggested that it was capable of appearing in numerous guises depending on time, circumstance, and persons.[5] What I found instead is that the condition follows a common course and produces common symptoms. Its ubiquitous sameness across diverse situations was not something I initially perceived. Finally I could no longer deny the data, and was attracted to ideas that had begun to emerge from certain of the biological sciences, especially from the study of hereditary mechanisms and genetic theories, and from new disciplines attempting to cross a traditional barrier between the study of human experience and behavior (psychology) and biology. These new disciplines have been variously called "psychobiology," "sociobiology," or "biosocial approaches." [6] Only recently have scientists begun to consider the possibility that over the course of biological history, certain social behavioral tendencies have evolved along with anatomy and physiological structures and systems. According to David P. Barash of the University of Washington, this view has produced what amounts to a "conceptual revolution" in which evolutionary theory will greatly influence the study of human behavior.[7]

In fact, the relationship between inborn tendencies and environmental (physical and social) influences is complex. Even among lower animals, learning may be involved in the development of basically instinctive reactions.[8] Very few complex behavioral reactions are fully programmed in the nervous system.[9] The mere existence of a reaction does not imply that it is inborn. On the other hand, evidence suggests a clear genetic base for certain human traits. For example, in a recent survey of sculpture and paintings from various parts of the world and different historical eras, it was found that roughly 93 percent were rendered with the right hand, a proportion maintained regardless of historical era or culture, supplying strong evidence that handedness is not learned but built in.[10]

At present, study of a possible biological base for limerence would be closely related to a growing scientific field called "ethology," a branch of biology traditionally concerned with the behavior of animals in natural settings from an evolutionary perspective, and increasingly applied to human beings.[11] First ethological attempts at theorizing about humans concern aspects of the reproductive process.[12] Courtship, mating, the nature and duration of the pair bonds (if any) that exist between partners, sexual behavior, child rearing—these have tended to be the focus of the many animal studies that are being looked at in light of sociobiological conceptions. Any behavioral pattern observed, whether it be salmon migration, the retrieval of pups that stray from the maternal rat's nest, courtship displays by certain birds, or limerence in humans, can be considered in the light of how the specific behavior was adaptive; in other words, how did the existence of this pattern increase—or at least not decrease—the chance that the genes controlling it survived in subsequent generations?

Evolution is *not* an ever continuing drive toward perfection, but an often bungling and inefficient (as well as cruel) series of essentially random accidents. The fundamental principle is disarmingly simple. The inherited you (or genotype) is the product of a "selection" of traits running in a continuous line back from your parents to theirs and on through all the organisms that were your progenitors to the primordial substance in which the spark of life first began on this isolated planet. Step by minute step across the eons of incredible duration, life proliferated and changed through the single essential principle of selection, whereby some hereditary substances endured and others were lost. The "best" was not necessarily the best by any standard except the happenstance of survival.[13]

The issue here is the possible usefulness of evolutionary concepts to the understanding of limerence. If a behavior or a state is genetically programmed, it is one which enhanced the "fitness" of organisms carrying its controlling gene or genes. Evolutionary theorizing wonders why. What is behind the irrationality that seizes otherwise reasonable human beings, forcing them to set aside other goals and strivings and to focus on a single other individual, who may be of little interest prior to limerence and also of little interest afterward?

In sampling evolutionary thinking, let us consider another type of experience, motion sickness. Psychologist Michel Treisman of the University of Oxford noted that vomiting induced by motion had been viewed as an evolutionary anomaly. Evolutionary theorists usually begin by speculating about hidden advantages, perhaps from a former time, with vestigial carry-over. Yet those species that experience motion sickness (some birds, horses, monkeys, and even certain fish) and those that do not (rabbits, guinea pigs) present a confusing array of possibilities. In what way is a monkey like a codfish but not like a rabbit?

Treisman reasoned that the phenomenon of malaise and vomiting in response to some forms of motion is unlikely to be the result of sheer accident and is in fact so disruptive—sometimes leading to death, as in the case of those people who are unable to hold out on a life raft until help arrives—that one would have expected natural selection to have eliminated it unless there existed positive reason for its persistence. Treisman reasons that the syndrome of malaise and vomiting is inappropriate in the case of motion but highly adaptive when it functions to eliminate ingested poisons. It turns out that certain types of motion create triggering conditions similar to those produced by the ingestion of toxins. Corroborating evidence that it is this fact which is responsible for the existence of an otherwise inexplicable phenomenon is supplied by the finding that motion sickness does not occur in infancy, when food is likely to be free of toxins and also when being carried about is frequent, or in species which subsist on highly specialized diets. Although the malaise that accompanies vomiting does not assist the process of toxin elimination, it serves to *teach* the organism to stay away from such substances in the future.

Thus vomiting and the malaise are part of an early defense and warning system inappropriate in the case of motion, but lifesaving in the case of toxin ingestion. Treisman's evolutionary hypothesis is that motion sickness is an accidental by-product of the organism's response to certain head and eye movements that occur in the case of food poisoning but unfortunately also in the case of certain types of motion.[14] Thus evolutionary thinking assists the scientific process of theorizing, and it may become far more complex than simply conjecturing about the "survival value" of the phenomenon observed.

The force behind the way a particular trait functions to permit its own survival through a continual supply of individuals who "carry" it is known as the ultimate cause of the adaptive process. The specific way the trait functions is known as the "mechanism" or proximate cause. For what ultimate cause is the state of limerence a mechanism or proximate cause? Why did limerence evolve and persist, that is, why were people who became limerent successful in passing their genes on to succeeding generations?

To explain why limerence occurs we might consider the behavior it induces. Some limerence-inspired actions, as we have already noted, are generally judged socially undesirable, even socially disruptive. It is often noted that limerence causes couples to remove themselves from the presence of other persons. It deflects interest from affairs of business, state, even family, and turns them instead toward LO. Limerence intrudes. In the midst of battle, the soldier's despair over the morning's letter of rejection from his LO back home is not forgotten. A king gives up his crown. An artist lets her career languish while she spends a year overseas accompanying him on a new assignment. But such visible disadvantages should not constitute the sole basis of judgment.

The most consistent result of limerence is *mating,* not merely sexual interaction but commitment, the establishment of a shared domicile, a cozy nest built for the enjoyment of ecstasy, for reproduction, and, usually, for the rearing of children.[15] Fear of rejection, an integral aspect of limerence, may have some adaptive value of its own. In other species, especially in birds, courtship tends to be something of a drawn-out process. In many species, it involves behavior that bears resemblence to the flirtations and game playing of limerents. Ethologists have guessed that the long period of courtship ensures a better ability of the individuals to be sure they have found a satisfactory partner. What we experience as fear of rejection may, in other words, be part of the process that ensures (or at least tends toward) making the process drag out a bit. The fear is the proximate cause. Since limerence goads one toward action, fantasy based in reality (as limerently perceived, but reality nevertheless) can be conceived as intricate strategy planning.

Limerence frees the young from too strong an attachment to the parents. It may not ensure in human beings the kind of permanent monogamy sometimes found in other species, but its average duration of about two years allows a female to become pregnant, bear a child, and begin the new family. The much longer duration of limerence-inspired relationships tends to keep both parents around and cooperating with each other in protecting and caring for the young, at least for a time.[16]

Not that limerence is the only mechanism in the human system to help the child on its way in life. There is for example an inborn response to characteristics of infants perceived as "cute," characteristics such as large eyes low in a head somewhat out of proportion, at least out of adult proportion to the rest of the body, a set of characteristics shared by most mammalian young.[17] Because human beings are not the only animals to respond favorably—and protectively—to these features, some species have actually capitalized on the reaction. Such responses to infants occur in men as well as in women. Even domestic animals such as dogs sometimes treat babies and young children with solicitude.

Mammologist Devra G. Kleiman of the National Zoological Park in Washington, D.C., has observed that the bush dog, like the human being, may develop emotional bonds which serve as a substitute for aggression and prevent adultery.[18] She further believes that while human beings may not have begun as monogamous creatures, monogamy was essential to the growth of human intellectual power, since mental development required a longer period of childhood dependency, dependency extending beyond the time of weaning and requiring assistance from the father or other adults.

Many animals also form pair bonds, and in some species partners remain monogamous for life. Others are monogamous for only a season. The type of pair bond formed, if any, is related to the species' overall reproductive pattern (or "strategy"). In some, by the time the young emerge from egg or pupa, the parents have long since departed, and the generations never even meet except perhaps by remote chance. The new generation fends for itself from the outset. But the range is wide. Wolfgang Wickler, professor of zoology at Munich University and ethologist, describes the behavior of the native European bird, the *Panurus biamicus* (the bearded tit):

The partners spend their whole lives in very close permanent monogamy and can only be separated by force. . . . Two or three days after the male has concentrated his attention on a particular female and she has tolerated it willingly, the matter is decided, and the two sleep closely clumped together at night and not with [their] brothers and sisters as before. During cleaning and drinking, foraging, bathing, and sleeping, the one will hardly leave the side of the other, and they continually preen each other's ruffled feathers. If one flies a grass blade farther away, the other will land beside it a moment later. If one loses sight of the other, it will call loudly until they have found each other again. About two months later the call-bond is enough . . . so that they can tolerate a separation of a few meters. But the marital partners sleep close together throughout their life. If one dies, the other will fly around excitedly, searching and constantly calling and becoming extremely agitated the moment it hears the call of another bearded tit or a sudden rustling in the bulrushes, as though hoping that at last its partner was about to land beside it.[19]

The duration of a typical limerence in humans is comparatively shorter than the lifelong attachment of these little birds. On the other hand who can say that what the bearded tit feels for its mate is not basically the same as what the human limerent feels for LO. The outward actions look very similar, and if limerence evolved because the monogamy it induces helps set the next generation on its course, it may have begun even before human biological development was quite finished.

IMPRINTING

Originally, the term "imprinting" referred to a kind of fast "exposure" learning postulated to explain the finding that young birds would thereafter follow in the wake of whatever it was they happened to see at a certain critical period during early development. Under natural conditions, that stimulus would be the mother bird; in the laboratory, chicks and ducklings have picked up and taken after red rubber balls, experimenters, toy trains, or whatever it is that has been substituted for the mother during the critical moment of life. This phenomenon is a good example of built-in potential for adapting to a particular environment. If something happened to the mother, the animal would come to "love" the father, foster mother, or whoever happened to be around at the time. (Even a predator, I presume, but that would be a shortlived love affair.)

The vision of little birds hopping along in the wake of an experimenter (ethologist Konrad Lorenz in a famous photograph) excited the imagination of many behavioral scientists, some of whom attempted—with varying degrees of success—to detect the phenomenon in other species and at other points in the life span. Controversy broke out in the scientific journals concerning appropriate use of the term when some seemed ready to apply the label wherever the faintest degree of resemblance appeared.[20] One investigator reported prenatal imprinting of the human infant to the mother's heartbeat which he felt might predispose the child to certain musical tempos in later life, but others contended that imprinting, when it occurred, was limited to visual, not auditory stimuli.[21] (At least one attempt to repeat the heartbeat research was unsuccessful.)

Inevitably, someone would wonder whether falling in love could be classified as imprinting. Utilizing findings in genetics, embryology, endocrinology, neuroendocrinology, psychology, and anthropology in an analysis of gender identity focusing on the interactions of heredity and environment, John Money and Anke A. Ehrhardt remark on romantic love (which by their definition includes prepossession and emotional dependency on the actions of the loved person) in a manner generally consistent with limerent theory. Not only do they speak of imprinting, but they do not, for example, find falling in love to differ particularly for the two sexes, and they assume that it is both involuntary and largely genetically determined. Although it may precede or follow the onset of hormonal puberty, Money and Ehrhardt clearly assume a biological basis for falling in love.[22]

There seem to be some obvious similarities between what researchers call imprinting and certain aspects of the limerent experience. When you become limerent about a particular person, there comes a point in the process at which the emotional gates close and you do not shift your feelings to another LO until your reaction to the first has subsided considerably. In the retrospective account of one interviewee, "I know that I would have fallen in love with any fairly decent-looking, unmarried man who showed interest in me. I was so ready, all I'd need was a look." Crystallization fashions an image of "perfections" from LO's actual attractive features, the process, as described earlier, being one of emphasis rather than complete invention. In the laboratory, it was found that prolonged exposure to the imprinting object or person was unnecessary. In fact, the attachment could be undermined by too much familiarity.[23]

An impressive case for a kind of negative imprinting and for the role of involuntary and unconscious (genetically programmed?) factors in limerence is provided by the findings reported by Yonina Talmon in an article on mate selection in Israeli kibbutzim published in 1973 in the *American Sociological Review*. Kibbutzim children reared together in the same infants houses during their first five years did not in later life, "regard each other as erotically desirable."[24] Despite parental preferences to the contrary, data on 2,769 marriages that took place in second-generation offspring of kibbutzim dwellers indicate that not one occurred between persons reared together uninterruptedly during the first five years. In other words, intimacy during early childhood seemed to have left an "imprint" that prevented limerence. This finding appears consistent with the idea that limerence is a genetically transmitted individual reaction rather than the result of a culture "saturated" with romantic love in its stories and songs.

The function of anti-incest imprinting is, of course, obvious; too close relatives tend to have inferior offspring when they mate. I think it is possible that the imprint functions in limerence more forcibly than in sexual attraction, at least at the human level. Recent observations of higher primates revealed disinclination toward mating on the part of mothers and male offspring. In one group, a female had been observed to copulate with every male except her two adult sons. It is also interesting to wonder whether the antipathy toward this form of incest operates mainly in the mother or in the sons. Among humans, and possibly among other primates, sexual activities between fathers and daughters is probably far more common than generally realized. For the most part, it appears, the man may experience jealousy of the daughter's other potential partners but little limerence. Indeed, a man unfortunate enough to develop limerence for his own daughter might be disinclined to try to seduce her or force her to submit to him sexually, although I must admit that here the ice is very thin indeed. My sample did not include any men who spoke of either sex or limerence in relation to minors, or adults of either sex who spoke of childhood limerence for a parent.[25]

Without limerence as a guide to mate selection, inbreeding might lead to genetic weakness, as has been suggested to have occurred among European royalty, which mated for centuries according to considerations of ownership of property and the development of royal lineages. Even if individuals themselves selected a partner rationally by true worth, there might still be insufficient mixing. The relative arbitrariness of limerent fixation promotes matings among persons outside the limerent's immediate group, who may have no reason to be acquainted. Cultures have differed in their reactions to limerence, in their approval and/or disapproval, as well as in relation to who is and is not an acceptable marriage partner or to whether the selection is made by the individuals or by their elders. The kibbutzim finding does not rule out cultural influence over some aspects of the limerent reaction, but it clearly supports the notion that limerence is at least partly governed by forces outside the influence of social, as well as conscious control.

PHYSICAL ATTRACTIVENESS

When in love you get very concerned about your lover's image of you. Thus you alter your posture and try, as you talk, to hide with your hands or clothing, your unattractive chin or nose, or other blemish. You might also, if especially unsure that your appearance is pleasing, make nervous gestures to distract the viewer from the ugly sight.
—From an interview

The role of physical attractiveness is one of the few aspects of romantic attachments and human courting behavior that have been researched with some thoroughness by psychologists and sociologists. In study after study, the result was the same: the better-looking people had the advantage. Looks count, and they count in nonsexually related as well as sexually related attractions. Although we claim that you can't tell a book by its cover and beauty is only skin deep, we fall for beauty. Psychologist Vernon Grant holds that "esthetic qualities" are all important to the arousal of the "amorous emotion."[26] Furthermore, the feeling that appearance is of importance reflects itself in limerent persons' intense concern about their own attractiveness. Hair dyes, makeup, attire, diet, and exercise regimens are regularly featured in popular magazines because they make the user feel more able to stimulate the limerent reaction in LO. No wonder so much print space is devoted to such topics. To the limerent at the height of the reaction, no aspect of living is as important as is hope of achieving the persistently envisioned goal of reciprocation. Surely it is no accident that the time of life during which, by group consensus, we are most attractive—post adolescence and early adulthood—is also the time at which most reproductive matings and marriages are initiated. But why biologically does physical appearance assume so potent a role in the development of the limerent reaction?

One possible answer is that physical attractiveness, and youth, in particular, may function as a rough indication of good health and other attributes that relate to breeding capability and thus genetic fitness. Perhaps this explains why youth and early adulthood are times in which limerence is most probable.

There are other issues as well. Sex differences in the importance of physical attractiveness to human beings is well documented. Is the greater reliance on appearance by males biologically rooted, or is it mainly a result of cultural pressures? Furthermore, given that physical attractiveness plays a role in mate selection, have people, and particularly women, become more "beautiful" over the course of evolutionary development? With current emphasis on the role of culture and/or society in the formation of human values, attitudes, and behavioral patterns, many people would point to the fact that there are fashions in what is considered beautiful, just as there are fashions in clothing styles. If beauty is, as many would contend, culturally decreed rather than inborn, then what is there to stop a culture from choosing, for example, extreme obesity as beautiful, despite the fact that obesity predicts a less healthy and well-functioning organism, one more subject to disease, disability, and early death, and not at all the best prospect for producing fit offspring?

And isn't it wasteful for standards of physical attractiveness to be universal within a society? Isn't one of the biggest problems of living that of trying to meet standards that can only be achieved by a few at the top? Wouldn't transmission of the most favorable genetic material to future generations be better served by a mate selection process that did not depend so much on stereotypes of appearance but rather depended on assessment of a possible mate's aptitudes and capabilities? In other words, wouldn't producing healthy and desirable children be more likely if it did not depend so heavily on admittedly superficial traits?

The answer might be that the large role physical attractiveness plays in mate selection permits traits uncorrelated with beauty to be selected randomly. That is, there may be greater genetic benefit from *not* allowing us to decide by rational means which individuals will mate with each other to produce the next generation. What appears to be a good match by "rational" criteria might in fact amount to a genetically unfit form of inbreeding. Physical attractiveness draws us to a mate who may be unlike ourselves in other respects. The ability of the culture to shift specific standards of beauty seems to occur only within a certain range. That it can occur at all suggests interplay between external influence and genetic makeup, something scientists have found in abundance wherever they have looked for it.[27]

Whatever factors cause an individual to "select" a specific LO, limerence cements the reaction and locks the emotional gates against further intrusion. This exclusivity, which always occurs in limerence, weakens the effect of physical attractiveness, since the most beautiful individual in the world cannot compete with LO once limerence has taken hold. Clearly, persons across a wide range of physical appearances secure mates.

8

Can Limerence
Be Controlled?

There is much in folklore and mythology about magic rituals which have the power to induce the state of limerence; there is considerably less on the issue of ending it. It seems reasonable that limerence should eventually just go away, but this situation is not what my limerent informants described. Limerence for a particular LO does cease under one of the following conditions: *consummation*—in which the bliss of reciprocation is gradually either blended into a lasting love or replaced by less positive feelings; *starvation*—in which even limerent sensitivity to signs of hope is useless against the onslaught of evidence that LO does not return the limerence; *transformation*—in which limerence is transferred to a new LO.

WHAT CAN A LIMERENT SUFFERER DO?

In the absence of effective limerence-inducing techniques for LO, sufferers have tried all variety of other means to free themselves from the "agony" side of the condition. Suicide attempts which "fail" may in fact be helpful to the limerent sufferer. Subsequent events might include a declaration of commitment by LO or distractions provided by the excitement that near brushes with death tend to generate, including hospitalization, physical discomfort, and psychoactive drugs that dull the ache even though they may be powerless against its cause. We have also seen the case in which violent physical activity provided a kind of catharsis. My research suggests strongly that the negative aspects of limerence have not been given the kind of recognition that they deserve.

As much as limerence may be overvalued in drama, it is still despised in those close to us, who may be desperate for our blessings and comfort and also completely unable to ask for them. Unless the subject is studied, we will not have available to us the tactics necessary to deal with some of the tragic situations with which it is associated—"accidents" (much fantasy involves situations in which the limerent is injured and LO is "sorry"), outright suicide (often with note left behind to LO), divorce, homicide, and a host of "minor" side effects which have been documented repeatedly in this book.

To recognize the negative is not necessarily to "take a position" in favor of or against limerence itself. When it is viewed as I have come to view it, as an involuntary reaction to a situation not yet understood, a reaction mediated by physiological mechanisms which are at present unknown, but which surely exist, it becomes as illogical to favor (or not to favor) limerence as it is to favor (or not favor) eating, elimination, or sneezing! Limerence is not the product of human decision: It is something that happens to us. Its intrusive cognitive components, the obsessional quality that may feel voluntary at the moment but that defies control, seem to be the aspect of limerence in which it differs most from other states.

It will be a matter of future research to determine just how much control over limerence can be assumed. Although many interviewees expressed the feeling that they could, and should, have prevented their limerent reaction from getting out of hand, it is not at all clear whether or to what extent it could have been controlled. There are clearly many circumstances in which such control would be beneficial to the afflicted individuals and to those who are sometimes the victims of the afflicted; for example, their children. When limerence for another person results in the breakup or disruption of a marriage, children can hardly be expected to "understand." Sometimes they wonder whether their own actions might have helped to bring about the tragedy. As has already been noted, limerence may cause parents to be distracted and hence to provide children with less than attentive care and concern. As Amanda, a middle-aged professional, admitted,

"Today my children are grown and gone. I'm lucky if they get here on Christmas and call on Mother's Day. I can tell you that I'd give anything to be back in the tiny apartment with my babies. The ironic and really tragic thing is that when my children were little, I was all wrapped up in my love affairs and unable to give them the time and attention I wish I could look back on.

"I remember the summer that Amelia turned three. She was an adorable child. Everyone commented. I was sitting on the porch. I had just received Jeremy's farewell letter and I was miserable over the rejection. For some reason I remember that Amelia tried to get up on my lap. She wanted me to read her a story. The painful part of the memory is that I turned her away and preferred to sit alone thinking of that horrible man than to care for and enjoy my little girl. How I wish I could get those days back again. Jeremy didn't care anything about me or my children. Why did it take me four years to realize it?"

I hope that it may be possible for limerents to cease that self-hatred that sometimes comes from being in the grip of so uncontrollable a force. When The Group looked back on recent "love relationships," 32 percent found they had been "foolish" at the time, and 26 percent said they "hated" themselves for "feeling so helpless and dependent." Forty percent never told members of their family when they were in love. Stendhal also felt shame and feared that the men in his social circle would learn of his intense passion and misery. To write of it directly, he felt, would require a courage that he might have only in old age.[1] And Byron, the ultraromantic symbol, after his limerent reaction to his cousin Mary Chaworth, seems never to have had another. His writings are replete with adverse criticisms of love, with respect to those for whom he was the LO and to himself his own "falling."

The popularity of "advice to the lovelorn" columns in newspapers and magazines attests to the condition of untold millions of persons for whom trying to find a way out of their misery is a top priority. The writers largely confine themselves to recommending a return to good sense, a recognition that hope is gone, a figurative pat on the head intended as a boost to the ego, and an expression of disapproval, more or less mild, that such a state was ever entered into in the first place. Recommendations for coping with lovesickness often include a panoply of possible distractions, such as the traditional hot bath, trip to exotic lands, or some unusual personal indulgence.[2] Mariellen described her attempts to follow similar recommendations after being counseled by a professional psychologist.

"My therapist suggested each of the following: take a hot bath (I did and thought only of him throughout), go on a journey (I saw his face reflected in the glass of the window of the train), attack my work with 'gusto' (it was my inability to work that had sent me to her in the first place), or visit a museum (literally everything reminded me of him, even the Egyptian mummies)."

There seems to be a certain point in the recovery process at which such recommendations can truly be helpful. Ginny did nothing but grieve for weeks after Carl broke their engagement, but as she described it later:

"Even when you think everything is completely meaningless and that you will never in your life have any fun again, feelings do change.

"At first, when friends suggested I go back to work I couldn't imagine it. Lucky for me they didn't give up on me but came back later after I had improved a little and was able to consider other alternatives to the life with Carl I had expected to lead."

Another highly reasonable sounding approach is the elucidation and enumeration of LO's faults, failings, and imperfections. Except that the recounting of LO's unfavorable qualities is notable mainly for its failure to put an end to limerence. As Will learned,

"I decided to make a list in block letters of everything about Elsie that I found unpleasant or annoying. It was a very long list. On the other side of the paper, I listed her good points. It was a short list.

"But it didn't help at all. The good points seemed *so much more important,* and the bad things, well, in Elsie they weren't so bad, or they were things I felt I could help her with."

One recent book recommended pouring one's soul into a personal journal.[3] In *Memories of Egotism,* Stendhal reports suffering great anguish while writing *Love.* I therefore fear that extensive writing about LO and your feelings of limerence might boomerang and result in intensification of the problem. Fred reached the conclusion that writing in his journal might have been better for my research than it was for his welfare. He began to feel that the writing embroiled him hopelessly in the quagmire of limerent revery. Several times he discontinued it only to weaken his resolve and return. At the time, the diary was the only companion to whom he could confide the feelings he most wished to express.

Some of my clients tried standard self-management strategies.[4] For example, Lucy attempted to "convert the emotion into a sensation":

"Every time it started I focused on the place in my body in which I felt the pain, right in the middle of my chest. I concentrated on feeling it as a physical feeling, not a desire. Although it seemed to help at first, I couldn't keep it up. After a few days I went right back to the same old obsessional desires."

Another client, Esther, kept records concerning her chest sensations:

"I tried to notice when the sensation was not there. When I felt a slight ache, I would concentrate until it receded, and sometimes it actually did! At other times, however, all effort was in vain. I think the main effect of the record was to show me how much time I spent thinking of Herb and, later, to provide evidence that I was improving."

Some of my other clients reported greater success with this method, but objective research is required to determine whether the help was lasting or not.

Another strategy was to keep records of the percentage of time spent in limerent fantasy. The idea, as in any self-management program, was to make improvement more visible in order to try to discover what particular situations produce it. Len kept daily records for several months. Although his limerence declined during the period, it cannot, unfortunately, be concluded that record keeping was a cause. Perhaps the best that can be said about record keeping at this point is that it shows some promise with some people in some situations.[5]

Miriams's strategy was based on the idea that if hope could be fully extinguished, limerence would be starved out of existence. She wrote the following note and sent it to her LO:

"Dear Phil,
This is to inform you that I have decided that you are not at all the sort of person I want in my life in any way. I would appreciate it if you would keep your rather distasteful self out of my presence in the future. I am in fact in love with someone else and plan to be married in the near future."

Of course, such a message to LO is exactly the opposite of what a limerent person ordinarily would send. But Miriam had already received considerable evidence that Phil was not interested. In fact, as she said, "One part of me hoped it would shock him into feeling something for me. It didn't, of course. The only result was that he never called again and I slowly got over the whole thing."

Sue, one of my later interviewees, used what might be called a "cognitive" approach. After we discussed the existence of non-limerence, she considered her LO's behavior toward her from that point of view. My description of nonlimerence seemed to fit George exactly. Sue decided to discuss the situation with him. She reported the results:

"When I described the characteristics of limerence he said he couldn't imagine it. The whole thing turned him off so completely that I was really scared of what he'd do if he thought I felt that way. Luckily, I had done my best to appear as free and happy-go-lucky as he. Of course, there's always the chance that he was also trying to hide his crazy feelings, but it didn't fit the way, for example, he really didn't mind it if I was busy, or the time I went out with Bill in what was clearly a vain attempt to get a rise out of him."

Sue concentrated on the vision of George as a nonlimerent until, as she said, "I lost hope. But it wouldn't have worked if he hadn't fit the pattern so perfectly." Understanding the nature of limerence—and nonlimerence—is essential if we are to find methods of helping its sufferers. Although I cannot at this time indicate specific, surefire procedures for dealing with it, cases like Sue's offer some indication that knowing the effects of limerence and the existence of nonlimerent individuals may reduce some instances of vain hope. Perhaps the best cure you can administer to yourself is to remove all contact and all possibility of contact between yourself and your unresponsive LO.

HOW TO RECOGNIZE NONLIMERENCE IN YOUR LO

Hope for better relationships between limerents and those who are not likely to get into that state can also come from the reaction of the limerent person. As long as you believe that everyone is a limerent or readily made into one, it is hard not to interpret a casual glance as a sign of limerent interest. But now that you know there are those (and your LO might be one) who don't and won't, and don't want to fall, but could perhaps bond affectionately, you might lose your hope and with it your limerence, or you might "settle" for affectional bonding.

WHAT TO DO IF YOUR LO BECOMES LIMERENT ABOUT SOMEONE ELSE

Weep. Sympathize. Feel terrible. But recognize that limerence is basically involuntary. Love vows reflect intense feeling and total sincerity, but there is no way that they can be *made* to stick when feelings change. Recognize, too, that once the gates of your LO's mind are closed on someone else—and against you— the hope you need to fuel your own passion must run dry. With this recognition you may end your limerence and reconstruct your life.

Does this mean that you are advised to forgive and forget when your partner is struck by limerent passion for another party? What if LO is your spouse? Is your relationship, and the memories you share, to be forgotten? What about bread and butter responsibilities? What about the children? Recognition of the nature of limerence should not in my view mean that commitments to the relationship, such as co-parenting and financial interdependencies, should not be honored. I hope that knowledge of just what limerence is will in fact help in dealing with breakups by preventing the usual faultfinding and substituting a more realistic approach. Although limerence demands a committed relationship, there can be commitments other than marriage. The effects of the current conditions under which marriages are ended produce great suffering that might well be avoided if limerence is understood for what it is. Even if limerence for a new LO disinclines you to maintain the same relationship you had with your spouse in all ways, understanding of the state as an involuntary reaction (at least after a certain point) should lead to (1) prevention of the development of limerence when possible and (2) a reduced tendency for limerence to cause total disruption of previous relationships. Perhaps promises made under the influence of limerence should not be treated as sacrosanct.

Indeed, the problems of stepparents and stepchildren are so enormous and well documented that we may wish to establish a legally binding co-parenting relationship that cannot be undone simply by divorce and remarriage. We may want to experiment with a variety of contractual forms, including forms designed primarily for affectional bonding. Certain aspects of the commitment usually associated with marriage (for example, assumption of a common surname and financial responsibility, or dependence) could be eliminated or limited. In other words, I would hope that social forms and customs could be changed to take account of the true nature of human beings and to reduce the dependency often established during limerence rather than to serve mainly the interests of patriarchy and property ownership as the forms in existence at present tend to do.

"RUNNING LIKE HELL"

Knowledge of limerence will not prevent its occurrence except, maybe, by encouraging those who wish to avoid it to hide away in monasteries or run at the first flicker of feeling. Several of my "nonlimerent" informants actually reported doing just that sort of thing. I would not expect Tin Pan Alley to change "Love, Love, Love" to "Limerence, Limerence, Limerence," or to have couples on park benches telling each other, "I limerence you. Do you limerence me?" On the other hand, I can conceive of the following dialogue:

"I love you."
"Have you read Tennov's book?"
"Yes."
"Well, do you mean limerence?"

Or even,

"I love you."
"Have you read Tennov's book?"
"No."
"Let me lend you mine."

Many informants in the throes of a severe reaction expressed the wish that they had acted differently at an earlier stage. There was a near unanimous feeling that limerence could be stopped voluntarily if it were "caught in time." Doris described her conviction that she could have kept herself from becoming limerent toward Vinny if only she had acted soon enough.

"On the first date, I kept saying to myself, 'This man will do me no good. He's too handsome, too much in demand by others, and entirely too charming.' I truly believe now that if I had simply cut it then, my feelings would never have reached the intensity that drove me out of my mind for the next three years.

"In fact, I met a man about a month ago who was very like Vinny in those ways, and did I ever run!"

"Running like hell" might not end a passion at its height, but it was cited by a number of persons who described themselves as voluntary nonlimerents. Carol was one:

"It's a basic policy. If anyone interests me more than casually, I stop it right there by avoiding him. I stay away from any place I think he might be. I've been playing it that way for a few years now, and so far it's worked. I had what you call 'limerence' once, and for me once was quite enough. I never want to go through that again!"

Only a few people expressed that conviction, but those who did were adamant about it. I think it significant that no one actually in the state of limerence at the time of the interview was among them, and I have tentatively drawn the conclusion that an aspect of limerence is a desire for limerence. Only when recovery is complete do people appear capable of rejecting limerence as one of their most urgent personal goals.

Some of the later interviewees, especially "involuntary" nonlimerents, those to whom limerence somehow had not occurred, but who had enjoyed the spectacle of limerent passion as portrayed in drama and song, voiced objections to the very idea of scientific study of limerence.

"You'll destroy romance," they said.

But those in the throes of limerence did not find that their analyses diminished their passion. What did happen was some relief of shame and guilt. Although they remained limerent, they no longer felt abnormal.

Stendhal's conclusions on "cure" have not been overturned. He said, "It is almost useless trying to stop love except in its very early stages," but if you are lucky, a kind friend might "apparently quite by chance" indicate undisputable signs that LO is not interested (thereby eliminating the needed element of hope and reducing the limerent desire).[6] For those who wish cure, the most certain course is prevention. Once you are in its grips your emotions are directed by the external situation, and the only effective action open to you is destruction of any opportunity for reciprocation to occur. An unendurable love-madness can drive its victim to outright self-destructive madness in the form of murder or suicide, as is often portrayed in drama.

WHAT ABOUT PROFESSIONAL HELP?

The writings of psychotherapists in their own professional literature give the impression that manifestions in their patients of the condition I have called limerence are a defect in the personality, an "addiction," "morbid dependency," "neurotic obsession," or "erotomania."

Psychologist Albert Ellis, however, attacks limerence head on for what it is and he does so logically. Therapists using his methods encourage their clients to "give up" what Ellis refers to as their irrational and damaging (limerent) "philosophies." Ellis's approach reflects a more general cultural swing toward lifestyles which might be called "nonlimerent" based on the assumption that it is possible, given appropriate human choices, to avoid sexual or limerent jealousies or needs for "exclusivity."

Ellis claims that his rational/emotive system:

enables an individual who accepts and works with its tenets to be intensely, and even romantically, in love or loving, and yet to avoid most of the serious disadvantages—especially the insecurity, the anxiety, and the grief—usually attendant upon romantic amour.

Ellis' clients "come to realize" that their basic problem is an "illogical interpretation" of LO's rejection. If Dr. Ellis can render you "sane," you'll feel a certain amount of expected (rational) discomfort, but you'll "never be grief-stricken, depressed, or seriously emotionally upset."[7] By achieving a state of *philosophical acceptance* if things don't work out as desired, the limerent need for exclusivity can be reduced. It must be admitted that Ellis' view represents an unmistakable challenge to limerence theory. If limerence is an uncontrollable, biologically determined, inherently irrational, instinct-like reaction, it could hardly be swayed, and certainly not quelled, even by such astute and competent clinicians as are those trained in Dr. Ellis' methods.[8] How can this head-on collision of ideas be resolved?

Ellis may have himself managed to be limerence-free in his personal life and therefore to have no better conception of what limerence is like as an experience than did my nonlimerent informants. Still, it must be admitted that the basic features of limerence have appeared to him again and again in the accounts of his clients, and they have been presented in Ellis' writings in highly discernible fashion in his descriptions of the conditions for which his clients consulted him. His own past experiences, whatever they were and whether or not they included limerence, do not preclude his believing that changing his clients' ways of thinking will help them control their limerence.

Like many of my formerly limerent interviewees, Ellis could be playing down in his memory any feelings of involuntariness he may have had. Human beings, and surely Dr. Ellis is not an exception, are eager to find causations among events. It is sometimes hard to avoid feelings that a causal relationship exists when events occur together or in close succession, and especially when the need for understanding of the phenomenon is urgent. Might his recovery from a limerent experience have coincided with the development of rational/emotive theory? And might that coincidence have given him the impression that his relief from limerence was related to his own abandonment of irrational, limerence-induced ideas?

Ellis' clientele may have comprised, as did my sample of informants, nonlimerents (whose experience would be compatible with his approach), reticent limerents who in their shame at getting into so "insane" and "self-defeating" a state, may have decided to cheat a little (just on this subject) to agree with a rational analysis, and happy limerents, for whom limerence seems a very satisfactory state in this most rational of ecstasy-providing universes. The nonlimerent would support Ellis' position, the bashful limerent would be reluctant to offer disconfirming confessions, and the happy limerent, if seeking help at all, would surely come to the rational therapist, not for help with limerence, but for assistance with unrelated problems.[9] It would be interesting to know how his clients have fared.

WHAT THE NONLIMERENT LO CAN DO

Most of my informants had at one time or another found themselves in the role of nonlimerent LO. As previously noted, they were in almost unanimous agreement that it was an undesirable situation in which to find oneself, and, in fact, their view of limerence was so effective in showing limerence's undesirable qualities that it tended to be remembered with what might even be termed a kind of horror. Part of that horror is the disinclination ever to be in the odious position of the limerent yourself.

What can be done about it should you find yourself in the role of the nonlimerent LO? Limerence has only one answer: Do whatever is necessary to eliminate any trace of hope. Informants repeatedly described the "I like you as a friend, but . . ." strategy, or worse, "I need some time alone to sort things out." Neither of these equivocal announcements can be relied on to provide the needed relief. Perhaps with the clarification of the state provided in this book, it will be possible to say, "I'm not limerent toward you. I don't wish to be limerent toward you." Or, "I am limerent about_____."

While knowledge of limerence as it emerged from the research is clearly incapable in itself of providing full control over its inception, it appears to have value in helping to clarify the condition of the nonlimerent LO.

Many of the LOs with whom I discussed limerence who had not themselves undergone the experience expressed a degree of relief when they learned that the reaction they had evoked in others was normal, and was not their fault. What they learned also helped them decide how to handle the situation. As Mary said:

"From now on, my whole approach will be quite different. If I suspect that anyone is beginning to become limerent about me, I will convince them immediately that the situation is impossible, that I do not wish to function as their LO, and that there is absolutely no hope for them. If that doesn't work, then we just won't be able to see each other anymore."

I think knowledge of the limerent state clearly suggests that the nonlimerent LO has certain responsibilities of an ethical kind. Better understanding of what the limerent person is undergoing and how your actions as LO influence that response will help to diminish the pain that the limerent person is experiencing, as well as the suffocating attention that is unpleasant for you.

It will also reduce the personal danger that you may find yourself in from a distraught limerent who does not understand that nonlimerence on your part is not a betrayal (the word so often used) but an inability to produce limerence that matches the limerent's inability to end it. Surely, the effect of limerence theory is beneficial if it increases the nonlimerent LO's awareness of the kind of desperate actions limerents have carried out, including violence and suicide. Instead of trying to help by offering friendly compassion (which is so easily taken as cause for "hope"), you will be resolute about not giving off any signals that could possibly be interpreted as signs of reciprocation. Let others offer compassion to the limerent. When possible, this will mean your ending the relationship altogether, unless you can nip the process in the bud.

Not that it hasn't been tried. Again and again, honest and sincere nonlimerents, recalling past problems, have begun new relationships with the declaration that they "didn't want to get involved," only to find that they might have saved their breath, for all the good it did.

One nonlimerent, on learning of limerent theory, felt that the pain of limerence may be great, but that it should not be forgotten that nonlimerents hurt, too. He expressed his feelings in a poem about his sadness over having to end a relationship that was dear to him because his lover had begun to demand the impossible in her limerence.

> We hurt, too, you know. It's not easy to be forced to give up a good friend, to see someone change before your very eyes from someone you feel knows and loves you to someone who is suddenly demanding the impossible, as if you were not you at all. This poem tells how strongly I felt the sadness of having to part.

I was allowed to keep a copy of the poem to show to others. I did. I explained the circumstances of its being written before reading it to a few interviewees. A limerent who was suffering the pain of nonmutuality, gave the following reaction:

"Okay, I understand what the poem is saying, and I can see that the writer really didn't like the relationship to break up and all, but, frankly, almost from the first line, my feelings were for the person addressed in the poem, the person being told to leave by a lover when the crime has only been that of loving.

"Furthermore, and I don't doubt the intensity of feeling expressed in the poem, but what the nonlimerent never realizes is that it is a unique kind of suffering because it is so inescapable. I can imagine that the next day the writer of the poem is sad, but the person the poem is addressed to is disconsolate, is in a state of grief and despair, because nothing can be done to make the thoughts go away. Nonlimerents don't know about that. They don't know how you can't control your own thought."

The more people I spoke to, the more apparent seemed the need for communication across this barrier, for understanding and identification of each state both by those who are experiencing it and by those who see it only from an external vantage point. Those who disparaged nonlimerence acted as though the nonlimerent was a cold, unfeeling individual who was both defective and exploitative. This is simply not true at all. Indeed, a case can be made for it being the limerents, with their intense preoccupation with LO, who are not responsive to the needs and wishes of others. Unfortunately, from the point of view of resolving conflicts, both states have their ardent champions and virulent detractors. I hope that classification of their true nature may put an end to such disparagement since the complaints from each side are based on misunderstanding.

If Don Juan is a nonlimerent and an exploitative person, it is his exploitativeness, not his nonlimerence, that constitutes a problem. Limerents are not immune to exploitativeness (even sexual exploitativeness, when sex is the only refuge from a painful and persistent state of nonmutuality). It is not nonlimerence as a general state, but nonlimerence with regard to a particular person, that is likely to be associated with sexual (or other forms) of exploitation.

Perhaps to the limerent the unforgivable characteristics of the nonlimerent are the failure to experience the intrusive inescapability of limerent pain, along with the nonlimerent's freedom to exercise skillfulness in social situations in which limerent fears of rejection can be paralyzing. Antagonism toward nonlimerents might also function to rationalize the insanity of the limerent state by idealizing it, even deifying it. The limerent is horrified to learn of nonlimerence as a normal state because, as Bruce put it:

"I might not have put all that energy into it when it was impossible from the start. If, as you say, there are people who do not fall in love, then there's no hope from the beginning, and that in itself would prevent falling in love, especially if it were known in time. It would be like not falling in love with a married person or a TV personality or someone who was extremely beautiful or anyone else who is absolutely unattainable.

"But what I wonder is how many times, with my active past

loves, I have been painfully and desperately in love with someone who was really telling the simple truth when she uttered
that awful sentence, 'I really like you, Bruce, *as a friend.*'

"Janice, for example. Now that I think of it, she seemed really
puzzled by my demands. Looking back at the situation, I think
she was simply nonlimerent. I was always trying to read deep
meanings into her every action when what must really have been
happening was simply her sincere attempt to maintain an important friendship. If I had known, I might have kept a valued friend
instead of accusing her of deliberately trying to keep me on a
string. I wouldn't have been jealous because there would have
been nothing to be jealous about. She probably liked me best,
and I'd have realized that was all I would ever get."

Bruce's reasonable attitude toward Janice came too late for
him to salvage that relationship, but he felt that he would in the
future be alert to the possibility of nonlimerence in a woman to
whom he was attracted. He felt that knowing this about her from
the beginning would enable him to prevent limerence toward
her from developing.

Limerent and nonlimerent persons may have difficulty in com-
municating with each other. If you are limerent, it may not be
true that you are blind to the mole on LO's chin, but imperfections are readily dismissed and not associated with any logical
consequences. If your bewildered nonlimerent friends try to offer
assistance to you, when you are clearly suffering because of your
limerence, try to understand them. They will ask questions about
the reasonableness of your choice of "this particular person."
They will stress either the rational unsuitability of the person or
the clear "evidence" that you are not that person's choice. You
prefer the first approach, of course. It is rather fun to see LO
taken down a peg or two. It diminishes the hurt a little, increases
your self-confidence. And LO *is* your favorite topic. That's why
even the second is not intolerable. Besides, how can you explain
to your friend that the "evidence" is not in words alone, but in
their meanings. And you find meanings, *know* of "certain" meanings, that defy description.

Now imagine yourself in the role of the nonlimerent friend.

You try to find a way to help. You say things like, "How can I help?" and the answer turns out to be that there's nothing you can do except listen passively, which gets boring and seems futile. Really, dealing with an active and miserable limerent is a job no one is fit for—the nonlimerent, non-LO, good-natured, well-meaning friend least of all. Not wanting to believe a person could be in the grips of such a madness, you must put the person down, or put *it* down, or both.

BUT WHAT STARTS IT?

As much as I have been able to pin down a description of what people feel and how they behave when they are experiencing this state I have called limerence, an important question remains unanswered: what starts it? What is it about the limerent person, about LO, or about the situation that sets off the reaction? Is it some delicate balance among a variety of factors? The ancient theories about love that focused on initiation by Cupid's arrow or a love potion or spell have yet to be replaced. Is the love potion a hormone? That so many of us have our first limerences around the time of puberty, as has already been noted, suggests that physiological processes occurring during normal development may have to reach a certain state of readiness, which, however, might be insufficient to stimulate a limerent reaction unless other factors are also favorable.

Can we find out what those factors are? While it is true that the person who becomes LO often shares certain similar traits or background, such as educational level, with the limerent, it is also true that the LOs of a significant number of my informants did not share either character traits or similar backgrounds. Why? Among the group of people generally like the limerent, what is the reason one particular person rather than another particular person becomes LO?

If there is one result that I hope this work will generate, it is the conviction that finding out more about limerence is desirable, that we can give up some of our awe concerning the marvelous miracle in exchange for assistance in dealing with it. My interviewees seemed unanimously grateful for what they felt would be a greater ability to deal with personal situations—especially with persons, including themselves, who might be suffering from some of limerence's less pleasant aspects, because, as one woman said, "Limerence was bad enough, but on top of that was the terrible feeling that I was also crazy to be feeling it. I mean literally crazy—hopelessly neurotic. Whatever term you want to use, I used them on myself." Or as the never-limerent parent of a very limerent teenager said, "I thought there was something wrong with her. I had absolutely no idea of what she was going through until now and it fits. That's exactly how she is acting."

Nor do I feel that a "cold" scientific eye will rob us of the ecstasy of reciprocation or of the artistic creations which limerence tends so often to inspire.[10] I do not believe that to know limerence is to destroy it any more than to understand the physics of ionization is to destroy the beauty of the Paris sky. To view Violetta in Verdi's opera as a woman undergoing a limerent reaction has neither impaired my pleasure in the music nor prevented empathic reaction to the anguish of the opera's characters. It is true that certain works will undergo reevaluation. For example, although Flaubert imparted certain limerence-like characteristics to her, Emma Bovary emerges, in the light of limerence theory, as a synthetic character. Materialism and romantic aspirations appear fused in her in ways that were not found in my informants. Perhaps reanalysis of fictional portrayals will cause us to see some authors as limerents excellently depicting its course as it is affected by its context, while others will be more satisfactorily interpreted as viewing the process from an external—or disbelieving—vantage.

Although, like anyone else, I am loath to talk about my own experiences in this sort of context, I feel it is necessary that I do so, and thereby lay the thing to rest. Had I not known the experience of limerence, it would have been harder for me to have discovered it in others. My own experience guided my questioning, gave me ideas to explore, and possibly kept me from seeing other things that were foreign to it. Whether my conclusions hold up depends on whether they are valuable in the furtherance of human understanding of human nature. The method of arriving at a discovery does not determine its relationship to reality, to what can be observed by other people as well.

It is more important to entertain the idea that we have inborn inclinations, including certain inclinations toward other persons, than to deny ourselves self-knowledge.[11] Although my studies have not found a way for limerents to manage the course of limerence according to individual volition, or even how to cure it once it has taken hold, surely we are closer to imposing our intelligence on the course of our lives than we were when limerence was believed to be entirely under the spell of magic or other supernatural influences. As we learn about our basic nature, including those aspects that seem resistant to voluntary control, we can put that knowledge to the service of our human social goals. We can be liberated from genetic tendencies known, admitted, and understood, far more than we can from genetic tendencies denied. Limerence theory is not merely a step toward understanding romantic love; it is also a step toward understanding how we can transcend those aspects of our inborn behavioral tendencies that inhibit our progress in the direction of self-determination.

If we may use the term "philosophy" to indicate the transitory values of a given time and condition, then it can be said that our philosophy has until now hidden limerence from our clear view. It may not be in contemplation of outer space that the greatest discoveries and explorations of the coming centuries will occur, but in our finally deciding to heed the dictum of self-understanding. In the past 50 or so years, we have watched the field of psychology succumb to invisible pressures to conform to what is now beginning to be recognized as an outdated and inhibiting philosophy, an inordinate and ultimately stultifying disinclination to view ourselves as biological creatures. I believe it is time to reject that philosophy in favor of a new humility which bends to the innermost voices of our fundamental nature, and, in so doing, to shape that nature in accordance with truly human values which can only be discovered when we learn truly what it means to be human.

Appendix
Future Research

In order to study "romantic attachment" I found it necessary to use methods that depart from what has become conventional in psychological research. I asked informants to tell me about their feelings in unstructured interviews. I did not manipulate independent variables, measure dependent variables, or conduct statistical correlations among traits.[1] In some of my other research, I have adopted, even championed, the behaviorist's tactic of exclusive focus on what can be seen readily and publicly. But behaviorist procedures and theories made no sense to me at all in the initial formulating of limerence theory.

Now, however, that the state of limerence has been recognized, research of many different types and purposes can be conducted. For example, we might be able to learn more about influences on the course of limerence by studying the amount of time spent in limerent revery throughout the entire reaction. Or, from data provided by many different persons, we might get a better idea about whether the experience changes over the life span.

Since limerence appears more often in adolescence, study of factors relating to how it is initiated might involve following adolescent volunteers physiologically, emotionally, socially, academically, and in other ways, over several years. The point here would be to discover the precipitating conditions by having them recorded prior to the appearance of the first limerence rather than retrospectively. It might prove feasible to obtain data by arranging for volunteers to type daily reports directly into a computer located conveniently in the school and/or workplace.

Why does limerence happen with this admirable person, not with another? Could it be mainly the state of the limerent person and certain aspects of the situation that induce limerence, not primarily the qualities of LO? [2] No individual is or could be "worth" the time and intensity of desire that limerence evokes. Do relationships initiated by limerence differ importantly over time from those initiated without limerence?

What is the relationship between sex and limerence? Is one biologically based reproductive system superimposed on another, as Carl Sagan suggests? [3] Are they based differently in the physiology? Sex and limerence don't "fit" together very well. Sex is generally viewed as more primitive, but limerence may also be influenced by primitive parts of the brain.[4]

Physical beauty influences the choice of LO. How do limerent objects differ from sex objects? Is physical attractiveness equally important to both?

What factors, if any, inhibit the development of limerence? Are people less likely to become limerent when they are distracted by serious life situations? [5] Some informants noted that limerence is itself a distractor. It sometimes occurs under conditions of adversity. Does adversity invite it?

Why are unrequited love stories so popular? When they end with reciprocation they resemble limerent fantasy. It would not be difficult to identify people's states at the time—limerent (and at what intensity), nonlimerent, or never limerent—and then record their reactions (physiological, behavioral, social, etc.) as a function of what sort of film they viewed or story they read. Which group would enjoy which type of story most? Is the "noble suffering" endured by limerents appreciated in fiction mainly by those personally familiar with the state, or mainly by those for whom it is "romance," or by both, but in different ways?

Comparing verbal reports with diary entries, I found that retrospective estimates of limerence underestimate intensity compared with reports given closer to the time at which the reaction was experienced. Is it true that the more intense and prolonged the suffering, the greater may be the degree of forgetting?

What is the role of affection in limerence? It has been said that human beings are the only species capable of combining sex and affection, reactions that can be and often are quite separable. Is it limerence that brings them together, when they are combined? Affectional bonding appears to combine affection and sex better than does limerence, especially over the long haul. When limerent you may feel intensely affectionate as well as desirous of the type of total union which includes the physical, but intense desire does not ensure successful sexual functioning. Is the fact that sex with LO was often reported to be difficult related to fear and shyness that inhibited "abandon"? Limerence was sometimes accompanied by increased interest in sex. What explanation underlies such seeming contradictions?

Are the various stages of limerence reliably associated with discernible physiological reactions? What is limerence's biochemistry?

Is limerence experienced differently depending on other factors (other than LO's behavior, on which we know it is dependent)? Do mentally ill or retarded persons experience limerence (or not) as do the rest of us?

Under what conditions does disappointment in limerence lead to self-destructive acts or violence toward others?

Do limerent lovers neglect birth control? Understanding limerence may have practical implications for population control and family planning.

Limerent people are traditionally teased. The nervous, lovesick adolescent and the schoolgirl crush are held as objects of amusement. Yet there are no "dirty jokes" about love. Why?

Why were so many interviewees concerned about secrecy? Is it related to the near-taboo status of love in the professional literature?

Are sex differences in limerence built into the genes or do they change with changes in custom? And, indeed, what, if any, are the sex differences?

Do the low in self-esteem, the lonely, the depressed, the generally unhappy and out-of-step fall more readily into limerence, as is so often supposed? Or does limerence occur equally often among those in all such categories?

Limerence can make you feel somewhat lessened in self-esteem, depressed, lonely, and so forth, even if other aspects of life are going well. Do socially adequate people hide the reaction better, idealize it, rationalize, it, fail to act on it, or what? Are more "romantic" persons more likely to become limerent—or less likely? Is there perhaps a form of "romantic love" that does not involve limerence?

It was surely my behaviorist background that inclined me to ask about specific details of the experience. Whatever it was it seems now to have been a lucky decision. I am also glad that I concentrated on the individual experience rather than on relationships. Many limerences occur outside of established relationships. It is, therefore, not surprising that researchers who restricted their inquiries to relationships missed the invariant aspects of the limerent pattern that I found.

Since interviews are subject to unconscious bias that can influence tone of voice, as well as the timing and wording of follow-up questions, it cannot be ruled out that the conclusions I have drawn are not those others would have arrived at even if they had interviewed the same people. I would like to hear directly from readers, especially about experiences that differ from those given by my informants and reported here.

This is a preliminary report. Its purpose is to open a field for investigation.

Notes

NOTES, CHAPTER I

The Beginning

Text Page

p. 6   1. Sidney M. Greenfield, "Love and Marriage in Modern America: A Functional Analysis," *The Sociological Quarterly* 6 (1965): 365.

p. 6   2. Sarah Cirese, *Quest: A Search for Self* (New York: Holt, Rinehart and Winston, 1977), p. 175.

p. 6   3. The problem of methodology appeared particularly acute in view of my behaviorist orientation. Although behaviorism is often thought of as a psychology of overt action, my own interpretation of behaviorism stresses the value of objective verification, without implying that the only useful observations that can possibly be made are of nonverbal, molar actions.

p. 15   4. In "Alternatives to Romantic Love," a paper presented at the American Psychological Convention, Washington, D.C., September 1971, Margaret Horton noted that the word "love" is not only ill defined, but also used to characterize a variety of interpersonal relationships. J. Richard Udry, in *The Social Context of Marriage*, 3rd ed. (Philadelphia: J. B. Lippincott, 1974), termed the various definitions of love given by college students and by writers of, for example, marriage and family texts, [as well as others] a "conglomeration", p. 133.

p. 15   5. Denis de Rougemont, *Love in the Western World* (New York: Harcourt, Brace, 1940), p. 310.

p. 16   6. Nora Budzilek and Lisa Cook. It was gratifying when Charles Ferguson, retired senior editor of *Reader's Digest*, wrote on May 19, 1978, in *The Patent Trader:* "A charming new noun has entered American English. It is 'limerence,' and it compresses into three pleasant syllables the stunning experience hitherto covered by the roundabout phrase of being or falling in love." In addition to his acceptance of the term, which had appeared by then in *The New York Times* and other places, as he noted, Ferguson clearly recognized the need for scientific study of the phenomenon.

NOTES, CHAPTER II

The Individual Experience of Limerence

p. 20   1. *The Oxford Dictionary of Quotations,* 2nd ed. (London: Oxford University Press, 1953), pp. 45–46.

p. 21   2. Ibid., pp. 26–32.

p. 21   3. Stendhal, *Love,* translated by Gilbert and Suzanne Sale (Middlesex, England: Penguin Books, 1957), p. 107.

p. 21   4. *The Oxford Dictionary of Quotations,* 2nd ed., p. 88.

p. 21   5. Robert Seidenberg, *Marriage in Life and Literature* (New York: Philosophical Library, 1970), p. 32.

p. 21   6. Liv Ullmann, "Changing," *McCall's* (February 1977), p. 205.

p. 29   7. John Money and Anke Ehrhardt, *Man and Woman, Boy and Girl* (Baltimore: Johns Hopkins University Press, 1972), p. 190.

p. 29   8. Elaine Walster and G. William Walster, *New Look at Love* (Reading, Mass.: Addison-Wesley Publishing Co., 1978), p. 139. Other authors who have emphasized visual features are Andreas Capellanus, *The Art of Courtly Love* (New York: W. W. Norton, 1969), p. 9; and Vernon W. Grant, *Falling in Love: The Psychology of the Romantic Emotions* (New York: Springer Publishing Co., 1976), p. 16. Alvin Pam, Robert Plutchik, and Hope R. Conte ("Love: A Psychometric Approach," *Psychological Reports* (37) 1975: 83–88) found attractiveness more important in a "love relationship than in dating and friendship," according to responses of college students.

p. 30   9. Stendhal, *Love*, p. 49. Stendhal, the French writer to whom the present book is dedicated, was writing as a limerent far ahead of his time and knew it. As he himself had feared, for the most part his critics did not forgive him the neologism of "crystallization."

p. 30   10. Ibid., p. 48.

p. 31   11. Sidney Greenfield, "Love and Marriage in Modern America: Functional Analysis," *The Sociological Quarterly*, 6 (1965): 364.

p. 31   12. Morton M. Hunt, *The Natural History of Love* (New York: Alfred A. Knopf, 1959), p. 357.

p. 32   13. Matthew Josephson, *Stendhal, or the Pursuit of Happiness* (Garden City, N.Y.: Doubleday, 1946), p. 246.

p. 32   14. Paul Bohannan, *Love, Sex and Being Human* (Garden City, N.Y.: Doubleday, 1969), p. 113.

p. 32   15. David Norton, "Toward an Epistemology of Romantic Love," *Centennial Review* 14 (1970): 442.

p. 32   16. Llewellyn Gross, "A Belief Pattern Scale for Measuring Attitudes Toward Romanticism," *American Sociological Review* 9 (1944): 464.

p. 32   17. Stendhal, *Scarlet and Black*, translated with an introduction by Jean Stewart and B. C. J. G. Knight (Middlesex, England: Penguin Books, 1969).

p. 33   18. Stendhal, *Love*, p. 61.

p. 34   19. Among writers on love who have stressed cognitive prepossession are Vernon W. Grant (in *Falling in Love*, p. 16), Llewellyn Gross (in "A Belief Pattern Scale," p. 464), Sidney M. Greenfield (in "Love and Marriage in Modern America," p. 363), Margaret Horton (in "Alternatives to Romantic Love," p. 4), Marian G. Kinget (in *On Being Human*, chapters 8 and 9), David Norton (in "Toward an Epistemology of Romantic Love," p. 438), and Denis de Rougemont (*Love in the Western World*, p. 146). The state of prepossession is well described by Mary Wollstonecraft, author of "A Vindication of the Rights of Women," who said in a letter to William Godwin on September 13, 1776, "You are not only in my heart, but in my veins, this morning. I turn from you half abashed—yet you haunt me, and some look, word, or touch thrills through my whole frame—yes, at the moment when I am laboring to think of something, if not somebody, else. Get ye gone, Intruder! Though I am forced to add dear—which is a call back" (quoted in *MS* magazine, February 1978, p. 42).

p. 41   20. William Shakespeare, *A Midsummer Night's Dream*, act I, scene I, line 132.

p. 41   21. Psychologists have often used numbers in describing sensations and have found that their experimental subjects could, for example, estimate distances, durations, and even intensity of color using numbers.

p. 42   22. It is interesting to note that Stendhal was also moved toward quantification of his feelings of love; for example, he often comments about how many hours in succession elapsed without his thinking of Metilde.

p. 48   23. Stendhal, *Love*, p. 211.

p. 49   24. Morton M. Hunt, *The Natural History of Love*, p. 54.

p. 49   25. Stendhal, *Love*, pp. 107–8.

p. 51   26. Ingrid Bengis, *Combat in the Erogenous Zone* (New York: Bantam Books, 1973), p. 178.

p. 51   27. Ibid., p. 179.

p. 54   28. Stendhal, *Love*, p. 77.

p. 56   29. Ellen Bersheid and Elaine Walster, "A Little Bit About Love." In *Foundations of Interpersonal Attractions*, ed. T. L. Houston (New York: Academic Press, 1974), p. 365. Bertrand Russell's quote was taken from *The Anatomy of Love*, edited by A. M. Kirch (New York: Dell Publishing Co., 1960), pp. 10–11, and given on page 365 of the Bersheid and Walster article.

p. 57   30. Richard Driscoll, Keith E. Davis, and Milton E. Lipetz, "Parental Interference and Romantic Love: The Romeo and Juliet Effect," *Journal of Personality and Social Psychology* 24 (1972): 1–10.

p. 57   31. Suzanne Brogger, *Deliver Us from Love*, trans. Thomas Teal (Copenhagen: Rhodes, 1973; New York: Dell Publishing Co., 1976).

p. 59   32. Margot Strickland, *The Byron Women* (New York: St. Martin's Press, 1975) p. 71.

p. 59   33. Josephson, *Stendhal*, p. 142.

p. 61   34. Simone de Beauvoir, *The Second Sex* (New York: Bantam Books, 1961), pp. 620–21. She calls it "paranoia," not in the psychotic sense, but in the everyday one of dedicating virtually all one's mental energies to one enterprise, hopefulness. The phenomenon to which she refers had been noted as an aspect of a pathological condition in a French medical treatise under the name of "the de Cléramboult syndrome." See G. G. de Cléramboult, *Oeuvre, Psychiatrique* (Paris: Presses Universitaires de France, 1942).

p. 61   35. Ibid., p. 621.

p. 61   36. William J. Goode, "The Theoretical Importance of Love," *American Sociological Review* 24 (1959): 24, 38.

p. 62   37. The Jacobean dramatist Phineas Fletcher wrote, "Love's tongue is in the eyes." For further discussion of the interpretation of gestures, posture, and other body movements see *Introduction to Kinesics*, by Ray L. Birdwhistell (Louisville, Ky.: University of Louisville Press, 1952), *Body Language*, by Julius Fast (Philadelphia: M. Evans and Co., 1970), and *Behavior in Public Places*, by Irving Goffman (New York: Free Press, 1969).

p. 63   38. Michael Argyle and Mark Cook, *Gaze and Mutual Gaze* (New York: Cambridge University Press, 1976).

p. 63   39. Desmond Morris, *Intimate Behavior* (New York: Bantam Books, 1973), p. 64.

p. 63   40. Zick Rubin, "Measurement of Romantic Love," *Journal of Personality and Social Psychology* 16 (1970): 265–73.

p. 64   41. Beatrice C. Lacey and John I. Lacey, "Two-Way Communication Between the Heart and the Brain," *American Psychologist* 33 (1978): 99–113. Called the "bradycardia of attention," this reaction is just one among complex relationships between physiological organs that have recently been revealed by research. See also Richard J. Davidson, "Specificity and Patterning in Behavioral Systems: Implication for Behavior Change," *American Psychologist* 33 (1978): 430–36.

p. 67   42. Similar deceptions occur in other forms of human interaction, often deliberately. See Peter Blau, *Exchange and Power in Social Life* (New York: John Wiley, 1964).

p. 67   43. According to biographer Joanna Richardson's *Stendhal* (New York: Coward McCann and Geoghegan, 1974), p. 88, Stendhal never quite forgave one of his lovers for yielding too soon and thereby preventing full crystallization and achievement of the most intense ecstasy.

p. 67   44. Josephson, *Stendhal*, pp. 157–58.

p. 68   45. Beauvoir, *The Second Sex*, p. 626.

p. 70   46. Peter Blau, *Exchange and Power in Social Life* (New York: John Wiley, 1964), pp. 77, 80.

p. 70   47. Beauvoir, *The Second Sex*, p. 619. Speaking of Marcel Proust, Beauvoir observed that "Albertine seems insipid when she is at hand and yielding; at a distance she becomes mysterious again and the jealous Proust reappraises her. But such maneuvers are delicate; if the man sees through them, they can only ridiculously expose the servility of his slave" p. 626.

p. 71   48. Cited by Morton M. Hunt in *The Natural History of Love*, p. 80.

p. 71   49. Andreas Capellanus, *The Art of Courtly Love*, p. 153.

p. 71   50. Alfred Stern, *Sartre: His Philosophy and Existential Analysis*, 1967.

p. 72   51. Rolf E. Muuss, *Theories of Adolescence* (New York: Random House, 1962), p. 48.

p. 73   52. John Money and Anke A. Ehrhardt, *Man and Woman, Boy and Girl*, pp. 182–84.

p. 73   53. Hunt, *The Natural History of Love*, p. 304.

p. 73   54. Evidence for the opinion that sex can be disassociated from romantic attachment or indeed love of any sort can be found in the sexuality textbooks used in college courses. Vernon Grant *(Falling in Love*, p. 17) notes that while sex begins with an urge or appetite that then seeks an outlet, the "amorous emotion" has a specific person as its object. Sex and limerence also differ in exclusivity. Although this is not the conclusion dictated by the limerence interviews, it is widely contended that simultaneous passion for more than one person is quite possible. See, for example, the discussion by sociologist Kingsley Davis ("Jealousy and Sexual Property," *Social Forces* 14 (1936): 395, 405). Probably, sexual interest in several persons has been confused with romantic (i.e., limerent) interests. Dramatic refutation of the idea that love and sex do not differ is contained in G. Legman's statement found in his voluminous compilation of dirty jokes: "With only the most minor exceptions, dirty jokes involving *love* have not been encountered. I repeat: DIRTY JOKES ABOUT *love* HAVE NOT BEEN ENCOUNTERED." See his *Rationale of the Dirty Joke: An Analysis of Sexual Humor* (New York: Grove Press, 1968) p. 331.

p. 77   55. *The Letters of Abelard and Heloise*, translated with an introduction by Betty Ladice (Middlesex, England: Penguin Books, 1974), pp. 113 and 133.

p. 78   56. Eugene J. Kanin and Karen Davidson, "Some Evidence Bearing on the Aim-Inhibition Hypothesis of Love," *Sociological Quarterly* (1972) Vol. 13, pp. 210–217.

p. 79   57. Morris, *Intimate Behavior*, p. 87.

p. 79   58. Interference with sexual functioning can also be interpreted to include difficulties in the use of contraceptives. According to Sylvia S. Hacker, high levels of anxiety interfere with the use of birth control measures during the early stages of a relationship. See *Behavior Today* 8 (1977): 3.

p. 81   59. Stendhal, *Love*, pp. 215–16. In "Sex with (and without) Love" *(Medical Aspects of Human Sexuality* 85, 1974: 32, 42), Arnold A. Lazarus indicated his belief that love is not a necessary requirement for "fulfilling" sex and that it can in fact detract from sexual pleasure. Women reported that their best orgasms were achieved during sex with men with whom they were less involved. They reported that their sexual experiences were more satisfying but less erotic with men for whom love and affection existed.

NOTES, CHAPTER III

The Other Sides of Limerence

p. 82   1. This survey was conducted with the assistance of Meir Hadar.

p. 90   2. André Maurois, *Seven Faces of Love* (New York: Didier, 1944), p. 56.

p. 90   3. *The Oxford Dictionary of Quotations,* p. 229.

p. 91   4. Stendhal, *Love,* p. 112.

p. 91   5. Fred's residence in France was inspired by Crosby Hall, Chelsea, London, where the first draft of the manuscript for this book was written.

p. 96   6. Stendhal, *Memoirs of Egotism,* trans. Hannah and Matthew Josephson (New York, Lear, 1949).

p. 106   7. Isadora Duncan, *My Life* (New York: Liveright, 1955).

p. 106   8. Edward S. Gifford, Jr., *The Charms of Love* (Garden City, N.Y.: Doubleday, 1962), p. 4. Gifford, who finds that romantic love keeps a considerable number of people "in a ferment," also emphasizes the importance of an exotic setting and an emotionally charged situation. Gifford attributes to philosopher Santayana the idea that in love nine-tenths is need in the lover and only one-tenth the attractions of the love object.

p. 107   9. Hunt, Morton, *The Natural History of Love,* p. 369.

p. 108   10. Martin Bloom, "Toward a Developmental Concept of Love," *Journal of Human Relations* 15 (1967): 250.

p. 110   11. Doris Lessing, *The Summer Before the Dark,* p. 250.

p. 111   12. H. E. Krehbiel, essay on the story of the opera, in Richard Wagner, *Tristan and Isolde* (New York: G. Schirmer, 1934), p. vi.

p. 112   13. Maurois, p. 197.

NOTES, CHAPTER IV

The Social Effects of Limerence

p. 120   1. I must confess to having examined only a limited number—French, German, Latin, Chinese, and Japanese. There are many thousands of human languages, and I often wonder if a synonym for limerence could not be found in at least one of them.

p. 121   2. These are some of the behaviors listed in the twelfth-century Code of Love by Andreas Capellanus. Of the 31 articles that constitute the code and that fit the limerent pattern, others are: "No One Can Surrender to Two Loves"; "Love Can Always Increase or Diminish"; "True Love Desires Caresses Only from the Beloved"; "Success Too Easily Won Soon Strips Love of Its Charm"; "Obstacles Enhance Its Value"; "New Love Drives Out the Old"; "Waning Love Dies Quickly and Seldom Revives"; "The Lover's Every Action Ends with the Thought of the Beloved"; "A Person in Love Is Unremittingly and Uninterruptedly Occupied with the Image of the Beloved"; and "Nothing Forbids a Woman to Be Loved by Two Men, or Man by Two Women" (Stendhal, *Love,* pp. 278–81).

p. 121   3. Ingrid Bengis, *Combat in the Erogenous Zone,* p. 180.

p. 122   4. William J. Goode, "The Theoretical Importance of Love."

p. 122   5. Stuart A. Queen and R. W. Haberstein, *The Family in Various Cultures*, 4th ed. (J. B. Lippincott, 1974), p. 105.

p. 122   6. Rosemary Haughton, *Love* (Baltimore: Penguin Books, 1970), p. 32.

p. 123   7. Laurence Veysey, "Communal Sex and Communal Survival: Individualism Busts the Communal Boom," *Psychology Today* 8 (1974): 75.

p. 123   8. This is from Plato's *Phaedrus*, cited by David Norton in "Toward an Epistemology of Romantic Love," p. 442.

p. 123   9. Nellie Ptaschkina (1903–1920) died at age 17, but not before writing in her diary about love. Her words were reproduced in Mary Jane Moffat and Charlotte Painter's *Revelations: Diaries of Women* (New York: Random House, 1974), pp. 65–66.

p. 124   10. Beauvoir, *The Second Sex*, p. 625.

p. 124   11. Desmond Morris, *Intimate Behavior* (New York: Bantam, 1973), p. 45.

p. 126   12. Cited by John Jay Parry, ed., in the introduction to Andreas Capellanus, *The Art of Courtly Love*, pp. 9–10.

p. 126   13. Josephson, *Stendhal*, p. 249.

p. 126   14. Seidenberg, *Marriage in Life and Literature*, p. 33.

p. 127   15. David Norton notes that the person in love tends to be in love with the environment of the beloved, not merely the person. This environment includes geographical location, lifestyle, and artistic taste. Cf. "Toward an Epistemology of Romantic Love," p. 440.

p. 130   16. Although to have been able to speak to both members of partnerships would have been very desirable from a research point of view, the reasons why this rarely occurred are intrinsic to the very nature of limerence. More often than not, persons interviewed talked about a LO who was not committed to a relationship with the interviewee, who sometimes was merely an acquaintance or a person with whom the interviewee had only a formal relationship.

p. 133   17. As to whether people can be categorized in terms of general sex drive, opinions vary from that of psychiatrist Hans J. Eysenck, who relates high and low "eroticism" to introversion and extroversion (Invited Opening Address, International Conference on Love and Attraction, September 6, 1977, University College of Swansea, Wales), to Kenneth R. Hardy's "appetitional" theory of sexual motivation ("An Appetitional Theory of Sexual Motivation," *Psychological Review* 71 [1964]: 1–18.)

p. 137   18. David Norton, "Toward an Epistemology of Romantic Love," p. 439.

p. 140   19. According to William N. Kephart, "romantic experiences" occur yearly beginning at "a very early age" and continuing throughout the teens and early twenties ("Evaluation of Romantic Love," in

Medical Aspects of Human Sexuality 7 (1973): 92–93, 98, 100). Money and Ehrhardt indicate that falling in love does not typically occur until after the onset of hormonal puberty *(Man and Woman, Boy and Girl,* p. 22). When I asked fourteen women who were enrolled in a college class to indicate anonymously age of first limerence, first sexual attraction, and first sexual intercourse, the average ages reported were, respectively, 13.5, 14.8, and 17.1. In other words, limerence preceded sexual intercourse by approximately three and a half years.

p. 142 20. One-third of 62 women who provided questionnaire data indicated the duration of their romatic love experience in years, with some estimates reaching as long as several decades. The estimates were consistently longer among those who met criteria of limerence in other answers to their questionnaires. That intense passion is of *short* duration has however, been suggested by many writers (e.g., G. C. Homans, *Social Behavior: Its Elementary Forms,* New York: Harcourt, Brace, 1961).

p. 143 21. Writing in the *American Sociological Review* in 1959, William J. Goode advanced the thesis that although "violent, self-sufficient love" is rare, it is a potentially disruptive force in society which must be controlled because it has the power to estrange individuals from their kinship and lineage groups. Furthermore, mating would be "random" if it depended on love for selection, and such mating is intolerable in societies in which power and property follow kin lines: That includes all known societies to a greater or lesser degree.

p. 146 22. Nena O'Neill and George O'Neill, *Open Marriage,* A New Life Style for Couples (New York: M. Evans, 1972)

p. 146 23. Mirra Komarovsky, *Dilemmas of Masculinity* (New York: W. W. Norton, 1976), p. 97.

p. 147 24. Charlotte Wolff, *Love Between Women* (New York: Harper and Row, 1971), p. 246.

p. 149 25. Hunt, *The Natural History of Love,* p. 311.

p. 149 26. Josephson, *Stendhal,* p. 248.

p. 149 27. Stendhal, *Memoirs of Egotism* (New York: Lear, 1949), pp. 431, 947, 948.

p. 150 28. For example, see James A. Knight, "Suicide Among Students," in *Suicidal Behaviors: Diagnosis and Management* (Boston: Little, Brown, 1968) pp. 228–40.

p. 150 29. This category was listed, but without further discussion, in *Clues to Suicide,* edited by Edwin S. Schneidman and Norman L. Farberow (New York: McGraw-Hill Book Co., 1957). But the authors stated that "many suicide attempts, especially in young persons, occur after the separation from a spouse or a loved one.... Frequently, these suicide attempts are successful as a form of

adaptation in that they do serve to bring the loved person back"
(p. 262). Although they found a love affair to be the official
"indicated" reason in only 2 percent of suicides and 4 percent of
attempts, limerence is likely to be a hidden factor in situations
categorized as "marital difficulties" and "depression," both of
which are among the reasons most frequently given for suicide.

p. 150   30.   For example, "Dyadic Crisis Suicides in Mental Hospital Patients," by Norman L. Farberow and David K. Reynolds, in the
Journal of Abnormal Psychology, 78 (1971): 77–85.

p. 150   31.   Although romantic love has tended to be a subject neglected by
suicidologists, among others, the trend appears to be changing.
See, for example, *Suicidology: Contemporary Developments*, edited by Edwin S. Schneidman (New York: Grune and Stratton,
1976); James A Knight, "Suicide Among Students."

p. 151   32.   Morton Hunt, *The Natural History of Love*.

p. 151   33.   Although such questionnaire responses may differ from actual
behavior, evidence of the implication of limerence in accidents
comes from many sources. David Phillips of the department of
sociology, University of California at San Diego, has noted the rise
in national suicides following a front page story of suicide in
major newspapers. Working with California motor-vehicle fa-
tality records, Phillips found that the number of "accidental
deaths" also rose significantly following "front page suicide" (*Behavior Today* 8 [1977]: 4). Furthermore, the phenomenon of disguised suicide in the form of accident has been found in other
cultures; for example, among the Semai agriculturists of Central
Malaysia (Ernestine Friedl, "Society and Sex Roles," in *Human
Nature* 1 [1978]: 68). My questionnaire was administered at the
Conference on Women and Mental Health, April 5–7, Kala-
mazoo, Michigan.

In addition to suicide and accident, I found unhappy love
affairs linked with schizophrenia, amenorrhea, depression, and
drug addiction.

p. 156   34.   As Kingsley Davis notes in "Jealousy and Sexual Property," it is
the meaningfulness of situations which determines whether or not
jealousy will be aroused.

p. 157   35.   That men are more likely to express anger was also found in a
study of "sexual jealousy" conducted by psychologist Jeff B. Bryson. From questionnaire responses by 102 female and 66 male
college students, Bryson found that males indicated that when
jealous they wanted to go out with others, try to make the partner
jealous, become sexually aggressive with other women, make critical remarks about the partner, and get involved in other things
besides dating. They felt guilty about being jealous, angry at
themselves, and desired to "get even." Women also reported

feeling angry and wanting to get even, but they more often described themselves as "emotionally devastated." Males were more inclined to want some form of confrontation. These findings are consistent with the fact that 60 percent of the women of The Group reported having felt "depressed about a love affair," compared with 48 percent of the men. Bryson's study was reported to the 1976 Convention of the American Psychological Association, and in *Behavior Today* (September 7, 1976) vol. 7, no. 34, p. 4. Male anger also seemed to be reflected in Melvin Wilkinson's finding that the word "fool" was high on the list of descriptions of males in popular songs, but missing for women ("Romantic Love: The Great Equalizer? Sexism in Popular Music," *The Family Coordinator*, 252 [1976]: 161–66).

p. 158 36. *Newsweek* (June 12, 1978) p. 56.

p. 159 37. Marvin E. Wolfgang reports that 84 percent of all female murderers slay males and 87 percent of all female victims are slain by males ("A Sociological Analysis of Criminal Homicide," *Federal Probation* 3 [1961]: 48–55). *Psychology Today* ("The Murder Boom," July 1975) reported that seven out of every 100 victims of murder were killed after a "lover's quarrel," many by husbands, who killed wives they believed no longer loved them. In a study of African murder and suicide, it was found that most suicides were related to illness, but that among those which were not, approximately 20 percent could have been linked to limerence. The figure for homicides was approximately 19 percent. See Paul Bohannon (ed.), *African Homicide and Suicide* (Princeton N.J.: Princeton University Press, 1960).

p. 160 38. Quoted by André Maurois in *Seven Faces of Love* (New York: Didier Publishing Co. 1944), p. 220.

p. 161 39. Hunt, *The Natural History of Love*, p. 342.

p. 161 40. Among the many writers who have taken this position are Yonina Talmon ("Mate Selection in Collective Settlements"), Suzanne Brogger *(Deliver Us From Love)*, and Hugo G. Beigel ("Romantic Love," *American Sociological Review* 16 [1951]: 332).

p. 162 41. *The Oxford Dictionary of Quotations*, 2nd ed., p. 168.

p. 162 42. David Horton analyzed 290 lyrics in four popular periodicals of the 1950s and found 83.4 percent concerned love ("The Dialogue of Courtship in Popular Songs," *American Journal of Sociology* 62 [1957]: 569–78). J. T. Carey examined popular songs and found that love portrayed as an emotional involvement decreased and sex became more prominent between the mid 50s and mid 60s ("Changing Courtship Patterns in the Popular Song," *American Journal of Sociology* 74 [1959]: 720–31). David H. Knox found no relationship between what he considered to be the "romantic conception of love" and the number of hours that high school students reported that they spent listening to music ("Attitudes Toward Love of High School Seniors," *Adolescent* 5 [1970]: 89–100). More recently, Melvin Wilkinson analyzed gender roles as depicted in popular songs. He noted that sadness over lost love was the most frequent category for both sexes and even more frequent for males than for females ("Romantic Love: The Great Equalizer? Sexism in Popular Music," *The Family Coordinator* 25 [1976]: 161–66). Vernon Grant, who used romantic love as at least partly an aesthetic reaction, has also noted the frequent comparisons of the romantic love experience to the appreciation of music (*Falling in Love*, p. 69). Although love is a dominant theme in all forms of song popular in the West, the amount of emphasis varies from time to time. William Kilpatrick has noted some recent fluctuations ("The Demythologizing of Love," *Adolescence* 9 [1974]: 25–30).

p. 163   43. Stendhal, *Love*, p. 65.

p. 163   44. *Twelfth Night*, Act 1, Sc. 1, lines 1–3.

NOTES, CHAPTER V

The Opinions of Philosophers, Psychologists,
and Other Experts

p. 166   1. John Dryden, Epilogue to *Mithridates, King of Pontus*.

p. 167   2. Hunt, *The Natural History of Love*, p. 365.

p. 167   3. Brogger, *Deliver Us From Love*, p. 8. The idea that love was invented by the culture is a common one and will be taken up in greater detail in the next section.

p. 169   4. Francis Bacon, "On Love," *Bacon's Essays and Advancement of Learning* (New York: Macmillan, 1900) p. 22.

p. 169   5. Maurice Valency, *In Praise of Love*, p. 174.

p. 169   6. "The Song of Solomon" 2:5.

p. 169   7. "Sex Differences in Romantic Love and Depression Among College Students," *Proceedings of the 81st Annual Convention of the American Psychological Association* 8 (1973): 421–22. Stendhal was also criticized for his attempt to analyze "passionate love." For example, biographer Matthew Josephson *(Stendhal, or the Pursuit of Happiness)* frequently comments disparagingly about Stendhal's "scientific approach" and "mathematical" categories.

p. 169   8. *Time* magazine (March 24, 1975) quoted Proxmire as follows: "I believe that 200 million other Americans want to leave some things in life a mystery, and right at the top of things we don't want to know is why a man falls in love with a woman and vice versa. Even if they could give us an answer, we wouldn't want to hear it."

p. 169   9. Ellen Berscheid, University of Minnesota psychologist and researcher in romantic love, noted the possible connections between understanding of infatuation and romantic love and such important social issues as the use of contraceptives with its effects on population control, the divorce rate, and other issues (from an article written for *The New York Times* by James Reston and quoted in the magazine *Psychology Today,* for June 1975). An analysis of the Proxmire criticism of the research proposed by Ellen Berscheid and Elaine Walster was recently presented as a "Case Study in Anti-Intellectual Behavior," by Leigh S. Shaffer of Pennsylvania State University ("The Golden Fleece: Anti-Intellectualism and Social Science," *The American Psychologist* 32 [1977]: 814–23).

p. 170 10. For a time I used *evol* (love spelled backward). The humorous response to which the topic of love gives rise was also demonstrated in Robert Perloff's column in the *APA Monitor,* the newspaper of the American Psychological Association (February 1977), in announcing the International Conference on Love and Attraction of September 1977.

p. 170 11. Especially that of Kinsey (Alfred C. Kinsey, Wardel B. Pomeroy, and Clyde E. Martin, *Sexual Behavior in the Human Male,* Philadelphia: W. B. Saunders, 1948) and the more recent work of Masters and Johnson (William H. Masters and Virginia E. Johnson, *Human Sexual Response,* Boston: Little, Brown, 1966). That scientific research on sexuality should antedate that on romantic love provides some confirmation to the proposition that love has been something of a taboo subject in this culture.

p. 171 12. For example, among the list of writers citing "prepossession" (or intrusive thinking), which may be the most central of identifying characteristics, are Andreas Capellanus, Ingrid Bengis, Paul Bohannan, Suzanne Broggen, Helen A. DeRosis and Victoria Pellegrino, Albert Ellis, Llewellyn Gross, Ronald P. Hattis, Marian Kinget, John Money and Anke Ehrhardt, Ortega y Gasset, Finn Tschudi, and many others (see Bibliography for citations).

p. 172 13. If human beings are not free and rational, then they are not "responsible," and the concepts of sin and of the inherent goodness or evil in certain forms of behavior, regardless of personal consequence or consequence to others, become nonsensical.

p. 172 14. That this issue is still lively within scientific writings is revealed in a review of a book edited by Gordon G. Globus, Grover Maxwell, and Irwin Savodnik, *Consciousness and the Brain: A Scientific and Philosophical Inquiry* (New York: Plenum Press, 1976). In his review, "Dualism Still Lives!" (in *Contemporary Psychology* 23: 292–94), Timothy J. Teyler referred to the issue as a "classical battle" without a clear winner. The issue of "inclusive fitness," that genes from close relatives as well as from the individual are passed on, is considered by some to have dealt an even harsher blow to humanity's favored conception of itself than did the original Darwinian conception.

p. 173　15. Among writers on love who have commented on the view held by the ancients, of love as a madness, are Rosemary Haughton *(Love),* André Maurois *(The Seven Faces of Love)* and Denis de Rougemont *(Love in the Western World)*.

p. 174　16. Andreas Capellanus, *The Art of Courtly Love,* p. 195.

p. 174　17. Ibid., p. 188.

p. 174　18. Ibid., p. 190.

p. 174　19. Ibid., p. 191.

p. 174　20. Ibid., p. 192.

p. 175　21. Ibid., p. 196.

p. 175　22. Ibid., p. 199.

p. 175　23. Ibid., p. 210. Like Ortega after him, Andreas Capellanus includes, in a major and highly influential work on the subject of love, an attack on the female sex. Are such writers nonlimerents, mystified by the strange and tormented condition of fond friends, a condition produced (in most cases) by a woman? Or are these men themselves limerents, but limerents who do not *love,* limerents who hate the condition, hate themselves for being in it, and most of all hate women for being, in their eyes, its perpetrators? See chapter V for further discussion of these issues.

p. 175　24. Hugo Beigel ("Romantic Love") and Morton Hunt *(The Natural History of Love)* are among those who assume that romantic love was invented by the culture, Beigel crediting eleventh-century France, while Hunt believes that love was invented by the ancient Greeks. De Rougemont *(Love in the Western World)* does not go that far, but instead asserts that without romantic-love rhetoric, the emotion would not be "avowed" (p. 174). Many writers clearly agree with the statement of La Rochefoucauld: "Very few people would fall in love if they had never heard of romance." Graham Spanier has recently emphasized the role of exposure to romantic love content through the mass media ("Romanticism and Marital Adjustment," in *The Journal of Marriage and the Family* 34 [1972]: 481–87).

p. 176　25. Erich Fromm, *The Art of Loving,* p. 48.

p. 177　26. Ortega y Gasset, José, *On Love,* trans. Toby Talbor (New York: Meridian, 1957), pp. 53, 55.

p. 177　27. Ibid., p. 22.

p. 177　28. Ibid., p. 36.

p. 177　29. Ibid., p. 25.

p. 177　30. Ibid., pp. 28–29. Ortega and Stendhal also disagreed on the subject of women. Ortega, by the end of his book, contributed his own brand of flagrant misogyny.

p. 178 31. Abraham H. Maslow, *Motivation and Personality* (New York: Harper, 1954).

p. 178 32. Robert C. Solomon, *The Passion* (Garden City, N.Y.: Anchor Press/Doubleday, 1976), p. 339.

p. 179 33. Paul Bohannan, *Love, Sex and Being Human,* pp. 112–113.

p. 179 34. George R. Bach and Ronald M. Deutsch, *Pairing* (New York: Avon Books, 1971), pp. 14 and 15.

p. 179 35. Ibid., p. 19.

p. 179 36. Ibid., p. 27.

p. 180 37. Robert Rimmer (ed.), *Adventures in Loving* (New York: Signet Books, 1973).

p. 180 38. For example, Paul Bohannan *(Love, Sex and Being Human,* p. 114) speaks of love as "willfully blind."

p. 180 39. William Kilpatrick, "The Demythologizing of Love." In 1956, Erich Fromm expressed the view that love was based on a polarity of the sexes *(The Art of Loving).* Recently, a similar position was taken by Joseph W. Critelli ("Romantic Attraction As a Function of Sex Role Traditionality," paper presented at the annual convention of the American Psychological Association, August 1977) and by Marian Kinget ("The Many Splendoured Thing in Transition or: The Agony and the Ecstasy Revisited," paper presented at the International Conference on Love and Attraction, held at the University College of Swansea, September 8, 1977).

p. 181 40. Stanton Peele, *Love and Addiction* (New York: Signet Books, 1976).

p. 181 41. "Emotional Trends in the Courtship Experience of College Students," *American Sociological Review* (1945): 619–26.

p. 182 42. See, for example, Sidney Greenfield's "Love and Marriage in Modern America: A Functional Analysis," *(The Sociological Quarterly* 6 (1965), no. 4; William J. Goode's "The Theoretical Importance of Love"; Bernard Ineichen's "The Social Geography of Marriage" (paper presented at the conference on Love and Attraction, Swansea, Wales, September 6–9, 1977); and Bernard I. Murstein's *Love, Sex, and Marriage Through the Ages* (New York: Springer Publishing Co., 1974). Sociologists have also tended to line up for or against marrying for love. Beigel asserts that love is good for marriage ("Romantic Love", p. 333); and Greenfield believes that the nuclear family which arises through romantic love is needed for economic reasons, that without it the social system would cease to operate ("Love and Marriage in Modern America: A Functional Analysis"). Another writer who believes that marrying for love is preferable to marrying "for convenience or convention" is Desmond Morris *(Intimate Behavior,* p. 73). But the bulk of the writers tend to view marrying for love the way society has so often viewed it, as hazardous. Goode mentions a number of sociologists who disparage love as a basis for marriage, including Ernest R. Mowrer, Ernest W. Burgess, Mabel A. Elliott, Andrew G. Truxal, Francis E. Merril, and Ernest R. Groves (p. 38).

p. 182 43. Although Margaret Mead *(Growing Up in New Guinea,* New York: William Morrow, 1930) found little evidence of love among the natives of New Guinea, Vernon Grant *(Falling in Love)* says that it is important to recognize that even among peoples in which "amorous fixations" appear to be rare, references to romantic love occur in the folklore and myths (Chapter 8, pp. 155–82). In *The Study of Man* (New York: Appleton-Century-Crofts, 1936) Ralph Linton points out that societies recognize that there are occasional violent attachments between persons of opposite sex (p. 174). In a recent cross-cultural study of 23 societies, Paul C. Rosenblatt found love magic, which he interpreted as a means of communication between lovers ("Communication in the Practice of Love Magic," *Social Forces* 49 [1971]: 482–87). Suzanne Lilar, in *Aspects of Love in Western Society* (New York: McGraw-Hill Book Co., 1965) also maintains the view that romantic love is a primitive fact of the human condition.

p. 182 44. Albert Ellis, *The American Sexual Tragedy* (New York: Grove Press, 1954), p. 113.

p. 183 45. Ibid., p. 122.

p. 183 46. Ibid., p. 128.

p. 184 47. Ibid., p. 130.

p. 184 48. Ibid., p. 134.

p. 184 49. A more recent statement by Ellis on romantic love is "Unhealthy Love: Its Causes and Treatments," in *Symposium on Love,* ed., Mary Ellen Curtin (New York: Behavioral Publications, 1973).

p. 184 50. Abraham H. Maslow, *Motivation and Personality* (New York: Harper, 1954), p. 235. The same complaint was made by Harry F. Harlow and Margaret Harlow in "Learning to Love" *(American Scientist* 54, no. 3 [1966]) and by Ellen Berscheid and Elaine Walster ("A Little Bit About Love"). For example, Zick Rubin said, "It is surprising to discover that social psychologists have devoted virtually no attention to love" ("Measurement of Romantic Love," *Journal of Personality and Social Psychology* 16 [1970]: p. 265).

p. 184 51. Among recent books on love by psychologists are *Falling in Love,* by Vernon Grant; *The Mystery of Love: How the Science of Sexual Attraction Can Work for You,* by Glenn Wilson and David Nias (New York: Quadrangle, 1976); and *A New Look at Love* by Elaine Walster and G. William Walster.

p. 184 52. For example, "The Effect of Self-Esteem on Romantic Liking," by Elaine Walster *(Journal of Experimental and Social Psychology* 1

[1965]: 184–97); and "Self-Esteem and Romantic Love," by Karen K. Dion and Kenneth L. Dion *(Journal of Personality* 43 [1975]: 39–57).

p. 184 53. Joseph W. Critelli, "Romantic Attraction As a Function of Sex Role Traditionality" (paper presented at the annual convention of the American Psychological Association, San Francisco, August 1977).

p. 184 54. From a report by sociologists David L. Larson, Elmer A. Spreitzer, and Eldon E. Snyder in *Human Behavior* 5 (1976): 49–50.

p. 184 55. "Correlates of Romantic Love," by Kenneth L. Dion and Karen K. Dion, in *The Journal of Consulting and Clinical Psychology* 41 (1973): 51–56.

p. 185 56. The coverage of social scientists' writings is not intended as a comprehensive review but only as a sampling. Although the overwhelming fact is that love has been ignored, there have been restricted references and limited theories. Only those that appear to bear on limerence are mentioned; opinions, comments, and theories that do not have any relevance to limerence or would be basically repetitive of other points made are not included. For example, Winch's psychoanalytic theory *(Mate-Selection* [New York: Harper, 1958]) that people in love have "complementary" personalities seems irrelevant here because (1) who falls in love with whom, or how LO is "selected," is not dealt with in this book and (2) Winch's theory has not received empirical support.

p. 185 57. Echoing Karen Horney, Helen A. DeRosis (a supervising analyst at the American Institute for Psychoanalysis of the Karen Horney Psychoanalytic Institute and Center), writing with Victoria Pellegrino in *The Book of Hope: How Women Can Overcome Depression* (New York: Macmillan, 1976), speaks of the "love-addicted" and "morbidly dependent" person. Dominick A. Barbara in "Masochism in Love and Sex" *(American Journal of Psychoanalysis* 34 [1974]: 73–79) applies the term "masochism" to "self-induced psychological suffering" and "dependent relationships." The implication that limerence is masochistic is also found in the writings of Abraham H. Maslow (e.g., in *Motivation and Personality*).

p. 185 58. See Dorothy Tennov, *Psychotherapy: The Hazardous Cure* (New York: Doubleday/Anchor, 1976, pp. 42–44) for a discussion on the tendency among psychotherapists, especially psychoanalytic psychotherapists, to place responsibility upon the patient.

p. 185 59. Capacity to love as a requisite for mental health is frequently mentioned in the psychological and personality literature. For example, see Morton Beiser, "Poverty, Social Disintegration and Personality" *(Journal of Social Issues* 21 [1965]: 56–78). Also see "The Origins of Human Bonds," by Selma Fraiberg *(Commentary* 44 [1967]: 47–57), in which she refers to "hollow people who lack capacity to love as the result of early childhood experiences."

p. 185 60. "Neurosis," a term bandied about with abandon in the old days, has now gone out of fashion, due mainly to the lack of reliable observable referents.

p. 185 61. Theodore Reik, *A Psychologist Looks at Love* (New York: Rinehart, 1944).

p. 186 62. For example, Helen Berscheid, Karen Dion, Elaine Walster, and G. William Walster ("Physical Attractiveness in Dating Choice: A Test of the Matching Hypothesis," *Journal of Experimental Psychology* 7 [1971]: 173–89) did not find personality types related to the matching process between members of couples in which persons of relatively comparable attractiveness will tend to pair off. In 1964, Dwight G. Dean published an article in which he reported that correlations in such matters did not seem to hold ("Romanticism and Emotional Maturity: A Further Exploration," *Social Forces* 42 [1964]: 302). David H. Knox ("Attitudes Toward Love of High School Seniors") did not find romantic love to be positively correlated with immaturity. William M. Kephart ("Evaluation of Romantic Love") went even further. He found that romantic experiences were actually more common among persons who were best adjusted. Ronald P. Hattis ("Love Feelings in Courtship Couples: An Analysis," *Journal of Humanistic Psychology* 5 [1965]: 22–53) reported that dependency was the least important component of love feelings listed by the subjects in the study. Finally, in a study on suicide, Norman L. Farberow and David K. Reynolds ("Dyadic Crisis Suicides in Mental Hospital Patients," *Journal of Abnormal Psychology* 78 [1971]: 77–85) showed that persons whose suicides had been precipitated by the breakup of a love relationship or other dyadic events had been less severely ill than were those whose suicides had occurred for other reasons.

p. 188 63. Some of my informants told how this pragmatic decision, that the woman should seek therapy, was later used against them during the process of divorce.

p. 199 64. Julie Roy's story was eventually published in a book written by Lucy Freeman and Julie Roy, *Betrayal* (New York: Stein & Day, 1976), and called "the true story of the first woman to successfully sue her psychiatrist for using sex in the guise of therapy."

p. 199 65. Subsequent to the publication of *Psychotherapy: The Hazardous Cure*, a number of books appeared for general readership (for example, *The Psychological Society* by Martin L. Gross [New York: Random House, 1978]). A very good source of documented comments on the deficiencies in psychotherapy can be found in *Coping with Psychiatric and Psychological Testimony*, 2nd ed. (Beverly Hills: Law and Psychology Press, 1975) by lawyer-psychologist Jay Ziskin.

p. 201   66.   See, for example, *A Beginning Manual for Psychotherapists* by Ernest Kramer (New York: Grune and Stratton, 1970).

p. 204   67.   See Sigmund Freud, *A General Introduction to Psychoanalysis,* New York: Simon and Schuster, 1969.

p. 205   68.   For a listing of other ways in which psychotherapy can be harmful, see *Psychotherapy: The Hazardous Cure,* pp. 87–98. They include an overdependency, egocentric passivity, disturbances in relationships with other persons, including family members, the financial burden, and discouragement of attempts to find real solutions to problems.

p. 205   69.   Edward C. Whitmont and Yoram Kaufman, "Analytical Psychotherapy," in Raymond Corsini (ed.) *Current Psychotherapy* (Itasca, Ill.: F. E. Peacock, 1973), p. 107.

p. 205   70.   Albert Ellis, "Rational-Emotive Therapy," *Current Psychotherapy,* p. 172.

p. 205   71.   William Glasser and Leonard M. Zunin, "Reality Therapy," in *Current Psychotherapy,* p. 293.

p. 205   72.   Psychotherapists Saul I. Harrison and Donald J. Carek, in their 1966 *A Guide to Psychotherapy* (Boston: Little, Brown) recommended complete termination rather than the more usual tapering off so as not to "keep open the wounds of therapy" (p. 226).

p. 205   73.   Richard D. Chessick, *How Psychotherapy Heals* (New York: Science House, 1969), p. 50. When the therapist develops limerence (or other emotional reactions) to the patient, it is called "countertransference." For Chessick, the "glue" consists of both transference and countertransference.

p. 205   74.   I believe that it behooves professionals to hold scientific procedures in higher regard than have psychotherapists as a group. By failing to define terms, and in other ways, they inhibited research that may have led to earlier discovery of the damage that was being done. See *Psychotherapy: The Hazardous Cure,* Chapter II, for a discussion of research methods and findings on the effectiveness of psychotherapy.

NOTES, CHAPTER VI

Limerence Among the Sexes

p. 207   1.   Valency, *In Praise of Love,* p. 154.

p. 207   2.   Beauvoir, *The Second Sex,* pp. 603–4.

p. 207   3.   Lord Byron, *Don Juan,* Canto I, Stanza 194. This idea is frequently expressed in one form or another, in poetry, in popular song, and in psychiatry.

p. 208   4.   Beauvoir, *The Second Sex,* p. 629.

p. 208   5.   Stendhal, *Love,* p. 57.

p. 208   6. H. L. Mencken. So called "locker room" humor is frequently based on similar misogynist and nonlimerent ideas.

p. 208   7. Humberto Nagera stated this theme in "Activity-Passivity; Masculinity-Femininity," *Basic Psychoanalytic Concepts of the Libido Theory*, vol. 1 (New York: Basic Books, 1969), pp. 129–45.

p. 208   8. Shulamith Firestone, *The Dialectic of Sex* (New York: Bantam Books, 1970), p. 138.

p. 209   9. Beauvoir, *The Second Sex*, pp. 618–621, *passim*.

p. 209 10. Ingrid Bengis, *Combat in the Erogenous Zone* (New York: Bantam Books, 1973), p. 159. A consistent finding in all questionnaires which I administered was that males' responses tended to fit the nonlimerent pattern more closely than did those of females.

p. 210 11. As Beauvoir said about women, "No other aim in life which seemed worthwhile was open to them; love was their only way out." *(The Second Sex*, p. 606.)

p. 210 12. This is an example of reality in blatant contradiction to common opinion. It is reported in *The Future of Marriage*, by Jessie Bernard (New York: World, 1972).

p. 210 13. Which is why parents traditionally want to see their daughters safely married. Socially and economically independent women are still relatively rare, a fact brought home to me repeatedly while traveling by automobile in France in 1977, when I was waved aside and my eighteen-year-old son asked to sign the hotel registration form.

p. 211 14. Seemingly trivial changes in the working of questionnaires and instructions can sometimes be associated with discernible shifts in group responses. Textbooks in methodology stress taking great care to keep such effects from obscuring the effects of variables which were supposedly amenable to independent manipulation.

p. 211 15. Sometimes unfounded opinion finds its way into strange and influential places. For example, the following statement was found in a medical textbook: "Women tend to love in a different way from men. The woman falls in love with the idea of being loved; whereas the man loves an object for the pleasure it will give." (From *Obstetrics and Gynecology* by J. Robert Wilson, Clayton T. Beecham, and Elsie Reid Carrington [St. Louis, Mo.: C. Z. Mosby, 1971]). An example of a study that found males to "fall in love" more easily is "A Research Note on Male-Female Differentials in the Experience of Heterosexual Love," by Eugene J. Kanin, Karen R. Davidson, and Sonia R. Scheck *(The Journal of Sex Research* 6 [1970]: 64–72).

p. 216 16. Walster and Walster, *A New Look at Love*, 1978.

p. 217 17. See, for example, Derrick Blakeley, "Love in the Executive Suite," *Chicago Tribune*, August 20, 1974.

p. 218 18. Ellen Berscheid, Karen Dion, Elaine Walster, and G. William

Walster, in "Physical Attractiveness and Dating Choice: A Test of the Matching Hypothesis," *Journal of Experimental Social Psychology* 7 (1971): 173–89.

p. 220   19. We have already seen how the limerent's uncertainty and insecurity can be manipulated by commercial interests, for example, in advertisements for clothing and other personal products and in gothic romances. Publishers of these popular novels, in which two people meet, overcome dark obstacles, then unite in marriage, claim that the public wants its gothic heroine to be simperingly feminine.

p. 220   20. Especially, "Love and Limerence" by Roy Reed, *New York Times*, Friday, September 16, 1977, Sect. B, p. 10.

p. 221   21. The nonlimerent, hypersexual pattern of conquest and desertion known as Don Juanism is a male pattern. Also found in a minority of males, and almost exclusively in males, are the so-called sexual "perversions" (e.g., fetishism, transexualism, transvestism, pedophilia, voyeurism, sadism, masochism, necrophilia, urophilia, coprophilia, and the scatological telephone caller) (Money and Ehrhardt, *Man and Woman, Boy and Girl*, p. 148). Fetishisms almost always involve a garment (underwear, shoes, etc.) of the female used by the male. A fetishist finds it difficult or impossible to obtain an erection in the absence of the object. Fetishism should not be confused with other types of attachments to objects that do not involve sexual arousal. The toddler who constantly clutches a favorite toy or blanket, the girl who collects dolls, the young woman who presses a flower into the pages of her Bible, the fan who collects memorabilia of the idol, the mother (or father) who saves and reveres their infant's shoes, or the Catholic who wears rosary beads or a religious medal—none of these are instances of fetishism because the objects are not sexually arousing but prized for other reasons.

p. 221   22. See "Cleared Sex Case Teacher Faints in Dock," in the *London Daily Express*, Saturday, September 3, 1977, no. 24007, p. 1. (Also *Guardian*, Saturday, September 3, 1977). I use the term "molestation" rather than rape because sexual interactions between child and man often do not include intercourse. "Molestation" does not necessarily imply coitus or even penetration. It does imply harmfulness. If the child is not harmed in any way, "molestation" is not the correct term. Whether sex between man and child is always, frequently, or seldom harmful, is a question for the researchers. Reports by adults who were molested as children indicate that, at the very least, harmfulness occurs *sometimes*.

p. 222   23. Gabrielle Russier, *The Affair of Gabrielle Russier* (New York: Alfred A. Knopf, 1971).

p. 222   24. It has been reported that of 2,500 psychiatrists polled, 52 percent felt that men want sex relations more often than their wives, as compared with only 7 percent who felt that wives' desires were stronger *(Behavior Today* 8 [1977]: 6–7).

p. 222   25. This was suggested by Stanley Schachter and Jerome E. Singer, ("Cognitive, Social and Physiological Determinants of Emotional States," *Psychological Review* 69 [1962]: 379–99). A recent study with supportive findings that related to sexual attraction was conducted by Donald G. Dutton and Arthur P. Aron ("Some Evidence for Heightened Sexual Attraction Under Conditions of High Anxiety," *Journal of Personality and Social Psychology* 30 [1974]: 510–17).

p. 224   26. For example, "Measurement of Romantic Love" by Zick Rubin *(Journal of Personality and Social Psychology* 16 [1970]: 267–73); and "Age and the Experience of Love in Adulthood," by Margaret Neiswender, James E. Birren, and K. Warner Schaie, paper presented at the 83rd annual meeting of the American Psychological Association, September 1975, Chicago, Ill. Melvin Wilkinson also reported that for the most part the lyrics to popular songs were the same for both sexes ("Romantic Love: The Great Equalizer? Sexism in Popular Music"). Such findings are important in view of the fact that conditions that would appear to encourage limerence are more likely in women: for example, time to think due to time spent engaged in simple activities that do not require intellect, the fact that men are deemed admirable by the culture even if homely, and the relative absence of distractions or other options. Note that the same conditions also apply to underprivileged males who have also been reported to be more "romantic."

p. 227   27. Oscar Wilde, *De Profundis,* ed. Rupert Hart-Davis (New York: Avon Books, 1962).

p. 227   28. Tennessee Williams, *Memoirs* (New York: Doubleday, 1975).

         29. Julius Lester, "Being a Boy," in *Men and Masculinity,* ed. Joseph H. Pleck and Jack Sawyer (Englewood Cliffs, N.J.: Prentice-Hall, 1974), p. 33.

p. 235   30. Although a number of writers have put forth similar views, my remarks here on the history of patriarchy and the civilizations that preceded its development are mainly derived from art historian Merlin Stone's recent book, *When God Was a Woman* (New York: Dial, 1976). Also, see the works of Elizabeth Gould Davis *(The First Sex,* Baltimore, Md.: Penguin Books, 1971).

p. 235   31. Merlin Stone, *When God Was a Woman* (New York: Dial Press, 1976). There is considerable controversy about whether ancient civilization actually placed power in the hands of women. To many, such an idea is inconceivable, and the absence of contemporary matriarchal societies, even among those few that are matrilineal, is cited as evidence against the possibility of female rulership.

p. 235 32. See "Witchcraft in Histories of Psychiatry: A Critical Analysis and an Alternative Conceptualization," by Nicholas P. Spanos *(Psychological Bulletin* 85 [1978]: 417–39.) for a recent analysis of the witch hunts; also Thomas Szasz, *The Manufacture of Madness* (New York: Harper and Row, 1970); and *Witches, Midwives and Nurses* 2nd ed. (Glass Mountain Pamphlet #1, The Feminist Press, Old Westbury, New York, 1978), by Barbara Ehrenreich and Deirdre English.

p. 235 33. For excellent discussions of misogyny in medieval and theological literature, see Rosemary Radford Ruether's *Religion and Sexism* (New York: Simon and Schuster, 1974) and Joan M. Ferrante's *Woman as Image in Medieval Literature* (New York: Columbia University Press, 1975).

p. 236 34. Heinrich Kramer and Jakob Sprenger, *Malleus Maleficarum,* trans. M. Summers (London: Arrow Books, 1971), pp. 114–15.

p. 236 35. Ibid., p. 133.

p. 236 36. Ibid., p. 112.

p. 236 37. Ibid., p. 122.

p. 238 38. Andreas Capellanus, *The Art of Courtly Love,* p. 18. The translator, John Jay Parry, notes that the misogyny expressed in Book III is in keeping with an anti-female viewpoint with "plenty of precedents in ecclesiastical tradition to justify his misogyny."

p. 238 39. Ibid., pp. 200–201.

p. 238 40. It should also be remembered that those writings which survive were those favored for selection.

p. 238 41. Andreas, p. 203.

p. 238 42. Ortega y Gasset, *On Love,* pp. 155, 162.

p. 239 43. Ibid., p. 164.

p. 239 44. Ibid., pp. 127–128. This view is also reflected in Jean Guitton, *Essay on Human Love,* 1976 (Salisbury Sq., London, Rockliff, 1951) pp. 95, 97.

p. 239 45. For an example of contemporary misogyny, see, for example, Wolfgang Lederer's *The Fear of Women* (New York: Harcourt, Brace, 1968).

p. 240 46. Maurice Valency, *In Praise of Love,* p. 20.

p. 240 47. Ibid., p. 20.

p. 240 48. For a discussion of medieval attitudes toward women, see Eleanor Commo McLaughlin's "Equality of Souls, Inequality of Sexes: Women in Medieval Theology," in *Religion and Sexism,* edited by Rosemary Radford Ruether (New York: Simon and Schuster, 1974), pp. 213–266. McLaughlin considers study of medieval attitudes toward women important because "These attitudes toward the female regarding her sexuality, her role, and her personality characteristics, reflected in medieval popular piety and theology, remain with us today." She believes that "true liberation from the androcentrism and misogyny of those assumptions can come only when the past is made explicit and clear in its implications" (p. 214).

NOTES, CHAPTER VII

Limerence and Biology

p. 241   1. Hunt, *Natural History of Love,* p. 257.

p. 241   2. Stendhal, *Love,* p. 49, 51.

p. 241   3. Maurois, *Seven Faces of Love,* p. 220.

p. 241   4. Greenfield, "Love and Marriage in Modern America," pp. 363–364.

p. 243   5. The general attitude is that love is so complicated and so individual that anything said about it is probably true for some people, or under some conditions (e.g. Wilson and Nias, *Mystery of Love,* p. 48).

p. 244   6. Alice S. Rossi ("The Biosocial Side of Parenthood," *Human Nature* 1 [1978]: 72–79) distinguishes between "biosocial science" and "sociobiology." The latter stresses cross-species analysis, while biosocial science is concerned with the physiological underpinnings to human behavior or "the impact of social and psychological factors on the body functioning" (page 72). Rossi is particularly concerned about "speculative leaps" across species.

p. 244   7. David P. Barash, "Behavior as Evolutionary Strategy" *(Science* 190 [1975]: 1084).

p. 244   8. Edward O. Wilson, *Sociobiology: The New Synthesis* (Cambridge, Mass. Harvard University Press, 1975), page 587.

p. 244   9. Ibid., page 152.

p. 244 10. Stanley Coren and Clare Porac, "Fifty Centuries of Right-handedness: The Historical Record" *(Science* 198 [1977]: 631–32).

p. 244 11. P. P. G. Bateson and R. A. Hinde *Growing Points in Ethology* (New York: Cambridge University Press, 1976): see part D, "Human Social Relations," pp. 425–536.

p. 245 12. Individual variability within the species is important for adaptation to changing conditions. It is precisely why sexual reproduction, as opposed to simple budding or otherwise dividing of some of the simpler organisms, developed through natural selection. For recent discussions of some of these issues, see François Jacob's "Evolution and Tinkering" *(Science,* 196 [1977]: 1161–66) and

Steven M. Stanley's "Clades vs. Clones in Evolution: Why We Have Sex" *(Science* 190 [1975]: 382–83).

p. 245 13. For an important discussion of "evolutionary thought," see George C. Williams, *Adaptation and Natural Selection* (Princeton, N.J.: Princeton University Press, 1966), p. 87.

p. 246 14. Michel Treisman, "Motion Sickness: An Evolutionary Hypothesis," *(Science* 197 [1977]: 493–95).

p. 247 15. In all the questionnaire surveys conducted during the course of the research on limerence, the most consistent finding was that limerence was associated with marriage, that is, those who answered questions more consistent with the limerent reaction were more frequently married than unmarried.

p. 248 16. Money and Ehrhardt, *Man and Woman, Boy and Girl,* p. 192; Desmond Morris, *Intimate Behavior,* p. 79; William J. Goode, "The Theoretical Importance of Love," p. 39.

p. 248 17. Wolfgang Wickler, *The Sexual Code* (Garden City, N.J.: Anchor Press/Doubleday, 1973), p. 256.

p. 248 18. Quoted by Michelle Galler Riegel in "Monogamous Mammals: Variations on a Scheme" *(Science News* 112 [1977]: 76–78).

p. 249 19. Wolfgang Wickler, *The Sexual Code* (Garden City, N.J.: Anchor Press/Doubleday, 1973), pp. 95–96.

p. 250 20. W. Sluckin, "Imprinting Reconsidered," *Bulletin of the British Psychological Society* 27 (1974): 447–51.

p. 250 21. Lee Salk, "Mother's Heartbeat as an Imprinting Stimulus," *Transactions of the New York Academy of Science,* 24 (1962): 753–63.

p. 250 22. Money and Ehrhardt, pp. 22, 191–92.

p. 251 23. Ibid., p. 190.

p. 251 24. Yonina Talmon, "Mate Selection in Collective Settlements," p. 501.

p. 252 25. Sexual molestation of children is done many times more frequently by men than by women, although actual percentages are difficult to estimate. It might be that an aspect of maternal "instincts" is the tendency not to be disposed toward sexuality involving children. Other theorists might argue that cultural conditions help to produce the effect.

p. 253 26. Vernon W. Grant, *Falling in Love,* p. 157.

p. 254 27. See E. O. Wilson, *Sociobiology,* for examples.

NOTES, CHAPTER VIII

Can Limerence Be Controlled?

p. 258 1. Josephson, *Stendhal,* page 268.

p. 258 2. Two recent books that provide somewhat more substantial suggestions are *How to Survive the Loss of a Love,* by Melba Colgrove, Harold H. Bloomfield, and Peter McWilliams (New York: Leo Press, 1976) and *How to Fall Out of Love,* by Debora Phillips (Boston: Houghton Mifflin, 1978). Advice columnists might do well to reconsider the rules for lovers initiated centuries ago in the Courts of Love in England and France by Eleanor of Aquitaine.

p. 259   3. *Letting Go: A Twelve Week Personal Action Program To Overcome a Broken Heart* by Zev Wanderer and Tracy Cabot (New York: Putnam, 1978).

p. 259   4. See, for example, my book *Super Self: A Woman's Guide to Self-Management* (New York: Funk and Wagnalls, 1977; Jove, 1978).

p. 260   5. As readers of *Super Self* know, record keeping is often exceedingly important in self-management and in coping. It may also prove valuable in helping to control limerence, but at this point, what sort of records should be kept and how they can be used are uncertain.

p. 265   6. Stendhal, *Love,* page 130.

p. 266   7. Ellis, Albert, *The American Sexual Tragedy,* page 158.

p. 266   8. Ellis does not deny a biological basis to the phenomenon, just that the condition is instinctive and involuntary. By "biological basis" Ellis means that the condition develops naturally and easily and is hard to change, but that does not mean it cannot be changed. His techniques are aimed at achieving rationality, even when the irrationality to be changed is rooted in biology. See "The Biological Basis of Human Irrationality" *(Journal of Individual Psychology,* 1976), pp. 32, 145–68.

p. 267   9. Dr. Ellis probably saw few of these. Happy limerents tend to be off in the lovenest. I found few wanting to take time off to be interviewed, except when LO was unavailable. In that case they were willing to talk, but primarily of LO's "perfections," the activity (talking about LO) rated by happy and unhappy limerents alike as second best to being in the divine presence. It may seem to be a poor second, but it is a consistent one.

p. 273   10. Marian Kinget was reported by the press to have said in a paper given at the Conference On Love and Attraction that the "sexual revolution" and women's liberation movement were "killing Cupid." Dr. Kinget's paper was in some ways a sensitive treatment of "romantic love," but she did not realize that free sexuality is not necessarily a threat to limerence since sexual intercourse is not itself the aim of the limerent yearning.

p. 274   11. As an unnamed book reviewer in *The Spokeswoman* put it, "It may be a question of facing up to stubborn biological patterns and dealing positively with them" (August 15, 1977, p. 12).

NOTES

Appendix

p. 275   1.   I can only attribute the hundreds of thousands of research reports of "significant correlations" in psychology journals to a peculiar type of "wiring" in the psychologist's brain. It is truly phenomenal how the mind goes all aquiver over the prospect of finding that limerents are more likely to be male than female, young than old, cross-eyed than wall-eyed, introvert rather than extrovert, low in self-esteem rather than high, reared in Nebraska rather than Ohio, European rather than Oriental, or both, in a year ending with an even number rather than odd. The problem is that the information obtained is of very limited usefulness. It can even set things back by leading to the feeling that more is known than is actually the case. Even a seemingly strong relationship between traits may not reflect a causal relationship. For example, liquor sales, the birth rate, and church-going all show a rise in the spring, which suggests little if anything about the probable causes of any of those events.

p. 276   2.   Several of my informants complained that the only role they ever seem able to play is that of (nonlimerent) LO. "What do I do that makes people fall in love with me?" they would ask. Although it's easy enough to say, as I did, "You give just the right mixture of attractiveness, hope, and uncertainty," it might be valuable to study such persons closely to determine exactly how they act, since the ability to induce limerence is the ability to control it.

p. 276   3.   Carl Sagan, *The Dragons of Eden: Speculations on the Evolution of Human Intelligence* (New York: Random House, 1977).

p. 276   4.   The behavior of certain birds, for example, bears resemblance to limerence as we have seen.

p. 276   5.   In *Sociobiology: The New Synthesis* (Cambridge, Mass.: Harvard University Press, 1975), page 543, Edward O. Wilson describes a society always on the brink of starvation in which limerence appeared not to occur.

Bibliography

Abelard and Heloise. *The Letters of Abelard and Heloise.* Translated with an introduction by Betty Ladice. Middlesex, England: Penguin Books, 1974.

Andreas Capellanus. *The Art of Courtly Love.* Translated with introduction and notes by John Jay Parry. New York: W. W. Norton, 1969.

Argyle, Michael, and Mark Cook. *Gaze and Mutual Gaze.* New York: Cambridge University Press, 1976.

Bach, George R., and Ronald M. Deutsch. *Pairing.* New York: Avon Books, 1971.

Barash, David P. "Behavior as Evolutionary Strategy." *Science* 190 (1975): 1084–85.

———*Sociobiology and Behavior.* New York: Elsevier North-Holland, 1977.

Barbara, Dominick A. "Masochism in Love and Sex." *American Journal of Psychoanalysis* 34 (1974): pp. 73–79.

Bateson, P. P. G., and R. A. Hinde. *Growing Points in Ethology.* New York: Cambridge University Press, 1976.

306

Beauvoir, Simone de. *The Second Sex*. Translated and edited by H. M. Parshley. New York: Bantam Books, 1961.

Beigel, Hugo G. "Romantic Love," *American Sociological Review* 16 (1951) 326–34.

Beiser, Morton, "Poverty, Social Disintegration and Personality," *Journal of Social Issues* 21 (1965): 56–78.

Bengis, Ingrid. *Combat in the Erogenous Zone*. New York: Bantam Books, 1973.

Berscheid, Ellen, Karen Dion, Elaine Walster and G. William Walster. "Dating Choice: A Test of the Matching Hypothesis," *Journal of Experimental and Social Psychology* 7 (1971): 173–189.

Berscheid, Ellen, and Elaine Walster. "A Little Bit About Love." In *Foundations of Interpersonal Attraction*, edited by T. L. Huston, pp. 355–81. New York: Academic Press, 1974.

Birdwhistell, Ray L. *Introduction to Kinesics*. Louisville, Ky.: University of Louisville Press, 1952.

Blakeley, Derrick. "Love in the Executive Suite." *Chicago Tribune*, August 20, 1974.

Blau, Peter. *Exchange and Power in Social Life*. New York: John Wiley, 1964.

Bloom, Martin. "Toward a Developmental Concept of Love." *Journal of Human Relations* 15 (1967): 246–63.

Bohannan, Paul (ed.). *African Homicide and Suicide*. Princeton: Princeton University Press, 1960.

————*Love, Sex, and Being Human*. Garden City, N.Y.: Doubleday, 1969.

Brogger, Suzanne. *Deliver Us from Love*. Translated from the Danish by Thomas Teal. New York: Dell Publishing Co., 1976.

Carey, J. T. "Changing Courtship Patterns in the Popular Song." *American Journal of Sociology* 74 (1969): 720–31.

Chessick, Richard D. *How Psychotherapy Heals*. New York: Science House, 1969.

Cirese, Sarah. *Quest: A Search for Self*. New York: Holt, Rinehart & Winston, 1977.

Colgrove, Melba, Harold H. Bloomfield, and Peter McWilliams. *How to Survive the Loss of a Love*. New York: Leo Press, 1976.

Coren, Stanley, and Clare Porac. "Fifty Centuries of Right-Handedness: The Historical Record." *Science* 198 (1977): 631-32.

Critelli, Joseph W. "Romantic Attraction as a Function of Sex Role Traditionality." Paper presented at Annual Convention of American Psychological Association, San Francisco, August 1977.

Davidson, Richard J. "Specificity and Patterning in Biobehavioral Systems: Implications for Behavior Change." *American Psychologist* 33 (1978): 430–36.

Davis, Elizabeth Gould. *The First Sex.* Baltimore: Penguin Books, 1971.

Davis, Kingsley. "Jealousy and Sexual Property." *Social Forces* 14 (1936): 395–405.

Dean, Dwight G. "Romanticism and Emotional Maturity: A Further Exploration." *Social Forces*, 42 (1964): 298–303.

DeRosis, Helen A., and Victoria Pellegrino. "The Love Addicts." *Working Woman*, January 1977, pp. 65–70. (Excerpt from *The Book of Hope: How Women Can Overcome Depression*, Macmillan, 1976.)

Dion, Karen K., and Kenneth L. Dion. "Self-Esteem and Romantic Love." *Journal of Personality* 43 (1975): 39–57.

Dion, Kenneth L., and Karen K. Dion. "Correlates of Romantic Love." *Journal of Consulting and Clinical Psychology* 41 (1973): 51–56.

Driscoll, Richard, Keith E. David, and Milton E. Lipetz. "Parental Interference and Romantic Love: the Romeo and Juliet Effect." *Journal of Personality and Social Psychology* 24 (1972): 1–10.

Duncan, Isadora. *My Life.* New York: Liveright, 1955.

Dutton, Donald G., and Arthur P. Aron. "Some Evidence for Heightened Sexual Attraction Under Conditions of High Anxiety." *Journal of Personality and Social Psychology* 30 (1974): 510–17.

Ehrenreich, Barbara, and Deirdre English. *Witches, Midwives and Nurses: A History of Women Healers,* 2nd ed. Old Westbury, New York: The Feminist Press, 1973.

Ellis, Albert. *The American Sexual Tragedy.* New York: Grove Press, 1954, 1962.

————"The Biological Basis of Human Irrationality," *Journal of Individual Psychology* 32 (1976): 145–68.

————"Rational-Emotive Therapy." In *Current Psychotherapy,* edited by Raymond Corsini. Itasca, Ill.: F. E. Peacock, 1973, pp. 167–206.

————"Unhealthy Love: Its Causes and Treatment." In *Symposium on Love,* edited by Mary Ellen Curtin. New York: Behavioral Publications, 1973.

Ellis, Havelock. *Studies in the Psychology of Sex.* New York: Random House, 1936.

Eysenck, Hans J. "Sex, Society and the Individual." Invited opening address at the International Conference on Love and Attraction, held at University College of Swansea, September 5–9, 1977, under the auspices of the Welsh Branch of the British Psychological Society.

Farberow, Norman L., and David K. Reynolds. "Dyadic Crises Suicides in Mental Hospital Patients." *Journal of Abnormal Psychology* 78 (1971): 77–85.

Fast, Julius. *Body Language.* Philadelphia: M. Evans and Co., Inc., 1970.

Ferrante, Joan M. *Woman As Image in Medieval Literature.* New York: Columbia University Press, 1975.

Firestone, Shulamith. *The Dialectic of Sex.* New York: Bantam Books, 1970.

Folsom, J. K. "Love and Courtship." In *Marriage and the Family,* edited by Rueben Hill and Howard Becker. Boston: D. C. Heath & Co., 1948.

Fraiberg, Selma. "The Origins of Human Bonds." *Commentary,* 44 (1967): 47–57.

Freeman, Lucy, and Julie Roy. *Betrayal.* New York: Stein & Day, 1976.

Freud, Sigmund. *A General Introduction to Psychoanalysis.* Translated by Joan Riviere. New York: Simon & Schuster, 1969.

———*Collected Papers.* London: The Hogarth Press and the Institute for Psychoanalysis, 1933.

Fromm, Erich. *The Art of Loving.* New York: Harper & Row, 1956.

Gifford, Edward S., Jr. *The Charms of Love.* Garden City, N.Y.: Doubleday, 1962.

Glasser, William, and Leonard M. Zunin. "Reality Therapy." In *Current Psychotherapy,* edited by Raymond Corsini, pp. 287–316. Itasca, Ill.: F. E. Peacock, 1978.

Globus, Gordon G., Grover Maxwell, and Irwin Savodnik. *Consciousness and the Brain: A Scientific and Philosophical Inquiry.* New York: Plenum Press, 1976.

Goffman, Irving. *Behavior in Public Places.* New York: Free Press, 1969.

Goode, William J. "The Theoretical Importance of Love," *American Sociological Review* 24 (1959): 38–47.

Grant, Vernon W. *Falling in Love: The Psychology of the Romantic Emotion.* New York: Springer Publishing Co., 1976.

Greenfield, Sidney M. "Love and Marriage in Modern America: A Functional Analysis." *The Sociological Quarterly* 6 (1965).

Gross, Llewellyn. "A Belief Pattern Scale for Measuring Romanticism." *American Sociological Review* 9 (1944): 463–72.

Gross, Martin L. *The Psychological Society.* New York: Random House, 1978.

Guitton, Jean. *Essay on Human Love.* Rockliff, Salisbury Square, London: 1951.

Hardy, Kenneth R. "An Appetitional Theory of Sexual Motivation." *Psychological Review* 71 (1964): 1–18.

Harlow, H. F. "The Nature of Love." *American Psychologist* 13 (1958): 673–85.

Harrison, Saul I., and Donald J. Carek. *A Guide to Psychotherapy.* Boston: Little, Brown, 1966.

Hattis, Ronald P. "Love Feelings in Courtship Couples: An Analysis." *Journal of Humanistic Psychology* 5 (1965): 22–53.

Haughton, Rosemary. *Love.* Baltimore: Penguin Books, 1970.

Homans, G. C. *Social Behavior: Its Elementary Forms.* New York: Harcourt, Brace, 1961.

Horton, D. "The Dialogue of Courtship in Popular Songs." *American Journal of Sociology* 62 (1957): 569–78.

Horton, Margaret. "Alternatives to Romantic Love." Paper presented at the American Psychological Association, Washington, D.C., September 1971.

Hoult, Thomas Ford, Lura F. Henze, and John W. Hudson. *Courtship and Marriage in America.* Boston: Little, Brown, 1978.

Hunt, Morton M. *The Natural History of Love.* New York: Alfred A. Knopf, 1959.

Ineichen, Bernard. "The Social Geography of Marriage." Paper presented at the Conference on Love and Attraction of the British Psychological Society, Swansea, Wales, September 5–9, 1977.

Jacob, François. "Evolution and Tinkering." *Science* 196 (1977): 1161–66.

Josephson, Matthew. *Stendhal, or The Pursuit of Happiness*. Garden City, N.Y.: Doubleday, 1946.

Kanin, Eugene J., and Karen R. Davidson. "Some Evidence Bearing on the Aim-Inhibition Hypothesis of Love." *Sociological Quarterly* 13 (1972): 210–17.

Kanin, Eugene J., Karen R. Davidson, and Sonia R. Scheck. "A Research Note on Male-Female Differentials in the Experience of Heterosexual Love." *The Journal of Sex Research* (1970): 64–72.

Kephart, William M. "Evaluation of Romantic Love." *Medical Aspects of Human Sexuality* (1973): 92–93, 98, 100, 106–8.

Kilpatrick, William. "The Demythologizing of Love," *Adolescence*, vol. 9, no. 33, 1974, pp. 25–30.

Kinget, G. Marian. *On Being Human*. New York: Harcourt, Brace, 1975.

————"The Many-Splendored Thing in Transition or: The Agony and the Ecstasy Revisited." Paper presented at the International Conference on Love and Attraction, University College of Swansea, Swansea, Wales, September 5–9, 1977.

Kinsey, Alfred C., Wardell B. Pomeroy, and Clyde E. Martin. *Sexual Behavior in the Human Male*. Philadelphia: W. B. Saunders, 1948.

Kirkpatrick, Clifford, and Theodore Caplow. "Emotional Trends in the Courtship Experience of College Students as Expressed by Graphs, with Some Observations on Methodological Implications." *American Sociological Review* 5 (1945): 619–26.

Knight, James A. "Suicide Among Students." In *Suicidal Behaviors: Diagnosis and Management*, pp. 228–40. Boston: Little, Brown, 1968.

Knox, David H. "Attitudes Toward Love of High School Seniors." *Adolescence* (1970): 89–100.

Komarovsky, Mirra. *Dilemmas of Masculinity: A Study of College Youth*. New York: W. W. Norton, 1976.

Kramer, Ernest. *A Beginning Manual for Psychotherapists*. New York: Grune and Stratton, 1970.

Kramer, Heinrich, and Jakob Sprenger. *Malleus Maleficarum*. Translated by M. Summers. London: Arrow Books, 1971.

Krehbiel, H. E. "Essay on Richard Wagner's Opera," in *Tristan and Isolde*. New York: G. Schirmer, 1934.

Lacey, Beatrice C., and John I. Lacey. "Two-way Communication Between the Heart and the Brain." *American Psychologist,* 33 (1978): 99–113.

Lazarus, Arnold A. "Sex with (and without) Love." *Medical Aspects of Human Sexuality* 8 (1974): 32–42.

Lederer, Wolfgang. *The Fear of Women.* New York: Harcourt, Brace, 1968.

Legman, G. *Rationale of the Dirty Joke: An Analysis of Sexual Humor.* New York: Grove Press, 1968.

Lessing, Doris. *Summer Before the Dark.* New York: Knopf, 1973.

Lester, Julius. "Being a Boy." In *Men and Masculinity,* edited by Joseph H. Pleck and Jack Sawyer. Englewood Cliffs, N.J.: Prentice-Hall. 1974.

Lilar, Suzanne. *Aspects of Love in Western Society.* New York: McGraw-Hill Book Co., 1965.

Linton, Ralph. *The Study of Man.* New York: Appleton-Century-Crofts, 1936.

Maslow, Abraham H. *Motivation and Personality.* New York: Harper, 1954.

Masters, William H., and Virginia E. Johnson. *Human Sexual Response.* Boston: Little, Brown, 1966.

Maurois, André. *Seven Faces of Love.* New York: Didier Publishing Co., 1944.

May, Rollo. *Love and Will.* New York: W. W. Norton, 1969.

McLaughlin, Eleanor Commo. "Equality of Souls, Inequality of Sexes: Women in Medieval Theology." In *Religion and Sexism,* edited by Rosemary Radford Ruether, pp. 213–266. New York: Simon and Schuster, 1974.

Mead, Margaret. *Growing Up in New Guinea.* New York: William Morrow, 1930.

Moffat, Mary Jane, and Charlotte Painter. *Revelations: Diaries of Women.* New York: Random House, 1974.

Money, John, and Anke A. Ehrhardt. *Man and Woman, Boy and Girl.* Baltimore: Johns Hopkins University Press, 1972.

Morris, Desmond. *Intimate Behavior.* New York: Bantam Books, 1973.

Murstein, Bernard I. *Love, Sex, and Marriage Through the Ages.* New York: Springer Publishing Co. 1974.

Muuss, Rolf E. *Theories of Adolescence.* New York: Random House, 1962.

Nagera, Humberto. "Activity-Passivity; Masculinity-Femininity." In *Basic Psychoanalytic Concepts of the Libido Theory,* pp. 129–45, Vol. I, New York: Basic Books, 1969.

Neiswender, Margaret, James E. Birren, and K. Warner Schaie. "Age and the Experience of Love in Adulthood." Paper presented at the 83rd Annual Meeting of the American Psychological Association, Chicago, Ill., 1975.

Norton, David. "Toward an Epistemology of Romantic Love." *Centennial Review* 14 (1970): 421–43.

Oppong, Christine. "Changing Family Structure and Conjugal Love." Paper presented at the International Conference of Love and Attraction, University College of Swansea, Swansea, Wales, September 5–9, 1977.

Ortega y Gasset, José. *On Love.* Translated by Toby Talbot. New York: Meridian, 1957.

Oxford Dictionary of Quotations, 2nd ed. London: Oxford University Press, 1953.

Pam, Alvin, Robert Plutchik, and Hope R. Conte. "Love: A Psychometric Approach." *Psychological Reports* 37 (1975), 83–88.

Peele, Stanton, with Archie Brodsky. *Love and Addiction.* New York: Signet Books, 1976.

Phillips, Debora, with Robert Judd. *How to Fall Out of Love.* Boston: Houghton Mifflin, 1978.

Queen, Stuart A., and R. W. Habenstein. *The Family in Various Cultures,* 4th ed. New York: J. B. Lippincott, 1974.

Reik, Theodore. *A Psychologist Looks at Love.* New York: Rinehart, 1944.

———*Psychology of Sexual Relations.* New York: Farrar, Strauss, 1945.

Richardson, Joanna. *Stendhal.* New York: Coward, McCann & Geoghegan, 1974.

Riegel, Michelle Galler. "Monogamous Mammals: Variations on a Scheme." *Science News* 112 (1977): 76–78.

Rimmer, Robert (ed.) *Adventures in Loving.* New York: Signet Books, 1973.

Rosenblatt, Paul C. "Communication in the Practice of Love Magic." *Social Forces* 49 (1971): 482–87.

Rossi, Alice S. "The Biosocial Side of Parenthood." *Human Nature,* 1 (1978): 72–79.

Rougemont, Denis de. *Love in the Western World.* New York: Harcourt, Brace, 1940.

———*Love in the Western World.* Revised and augmented edition; translated by Montgomery Belgion. New York: Pantheon [1940], 1956.

Rubin, Zick. "Loving and Leaving." Paper presented at the 84th Annual Convention of the American Psychological Association, Washington, D.C., September 3–7, 1976.

———"Measurement of Romantic Love," *Journal of Personality and Social Psychology* 16 (1970): 265–73.

Ruether, Mary Radford. *Religion and Sexism.* New York: Simon and Schuster, 1974.

Russier, Gabrielle. *The Affair of Gabrielle Russier.* Preface by Raymond Jean and Introduction by Mavis Gallant. New York: Alfred A. Knopf, 1971.

Sagan, Carl. *The Dragons of Eden: Speculations on the Evolution of Human Intelligence.* New York: Random House, 1977.

Salk, Lee. "Mother's Heartbeat as an Imprinting Stimulus." *Transactions of the New York Academy of Science* 24 (1962): 753–63.

Schacter, Stanley, and Jerome E. Singer. "Cognitive, Social and Physiological Determinants of Emotional States." *Psychological Review* 69 (1962): 379–99.

Seidenberg, Robert. *Marriage in Life and Literature.* New York: Philosophical Library, 1970.

Selye, Hans. Quotes from *Behavior Today,* 8 (1977): 4–5.

Shaffer, Leigh S. "The Golden Fleece: Anti-Intellectualism and Social Science." *American Psychologist* 32 (1977): 814–23.

Shneidman, Edwin S., Norman L. Farberow, and Robert E. Littman. *The Psychology of Suicide.* New York: Science House, 1970.

Shneidman, Edwin S., Norman L. Farberow, and Robert E. Littman (eds.) *Clues to Suicide.* New York: McGraw-Hill Book Co., 1957.

Sluckin, W. "Imprinting Reconsidered." *Bulletin of the British Psychological Society* 27 (1974): 447–51.

Solomon, Robert C. *The Passions.* Garden City, N.Y.: Anchor Press/Doubleday, 1976.

Spanier, Graham B. "Romanticism and Marital Adjustment." *Journal of Marriage and the Family* 34 (1972): 481–87.

Spanos, Nicholas P. "Witchcraft in Histories of Psychiatry: A Critical Analysis and an Alternative Conceptualization." *Psychological Bulletin* (1978): 418–39.

Spaulding, Charles B. "The Romantic Love Complex in American Culture." *Sociology and Social Research* 55 (1977): 82–100.

Stanley, Steven M. "Clades versus Clones in Evolution: Why We Have Sex." *Science* 190 (1975): 382–83.

Stendhal. *Love.* Translated by Gilbert and Suzanne Sale; Introduction by Jean Stewart and B. C. J. G. Knight. Middlesex, England: Penguin Books, 1975.

Stendhal. *Memoirs of Egotism.* Translated by Hannah and Matthew Josephson. New York: Lear, 1949.

Stendhal. *Scarlet and Black.* Translated with an introduction by Jean Stewart and B. C. J. G. Knight. Middlesex, England: Penguin Books, 1969.

Stern, Alfred. *Sartre: His Philosophy and Existential Analysis.* New York: Liberal Arts Press, 1967.

Stone, Merlin. *When God Was a Woman.* New York: Dial Press, 1976.

Strickland, Margot. *The Byron Women.* New York: St. Martin's Press, 1975.

Szasz, Thomas *The Manufacture of Madness.* New York: Harper and Row, 1970.

Talmon, Yonina. "Mate Selection in Collective Settlements," *American Sociological Review* 29 (1964): 491–508.

Tennov, Dorothy. "Sex Differences in Romantic Love and Depression Among College Students." *Proceedings* of the 81st Annual Convention of the American Psychological Association, Montreal, Canada, 8 (1973): 421–22.

Tennov, Dorothy. *Psychotherapy: The Hazardous Cure.* New York: Doubleday/Anchor, 1976.

——*Super Self: A Woman's Guide to Self-Management.* New York: Jove, 1978.

Treisman, Michel. "Motion Sickness: An Evolutionary Hypothesis," *Science* 197 (1977): 493–95.

Udry, J. Richard. *The Social Context of Marriage*, 3rd ed. Philadelphia: J. B. Lippincott, 1974.

Valency, Maurice. *In Praise of Love*. New York: Macmillan Co., 1961.
Veysey, Laurence. "Communal Sex and Communal Survival: Individualism Busts the Commune Boom," *Psychology Today* 8 (1974): 73–79.

Walster, Elaine. "The Effect of Self-Esteem on Romantic Liking." *Journal of Experimental Social Psychology* 1 (1965): 184–97.
Walster, Elaine, and Ellen Berscheid. "Adrenaline Makes the Heart Grow Fonder." *Psychology Today* 5 (1971): 47–50, 62.
Walster, Elaine, and G. William Walster. *A New Look at Love*. Reading, Mass.: Addison-Wesley, 1978.
Wanderer, Zev, and Tracy Cabot. *Letting Go: A 12-Week Personal Action Program to Overcome a Broken Heart*. New York: Putnam, 1978.
Washburn, Sherwood L. "Human Behavior and the Behavior of Other Animals." *American Psychologist* 33 (1978): 405–18.
Webster's Seventh New Collegiate Dictionary. Springfield, Mass.: G. & C. Merriam, 1967.
Whitmont, Edward C., and Yoram Kaufman. "Analytical Psychotherapy." In *Current Psychotherapy*, edited by Raymond Corsini, pp. 85–118. Itasca, Ill.: F E. Peacock, 1973.
Wickler, Woflgang. *The Sexual Code*. Garden City, N.J.: Anchor Press/ Doubleday, 1973.
Wilde, Oscar. *De Profundis*. Edited by Rupert Hart-Davis. New York: Avon Books, 1962.
Wilkinson, Melvin. "Romantic Love: The Great Equalizer? Sexism in Popular Music." *The Family Coordinator* 25 (1976), 161–66.
Williams, George C. *Adaptation and Natural Selection*. Princeton: Princeton University Press, 1966.
Williams, Tennessee. *Memoirs*. New York: Doubleday, 1975.
Wilson, Glenn and David Nias. *The Mystery of Love: How the Science of Sexual Attraction Can Work for You*. New York: Quadrangle, 1976.

Wilson, Edward O. *Sociobiology: The New Synthesis.* Cambridge, Mass.: Harvard University Press, 1975.

Winch, R. F. *Mate-Selection.* New York: Harper, 1958.

Wolff, Charlotte. *Love Between Women.* New York: Harper & Row, 1971.

Wolfgang, Marvin E. "A Sociological Analysis of Criminal Homicide." *Federal Probation* 23 (1961): 48–55.

Ziskin, Jay. *Coping With Psychiatric and Psychological Testimony,* 2nd ed. Beverly Hills: Law and Psychology Press, 1975.

Index